"Shamanism is alive and well in the twenty-first century. Anyone who doubts this should read *Traveling between the Worlds*, which paints a vivid picture of contemporary shamanism with all of its harmony and its contradictions, its fantasy and its rigor, its inner journeying and its devotion to community. Hillary S. Webb has collected a series of interviews that is as provocative as it is fascinating, and she mirrors the shamanic devotion to service by sharing these stories with her readers."

—Stanley Krippner, Ph.D.
Co-author, *Extraordinary Dreams and How to Work with Them*

". . . a precious harvest of answers concerning the under-studied, multi-faceted phenomenon of neo-shamanism."

—Jeremy Narby
Author, *The Cosmic Serpent* and *Shamans Throughout Time*

"*Traveling between the Worlds* is a remarkable opportunity to 'sit with' modern teachers and healers walking the path of shamanism, and learn from them to awaken those same innate abilities within you. Each one expresses with dedication how important it is to love the Earth, to serve All Our Relations, to dance with joy in the presence of such power and beauty. Reading this book can open you for some wonderful journeys of your own."

—Brooke Medicine Eagle
Author, *Buffalo Woman Comes Singing*

"This is an inspiring rainbow of experiences showing the various and colorful entries into the realm of the otherworld. Anyone should find his/her point of entry by knocking at the plethora of doorways available in this compilations. Each one takes us into the realm of otherwordliness with assurance and gentleness. This is a testimony of hope for those who think that spiritual experiences are for others and a gift to those who yearn to broaden their horizons."

—Malidoma Somé
Author, *The Healing Wisdom of Africa*

Also by Hillary S. Webb

*Exploring Shamanism: Using Ancient Rites to Discover
the Unlimited Healing Powers of Cosmos and
Consciousness*

Traveling *between* the Worlds

CONVERSATIONS WITH CONTEMPORARY SHAMANS

HILLARY S. WEBB

HAMPTON ROADS
PUBLISHING COMPANY, INC.
for the evolving human spirit

Cover design by Jane Hagaman
Cover painting © 2004 "Journey Into Ancestors"
Susan Cohen Thompson

Hampton Roads Publishing Company, Inc.
1125 Stoney Ridge Road
Charlottesville, VA 22902

434-296-2772
fax: 434-296-5096
e-mail: hrpc@hrpub.com
www.hrpub.com

If you are unable to order this book from your local
bookseller, you may order directly from the publisher.
Call 1-800-766-8009, toll-free.

Library of Congress Cataloging-in-Publication Data

Webb, Hillary S., 1971-
  Traveling between the worlds : conversations with contemporary
shamans / Hillary S. Webb.
      p. cm.
  ISBN 1-57174-403-7 (pbk. : alk. paper)
  1. Shamanism. 2. Shamans--Interviews. I. Title.
  BF1611.W4 2004
  201'.44--dc22

                                    2004007804

                    ISBN 1-57174-403-7

                10 9 8 7 6 5 4 3 2 1

      Printed on acid-free, recycled paper in Canada

To Derek
with whom I travel.

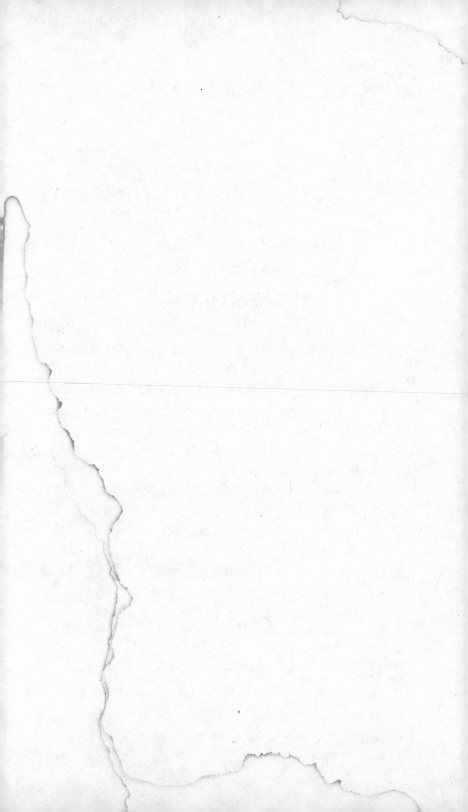

Author's Note

   The chapters that follow come from more than forty-five hours worth of taped conversations with shamans from a variety of traditions around the world. Needless to say, the transcripts in their entirety would fill up several volumes. Due to space constraints, as well as for ease of reading, the conversations that follow have been edited. In cases where even the slightest editing was needed, I contacted the subject of the interview so that both of us could be assured that the meaning had not been altered in any way. I would like to thank all of them for their help with that process.

Table of Contents

Acknowledgments

Over the course of the three and a half years that it took me to compile these conversations, I always remained aware of what unique and wonderful teachings I was receiving. Very early on in the project, I discovered that I no longer cared whether or not the collection ever found its way to the bookstore shelves. Somewhere along the line, my original goal of publishing the conversations became secondary to the experience of just talking to these adventurers of the spirit.

That said, I was, of course, still thrilled when Frank DeMarco of Hampton Roads Publishing enthusiastically agreed to publish the book. Thank you, Frank, for your vision and faith in taking on a project that was, admittedly, a little bit "out of the box." (And thanks to Ken Smith for introducing me to Frank in the first place!)

As always, the insights of many people helped me to express myself as fully and clearly as possible in the writing and editing of the book. Thank you to Pam Broido, Carl Hyatt, Mark Towle, and Stephany Evans for your feedback on the manuscript in all its various stages. Special thanks go to my mother, sister, and to Maddi Wallach for their enduring support and wisdom. And to you, Derek, for being your wonderful self, and for continuously challenging me in all the best possible ways. When two truths come together, new worlds are revealed.

Traveling between the Worlds

To each of the shamanic visionaries featured here, I want to express my most sincere and heartfelt thanks for taking the time to share your thoughts. Each of you has played a distinct role in the way I now look at the world and my place within it. To me, there is no greater gift than that of sharing one's experience of the Sacred. Those who have the courage to do so in a world that does not always hold a space for such things give a gift to us all. Thank you to all of our teachers who blazed the trail for us, giving us the courage and context with which to share our stories. Thank you to the Great Spirit and all our allies, both in physical and nonphysical form, who every day help us to blaze new trails of our own, clearing the path for adventurers yet to come.

Introduction

As I write this, I am sitting in the reading area at the public library in Portsmouth, New Hampshire. It is snowing outside. White, feathery puffs of ice dance past the windows, riding on the February wind. Across from me, a man is asleep in one of the chairs. He is snoring slightly; his eyelids twitch as his eyeballs flutter back and forth in their sockets. The man is deep into REM sleep, that fertile state of being where the dream world opens and the unconscious mind is given free rein over the psyche.

Though he probably is unaware of it, this man has entered what some practitioners of the ancient art would call a "shamanic state of consciousness" also referred to as a "shamanic journey," ecstasy, or trance. The methods for inducing this state—called "techniques of ecstasy" by historian Mircea Eliade—include dreamwork, the ingestion of hallucinogenic plants, chanting, drumming, fasting, and various kinds of ordeals. Once released from the constraints of the "logical" mind, the shaman's soul is free to journey into alternate realities and dimensions; places full of symbols and archetypes, myth and divine meaning. In these states, the shaman undergoes a visionary experience in which he or she comes in contact with his or her spirit guides who provide the shaman with otherwise unavailable information to bring back to "ordinary" reality. Unlike the dreamstate of the man sleeping in the chair, the shaman—who can access these states consciously and at will—goes into the journey with a specific goal to be accomplished before returning to his or her ordinary state of consciousness.

These techniques for altering consciousness have been used by tribal people from around the world to bring balance and harmony both to the community and to the individual. But while such practices are commonplace in most indigenous settings, the concept of such a magical journey may be a hard one for those of us brought up in the linear Western* mind-set to conceive of—much less believe.

This was not always so. Tens of thousands of years ago, our ancestors experienced the world very differently. Their reality was animated by spiritual intelligences. Through their experiences, they discovered that one could communicate with the trees, with rocks, and with the elemental spirits of nature, called *faeries* in the Celtic tradition, the *kontomble* by the Dagara tribe in West Africa, and the *malkis* by some South American cultures. According to their worldview, divine power permeated the physical world. Divinity was everywhere and in everything, and all things that existed were parts of a whole, bound together as one in the great web of life.

It wasn't until the early part of the seventeenth century and the emergence of the Cartesian worldview that these experiences became labeled as "superstition." With the Age of Reason came a new belief system: science. Science could explain away all the old fears and myths: The rumblings of thunder were not caused by angry gods but were acoustic shock waves caused by a sudden expansion of air. "Rationalism" was the new faith, and anything that could not be experienced through the five senses became suspect. Suddenly nature became something that needed to be whipped into shape. The further we got from a symbiotic relationship with

---

*I use the terms "Western" and "West" throughout this book not as a geographical distinction, but rather to refer to the state of mind that tends to develop with technologically advanced cultures. In this day and age of airplanes, e-mail, and other machinery that can connect and transport us to every corner of the globe, we are experiencing a global "modernization" across the planet. Geographical and economic boundaries are no longer so clear.

nature, the greater became the chasm between the sacred and the mundane, until the physical realm became a dead world of inanimate objects. The ideas of magic, of fairies, and of talking trees all were banished from everyday belief and placed in the land of myth and fairy tale. In my opinion, the Book of Genesis got it wrong. Divinity did not cast us out of the Garden. On the contrary—it was *we* who cast out Divinity, removed it from all things material, and placed it far, far away from the physical world into some great, untouchable Heaven, well removed from the physical world of sin and suffering.

With this new philosophy of logic came amazing scientific achievements. Today we have harnessed the atom and can create wondrous technology to transport us to other planets. Science has rendered harmless what once were fatal and debilitating illnesses with a mere manipulation of chemicals. We in the Western world have more technological comforts than at any other time in history. We have charted most of the world and even a bit into the universe beyond it.

And still we ask, is that all there is?

If the widespread use of antidepressants, the increase of violent acts committed by young people, and a growing dependency among all groups on drugs and alcohol is any indication, it would seem that a deep malaise has struck modern society. Despite our achievements and material affluence, something is lacking. From a shamanic point of view, this malaise is a symptom of our disconnection from the numinous, from the sacred aspect of life that resides within all things. So great is our disconnect that today most people cannot even conceive of the possibility that worlds unseen by our commonly acknowledged five senses could exist, much less that we could have access to those worlds and use them as sources of guidance and wisdom. What we are left with is a longing. For what, we don't know. A loneliness. For whom, we haven't a clue. In spite of the discoveries we have made, many of the most fundamental mysteries of life remain unexplained. Science has not yet answered for us the question of where we go when we die, or for that matter, where we come from just before we appear as an explosion of rapidly shifting cells within our mothers' wombs. We have come to rely on science so much that we feel that if science cannot explain it, there is nowhere else to turn. Disconnected from the sense of something bigger than ourselves, we are like children separated from their parents in the supermarket, walking vaguely up and down the aisles in a panicked daze, feeling disoriented, helpless, and utterly alone.

In a belief system based in the rational, secular myth of science, the sacred is split from the mundane. In shamanism, the two merge and dance like lovers, in a liquid and flowing state. In many indigenous societies there is no word for loneliness. The very concept is inconceivable to them. How can there be loneliness, knowing that the universe is a kind place and that there are spiritual intelligences assisting each one of us along our paths? Shamanic cosmology teaches the theory of Oneness, that there is an energetic link connecting all things in Creation. What, then, is loneliness if you know you can never be separate from the other?

My own personal spiritual awakening to this idea came about a year into my study of shamanism. That fall, I attended a weeklong workshop dedicated to learning how to enter these altered states of consciousness using simple guided meditations. For the better part of a week, we lay on our backs in the middle of the woods, practicing shamanic journeying techniques. One day, before we began our meditations, the leader directed us to go into the woods to find a trail that we had never been down before. We were instructed not to walk down the trail, but simply to take note of it. Back at the workshop site, the leader then led us through a journey in which we were, in our mind's eye, standing at the head of the trail we had just been to. We were instructed to envision ourselves walking down it, taking in all the things we "saw" there. In my journey, I found myself walking down a tree-lined path that then suddenly opened up to . . . a beach. I felt frustrated with this image because, as my logical, linear mind reasoned, there was no ocean out here in the middle of the woods. The instructor had warned us that some of the images might not make sense at first and to ignore the part of our minds that told us so. Taking this advice, I kept going and let myself enjoy the experience. The beach was lovely and warm, with sand that was soft between my toes. Sparkling ocean crashed next to me. As I walked, I looked down and found a large oyster shell at my feet.

The journey continued for several more minutes until the facilitator brought us out. He then instructed us to go back to the trail and, this time, physically walk down it. I did so, not feeling too confident that my journey was anything more than the aimless ramblings of my own imagination. As it turned out, the trail, which was like any trail in any woods one would find, opened up onto a large stream. On the banks of the stream, half-buried in the mud, I found the same oyster shell I had seen in my journey.

A feeling, a lot like relief, poured through me. I ran back to the workshop space with the shell, jumping up and down and hugging the facilitator. I was elated. I didn't know exactly what the experience meant, or how it had happened, but it gave me an inkling that there might be more to life than what I had been taught in school. Like many of us, I had always suspected it; now I knew for sure. And not only did it confirm that there was something "other" out there, but I had tapped into it. Little old me. In hindsight, I realize now that the feeling that went through me during that experience was the same as that of the child lost in the supermarket when she finally finds her mother again. Though it can be a challenge to hold on to that feeling of oneness during my day-to-day life, I think of that experience, and I am at peace.

I was at a party recently and got into a conversation with a man I had just met. He was intrigued when I told him about the book I was compiling. He knew nothing about shamanism and wanted to know more. I told him the story of finding the shell, citing it as one of my most life-changing experiences in this work. When I finished telling it, I waited for his response. He said nothing for a few uncomfortable moments, and just stood there blinking at me. I began to suspect he thought I was a little crazy. I was about to say something to try to put him at ease, when he cleared his throat and shook his head. "Do you know how lucky you are?" he asked me.

His eyes glistened as he thought of it. "I would give anything to have an experience like that," he said.

He *could* have that experience, I told him. In fact, I insisted, anyone sitting in this restaurant could have it, or one even more profound. He looked doubtful and shook his head. "No. I don't believe I could. Maybe someone else could. But not me."

His doubt made me sad. I wasn't being kind—he absolutely *could* have that experience. Anyone could. It is only because we are not taught these things from birth that we doubt such an experience is possible. Like anything, repatterning the brain to understand the spiritual experience takes perseverance. Though I've never heard any of them describe themselves in such a way, those who teach workshops on shamanic spirituality are, in a very real way, teaching language courses. And that's where most people get stuck. What is missing is not lack of ability, but lack of context. Learning to talk to a tree, to a rock, or to Spirit is like learning any other language. The tree does not just suddenly grow lips and start speaking in words, as you and I would speak to one another. Like any skill, learning to speak the language of Spirit takes time and practice. It also takes trust. It takes trial and error to understand the subtleties of metaphorical language. Anyone can achieve fluency if he is motivated enough to learn the intricacies of the language of Spirit.

To illustrate this idea, I'll give another example from my own experience. One morning I woke up with a deep, burning pain in my stomach. The pain lasted for several days without relief. I took myself into a journey in order to try to pinpoint the cause of the pain. Once in a deep meditative state, I found myself walking through a garden filled with leafy green plants. The plants spread out around me in every direction, as far as my eyes could see, and had an overwhelmingly pungent smell that was almost too much to bear. I found myself slightly nauseated by it. Though the smell was familiar, I couldn't place it. Before I could take a step, I heard a thump in front of me. A large tomato rolled out from under the plants and settled at my feet. It was then that I recognized the pungent smell as that of the tomato plant. Suddenly there were more thumps. Dozens of tomatoes came rolling at me, filling the space from all directions. Though I was somewhat amused by this surrealistic vision of this strange tomato world that my psyche had created, I was again frustrated that my mind wasn't cooperating to give me any answer to my question. I tried to will the tomatoes away, but they kept coming, until they filled the space completely. Frustrated, I ended the journey feeling I hadn't accomplished much at all. I certainly didn't have an answer to my question.

The next day, my doctor easily diagnosed the pain as the beginnings of an ulcer, most likely caused by stress and eating too many spicy and acidic foods. I took this news in stride and didn't try to make any connections between it and the images I had seen in my journey.

Later that same afternoon, I spoke with a close friend of mine and told him about the diagnosis. He was sympathetic. As it turned out, he had had a similar problem a few summers earlier. That year he had decided to plant a vegetable garden in his backyard. While most of the vegetables he had seeded in had not been successful, the tomato plants grew out of control until they took over the entire garden. Soon he had more tomatoes than he knew what to do with. Not wanting to waste them, he spent the summer eating tomato sandwiches, tomato soup, spaghetti sauce—any tomato concoction he could think of—for every meal. After a few months of this diet, his stomach began to burn ferociously until he was diagnosed—sure enough—as having the beginnings of an ulcer. When he told his doctor about his recent diet, the doctor pinpointed the tomatoes with their high acid content as being the cause.

Again, I was amazed. And also a little confused. Obviously, I had gotten the answer to my question, though the answer came in the way the psyche speaks best—in symbols and metaphor. But why? Why didn't my guides send a jaunty little green elf to skip by and just say, "It's an ulcer, kiddo, lay off the jalapeños for a while"? Why the obscure symbolism? And not just the question of language put me in awe. How and why had I connected to my friend's experience during that journey? Was it just a coincidence that I would be telling this story to my friend who had his own connection to the tomatoes? No, that was impossible. This was way too much of a coincidence to *be* a coincidence.

Experiences such as this showed me the power of this process. Using shamanic tools and techniques, I was having experiences that gave me empirical proof of something "other," instead of just the theoretical philosophies that I had heard all my life. One of the most powerful things about shamanism as a personal spiritual practice is that it takes the middleman—the priest, the theologian, the philosopher—out of the equation and sends the seeker straight to Divinity itself. I could feel the difference having these experiences made in my own life. No longer did I feel that disconnect, that existential despair of being alone in the universe. I had found a way to step into Creation and take an active part rather than feeling like a helpless by-product of it.

What followed was an insatiable hunger. I wanted to know more—more about the process, more about the philosophies of these teachings, more about expanding my perception in order to "see" what lies beyond the five senses, more about the incredible stories of shamans being able to cure normally fatal illnesses using shamanic healing techniques.

And so I started this book. I'll admit it—it began partly as a selfish effort. It was an excuse to sit down with some of the most highly respected shamanic writers, teachers, and visionaries of our time and talk to them about this work and the ways in which it can help us help ourselves, each other, and the world. I specifically decided to focus on shamans who live and work in the Western world; first, because they know from firsthand experience the struggles faced by technologically advanced societies. These people—many of whom are originally from tribal settings or have lived extensively in that setting—can act as a bridge between the two ways of life, translating old rites and customs to suit a new world. The second reason was one of practicality. It was important to me that I provide the reader with the words of teachers who are accessible to them, those who are only a book, a workshop, or a phone call away.

Collecting these interviews was like a treasure hunt. Although I had direct affiliations with a few of these teachers, either through having attended their workshops or through various personal connections, with many I did not. I began a vast emailing and letter-writing campaign explaining my idea and practically begging for an hour or two of their time. Many, because of their fame, I had little hope of hearing from.

To my amazement, almost all of the people I contacted responded with eagerness at the idea of such a book and were incredibly generous with the time they gave up in order to talk with me during our interviews. To me, that is indicative of the dedication they have to bringing indigenous teachings to the West, and their firm belief that these teachings are desperately needed to move us into the next state of consciousness.

I am very grateful for the opportunity to have talked with these adventurers of the spirit. Not only did their words inspire me, but each conversation changed me forever. With each interview came a new idea, a new piece of the puzzle, a new concept that forced me to reconsider the way I look at the world. Most of all, I began to feel a sense of optimism that, through this work, things can change for the better. I was amazed by the variety of positive ways in which shamanism can be applied to the world, as well as to the individual within it. I think of John Perkins who, with his nonprofit organization Dream Change Coalition, brings multi-million-dollar corporation executives down to the Ecuadorian Amazon to teach them ways of merging business and eco-philosophy. There is Rabbi Gershon Winkler, who uses these ancient beliefs and techniques to bring Arabs and Jews together on common, and more peaceful, ground—their indigenous roots. There is Celtic shaman Geo Trevarthen, who combines shamanism with the search for romantic love. Also featured is "renegade shaman" Ken Eagle Feather from the Toltec tradition, who explains how technology itself will help us move to the next level of expanding our perception. And Oscar Miro-Quesada, whose ideas on the difference between life and death challenged my view on reality itself.

And that is just the beginning.

Words cannot accurately describe the numinous. The numinous can only be experienced. In my attempts to describe the spiritual process, I most often find myself fumbling over ways to explain these things. Because of my familiarity with this difficulty, I have great respect for the individuals featured here. In their writings and teachings, as well as in the conversations that follow, they have come as close to revealing and explaining the numinous experience as anyone possibly can. While this book is not intended to be an instruction manual on how to become a shaman, my hope is that hearing the words of these visionaries will help all aware and searching people to live a little more deeply with Spirit—whether they be on a mountaintop or in a mall. This book has certainly been an education for me in many ways and on many levels. If one reader takes away even a fraction of what I have gotten out of compiling it, I will consider it a success.

At a time when we as a culture are drawing further and further away from the Spirit-That-Moves-Through-All-Things, and we find ourselves at the brink of self-imposed environmental destruction, we in the West are desperately in need of a reawakening of the numinous within ourselves and a reanimation of the world around us. That is where these people can be our greatest mentors in showing us how to awaken those parts of ourselves that have atrophied, giving us a chance to roll around in the mystery and experience it ourselves. These people act as spiritual tour guides, inviting us to go to places not hidden but disguised as dreams, as imagination, as play. They are training us in the art and science of traveling between the worlds.

Conversations with Contemporary Shamans: The Interviews

Oscar Miro-Quesada

© Carl A. Hyatt

The farthest we'll ever have to travel is from our heads to our hearts. If people start down this path using just their head, it can take a lifetime. *Two* lifetimes. *Three* lifetimes. *Four* lifetimes. But if people wake up to this path with their heart, they don't need to study with any teacher. They are already there.

—Oscar Miro-Quesada

Some people are born to have their own unique vision of the world; others are born to use other people's vision as a jumping-off place from which to delve far deeper into new concepts and creations. Without a doubt, Oscar Miro-Quesada has done both.

As a child, this Peruvian-born psychotherapist and medical anthropologist suffered from severe asthma. At age ten, he underwent an attack during which he died, and experienced himself leaving the physical plane.

"Three very wizened old beings called me back and told me a lot of things about where I came from and where I was heading to," Miro-Quesada recalls. "After that I was healed and never had asthma again."

As he grew older, the experience was forgotten, lost to the mundane interests of the teenage years—including one in the preparation of the hallucinogenic San Pedro cactus. At age eighteen, Oscar and a group of friends traveled to the northern coast of Peru, looking for don Celso Rojas, a curandero *(healer) who was reputed to be the best San Pedro maker in the world. When they arrived at his home, don Celso dismissed Oscar's friends immediately, and made him stay. Later, during a San Pedro ceremony, the same three wizened old men rose out of don Celso's* mesa *(the shaman's altar).*

"They reminded me of everything they had told me before regarding what my future was about—the marriage I was going to have, the schools that I was going to go to, the children I was going to have," Miro-Quesada says. "I was hooked, and started an apprenticeship with don Celso."

Drawing from both the spiritual teachings of don Celso and those of his own diverse educational background (which includes degrees in everything from humanistic clinical psychology to microbiology), today Oscar Miro-Quesada facilitates experiential workshops on the integration of indigenous shamanic practices into the contemporary world through the Heart of the Healer Foundation. His visionary work and unique self-transformational journey programs to sacred sites around Peru, Bolivia, England, and Egypt have caught the attention of a number of television stations, including CNN, A&E, and the Discovery Channel. His teachings are heavily featured in the book Peruvian Shamanism: The Pachakuti Mesa *by Matthew Magee.*

4

Hillary S. Webb: What do you mean when you say, "Part of shamanic mastery is learning to swim in this liquid universe"?

Oscar Miro-Quesada: Anyone who has done any work in shamanism knows that the universe is not a static state. It is more like an ocean—very liquid, very fluid. When doing magical flight or shamanic journeying, the soul or consciousness is actually separating from the physical vehicle and entering into that ocean of possibility. The shaman needs to learn to disengage his or her consciousness from the body and float freely in that ocean. The trick is in embracing the great mystery and in trusting that the universal world is a safe place to float. In a true shamanic journey, you need to put your personal will aside and allow Divine will to take over.

HSW: Which is probably one of the hardest parts of this work. The death of one's attachment to being in charge.

OMQ: A true practitioner of shamanism learns to trust that there is a larger source that is guiding you and directing your journey. Otherwise, you are constantly fighting it. The currents then become very threatening, and you feel like you are drowning. When you realize that there is no reason to hang on, because you realize that you are already dead, then you can just surrender and become the liquid universe itself.

HSW: Hold on a second. What do you mean we're "already dead"?

OMQ: Didn't you know that?

HSW: I guess I wasn't aware of that. Does this mean I don't have to go to work tomorrow? Seriously, though, what is all this about being dead?

OMQ: There is no difference between death and life. When you die and cross over, you are going to come to a place where you think that you are still alive. The Tibetan Book of the Dead talks about various *Bardos*—intermediate states in which you exist before you incarnate again. Let's say you have a car accident. You've hit a tree and you are on the floor. You look at yourself and there's not one scratch on you. You get up and you say, "Jeez, I'm fine. I guess I'll go home."

5

In reality, you are physically dead, but you are back in the same reality that you were before you died. Then, little by little, life starts shape-shifting around you and synchronicities start to abound. Your waking dream, your daydream, and your sleeping dream all become one and the same. You think about someone and immediately they call you up on the phone or perhaps show up at your door. Then, you start thinking about people who have already passed over, and *they* show up, too. At that point you start to say, "Oops, something's different here." Then, little by little, with very much gentleness, the Elders of the various *Bardos* start introducing you to the fact that you have passed over. At first you panic and life becomes unbearable, because the minute you experience fear, love becomes constricted and you attract lower astral forms. That's what Hell is. But when you learn to just surrender and accept it, it becomes a very luminous experience. Some people take a long time to wake up when they are on the other side, and some people are very quick at it. Get my drift?

HSW: *I'm not sure I do. If there is no difference between life and death, then why do we make a distinction between the two?*

OMQ: The difference is the mind. During my most tortuous period of initiation, I had a severe auto accident that resulted in a near-death experience. When I returned to my body I was given a choice to continue and transcend, or to return to physical form. Once I came back, the synchronicities and acausal coincidences were so rampant that I was convinced I had not returned at all; that I was in some other realm. Encounters were being provided that were beyond bizarre. For two years I did not know if I was dead or alive. I almost went mad trying to figure it out, until one day I realized, shit, whether I'm dead or alive, I still have to get up and go to work in the morning. I still had to live in whatever reality was being presented to me. So why freak out over understanding who's in charge, right? At the point that that "aha" came to me, I no longer had to struggle with the need to understand. I let go of the need to know and just embraced the great mystery. That was a major rite of passage.

HSW: And, I would imagine, a major lesson in detachment.

OMQ: Right. And it helps to understand that even the striving for enlightenment is attachment.

HSW: So when a shaman goes on a journey, is he or she experiencing a kind of death?

OMQ: Yes and no. The aspect of consciousness that goes on a shamanic journey is the same one that leaves the physical body at the moment of death. The shaman understands that he or she can travel through the same realms that are presented at the moment of one's physical death without having to physically die. In that sense, in having that experience, one realizes that there's no separation between life and death, spirit and matter. All duality is dissolved.

HSW: So the answer, then, is not to look for an answer?

OMQ: Well, the answers will come when the time is right. When the person is ready to apply them in a concrete way to help our planet, there will be many, many answers. They've always been there and they always will be.

HSW: During our conversation, Toltec shaman Ken Eagle Feather said to me, "You have to know that you don't know anything and be comfortable with that."

OMQ: That's exactly right. Unfortunately, I wasn't that clear in my earlier years. I really tried to explain God and Creator through academic means. Finally, I realized that a donkey with a load of books is still a donkey.

HSW: That makes me feel silly putting this book together. This whole project has been, in many ways, my quest for answers.

OMQ: Well, what I see you doing, regardless of what *you* personally want, is documenting certain people who are committed to a path of service and who can speak about where we are as a planet of people right now. And that is very important in waking people up.

HSW: Do you think that the current resurgence of interest in indigenous spirituality is part of our waking up? Are we experiencing a true shamanic renaissance, or is this just a fad that will die out within a few years?

OMQ: The way I view the current emergence of a shamanic global culture taking place on our beloved Pachamama* is simply the result of people having lost their connection to the sacred dimensions in life. Most of our psycho-spiritual traditions and religions have focused more on transcending the physical world and welcoming the afterlife than actually living the spirituality here and now in the *kay pacha*, the Middle World. Because of this, they have disconnected from our planet, from our beloved mother. Hence, the devastating conditions that we now witness on our planet.

I see the indigenous wisdom teachings, especially those of South America, as being very relevant for all humanity for a return to an intimate, reverent relationship with Pachamama. This is mainly because they focus on becoming as sensitive as one can to the touch, taste, and sounds of everything that is born from the Earth. You've probably heard this thousands of times from the people that you have interviewed, but in these traditions there is a very clear understanding that human beings are not separate. We are but luminous strands in the great web of life.

I find in my teaching that most of the people that come to these trainings are looking for a change. They realize that everything that they have accumulated and felt a sense of ownership of is no longer cutting the mustard. So, initially, they come for self-gain and self-healing. Little by little, however, they realize that they are an inextricable part of the greater whole and start working more for the Earth than for themselves, moving out of a narcissistic self-identity to more of a global consciousness. That's what I find is the relevance of these native traditions to the modern world. That is, helping us wake up to our sense of being a global family, rather than isolated individuals.

HSW: So is there a definite shift happening? This isn't just a fad?

---

* The word "Pachamama" in Quechual can mean "Mother Earth," "Mother Time," or even "Mother Universe."

OMQ: I find it is both. And I think that there is value in it being both a fad and an inevitable option for our people. Even those people who are transforming the indigenous ways into a commercial enterprise are still touching the hearts of many. And out of those many, maybe one may truly wake up and feel that they can do something at a grassroots level. Being a fad, it becomes mainstream, and being mainstream, we begin to see what we are seeing now throughout America. For example, everyone is talking about having altars in their home. So a fad is good in that sense. The more altars in the home, the more of a personal connection to the sacred is established, and the more one will venture out and feel like doing service for others. The more people that hold a common vision, especially a sacred vision, the greater the impact on the planet.

And this trend *is* having global implications. I just got back from Tibet and Nepal. Despite all the oppression and the attempted destruction of their traditions by the Chinese, the Chinese are now rebuilding all the monasteries and temples that they had once destroyed. A similar thing is happening in Peru, where there has been a resurgence of a respect for the Indian, who before was considered a lesser being. There are some major structural social political changes occurring as a result of people, especially from developed nations, honoring the teachings of our ancestors. To me, that is an indication that it is more than just a fad.

HSW: *It is ironic that once upon a time the white Europeans wiped out so much indigenous spirituality and now we're paying these same people thousands of dollars to teach us their beliefs.*

OMQ: Well, yes, it's all cycles, right? We are currently moving out of what the Hindus call the *kaliyuga*, the Age of Crisis, and moving into what's known as a *Satya*. This is an elaborate system of eras that is shared by various metaphysical traditions around the world. In the Andes we have a similar notion. According to Andean cosmology, we are currently living in Hell.

HSW: *How so?*

OMQ: The conquest by the Spanish five hundred plus years ago marked the beginning of the *uhu pachacuti*, the turning of the Lower

World, in which all of the repressed shadow of humanity began to come to the surface. That's what we have been living in since then, and that's why people are grasping to find meaning by having things and then feeling horrible even if they have money and property and material ownership. There is an imbalance, and that imbalance is reaching a critical point. A turning is going to have to happen, and that turning is going to create a major cataclysm. Not so much a geo-physical cataclysm, but an inner cataclysm. *Uhu* itself means "inner space." The earthquakes that are going to occur are going to be within the hearts of human beings more than on the planet. Individually, people are going to feel really off-balance, uncentered, and bewildered. On a global scale, it is going to mean a lot of crisis and chaos until we hit bottom. At that point, it is going to be a lot like a Twelve Step recovery program, where you realize that you can't do it on your own, and that anything is better than what you are experiencing now. Even those people who don't believe in God begin to call upon a higher power. In the same way, our consumer society is reaching that critical bottom. Through that internal pain, they are going to develop a relationship with the *hanaq pacha*, the upper realm, the more divine and spiritual dimension.

We're getting there. Regardless of all the shitty news that we see out there, there is an inherent transformation occurring in the hearts of people—in our political leaders, in our techno-industrial monopolies, in our multinational companies. There is a change occurring. As people who have woken up to the power that can be harnessed by tapping into these unseen forces and energies, our role is to avert many of the negative prophesies that were put out by Nostradamus, as well as the more recent prophets like Elizabeth Claire Prophet or Gordon Michael Scallion types.

HSW: So there is a little bit of free will versus determination at work here?

OMQ: Oh, most definitely. God works with us, not for us. It's our time to do it. We need to leave this planet a better place than how we found it for our children's children. That's the focus.

HSW: You sound optimistic.

OMQ: I'm very optimistic. Not optimistic in a Pollyanna sense, but optimistic in the sense that we can make it rain, or we can make it stop raining. We can master fire or not, simply by disciplining our imagination and our vision of what we want for the planet.

HSW: In terms of truly mastering this work, how far can someone not raised in an indigenous culture go with shamanism? Unlike those people who are raised with these beliefs, we in the West have to go back and erase all the paradigms that we were brought up with that, for example, reject the idea of a spirit world.

OMQ: As far as they want to go. Really, the furthest we'll ever have to travel is from our heads to our hearts. If people start down this path using just their head, it can take a lifetime. *Two* lifetimes. *Three* lifetimes. *Four* lifetimes. But if people wake up to this path with their heart, they don't need to study with any teacher. They are already there. I always encourage the people who come to my trainings to develop their own medicine way and to trust in their own intuitive self-directed call. I am here to provide them the tools, and yet ultimately, they have their hands and their heart with which to do healing. That's it. That's all that is needed. Sure, shamanism involves other things, but ultimately, prayer is just as powerful. So if there is heart in a person's calling and path, it makes no difference where they were born. They are already there.

HSW: Where? At the level of shamanic mastery?

OMQ: What's happening in our culture is that people are confusing shamanism with medicine man or witch doctor or just healer. Shamanism is much more than just being a healer, you see? Shamanism is living life in reverence, giving gifts of Spirit to people, and developing a reverent, intimate relationship with our beloved Pachamama. It is about being anonymous, not needing to be recognized for your shamanic gifts. Shamanism involves talking to the *malkis*, the tree spirits, to the *alkis*, the nature spirits, to the *tiracuna*, to the watchers, to the *machcuna*, to the benevolent ancestors, and to the *apu*s, the mountain spirits. That's really shamanism, whether you apply it in a healing practice or not. As a writer, your path is one of teaching, of making information available to others. And teachers are just as much needed as healers. As long as you are

11

sharing what you know with others, and as long as your information has heart at its core, you are living a good life, whether you call it shamanism or not. That's what people are waking up to. Most of them at first come to learn powers, but if they have good teachers they learn that that is only one part of it.

More important than being a shamanic healer is to be able to do an offering to the Earth. That is more important than anything. When we repay the Earth, we are doing more to restore balance to a neglected part of Spirit than we would by being on a path of service to human beings. By doing Earth-healing rites and ceremonies, you are reestablishing a conscious, awakened, sacred relationship with the Earth, allowing all of the unseen world that inhabits it to feel more comfortable to reveal themselves to those who are still asleep. Feed the Earth first and then you will have the strength to go out on the healing path.

HSW: Our conversation so far has been all about the benefits of shamanism. Are there any drawbacks to being on this path?

OMQ: There is a danger if someone does this work without a community. Being on this path without community, without a sense of belonging, can be a very, very isolating and alienating experience. It's hard to perceive reality in a very altered way such as this and not have people to share that vision with.

HSW: As Lily Tomlin says, "Reality is nothing more than a collective hunch."

OMQ: I love it! Really, that is beautiful. There is another great one that goes, "Why is that when we talk to God it's praying, and if God talks to us we are schizophrenic?"

HSW: Could this be the cause for much of mental illness? That these people are having a shamanic experience but don't have a community to share their vision with?

OMQ: Absolutely. As a clinician myself, I have found that about seventy percent of all sociopsychotic states are spiritual emergencies. The other thirty percent are psychopathological illnesses. But in the rest of these cases, if you help the client or the patient interpret his or her experience as a spiritual awakening rather than a sickness, they find purpose and meaning in the experience, rather than condemnation by societal norms. And if you then introduce them to a community of weird shamanic types, they recover even quicker. So, yes, if they had a community of like-hearted souls to offer nurturance for their shamanic initiation to run its course, seventy percent of Western psychopathology could be shape-shifted into a spiritual awakening.

That's what it is. Have I confused you enough?

HSW: Just enough to make me want to know more.

John Perkins

© Jessica Perkins

The role of the industrial shaman is the same role as it always has been. It's shape-shifting. It's leading the people into the next shape. It's helping the culture as a whole to visualize the next dream and to apply the energy that is necessary to have that dream manifest.

—John Perkins

John Perkins

Author-environmentalist John Perkins is committed to changing the dream that we in the West have for our world. In the summer of 1999, during the opening ceremonies for the first annual Gathering of Shamans in upstate New York, he told audiences:

"We are one of the wealthiest nations ever in the history of the world. We've also got the highest rates of suicide, family abuse, drug abuse, violence—you name it. We've got incredible statistics that show that we are very unhappy people. So what do we need to do? We need to move deeper into our hearts, into our happiness, into our ecstasy, into our feeling of connectedness and oneness with the elements, with the plants, the rocks, the rivers, the mountains, the animals, and each other."

Perkins had his first introduction to shamanism in 1968 when, as a Peace Corps volunteer, he came to live with the Shuar tribe, the famous "headhunters" of the Ecuadorian Amazon. During his stay, the young business school graduate from New Hampshire became violently ill and came close to dying. A Shuar shaman performed a healing on him that saved his life, making him rethink the way he viewed their "primitive" lifestyle.

"John Kennedy, the founder of the Peace Corps, had said, 'We're going to send young people off to these countries to teach [the natives] things,'" Perkins says. "Well, I learned very quickly that I had absolutely nothing that the Shuar needed. There was nothing I could teach them. Nothing. But they had a tremendous amount to teach me."

In the more than three decades since, Perkins has visited, lived with, and learned from indigenous shamans throughout the world. The lessons that he learned from them about living in harmony with nature prompted Perkins to found Dream Change Coalition, a nonprofit organization dedicated to inspiring Earth-honoring changes by applying indigenous shamanic wisdom. In his workshops and study programs throughout the world, Perkins teaches techniques of shape-shifting and shamanic dream change. He is the author of a number of books on shamanism, including Shapeshifting, Psychonavigation, The World Is As You Dream It, *and* The Spirit of the Shuar.

Hillary S. Webb: There seems to be an interesting thing happening. The shamans of the indigenous cultures around the world are disappearing—mostly

due to the influence of Western culture—and yet Westerners are becom-
ing increasingly interested in learning the ways of these Earth-honoring
traditions. Why do you think this shift is happening?

John Perkins: That's a really good question. Over the last century the influence of the industrialized world has gotten steadily stronger in indigenous cultures. Cultures like the Shuar of the Amazon, the Bugi people of Indonesia, and the Bedoin of the Middle East have been exposed to this whole new way of thinking that debunks the traditional wisdom and teachings of shamanism.

Whenever the priests and missionaries and medical doctors have gone into indigenous communities, they have brought with them the teaching that shamanism isn't important, isn't necessary, and in many cases, that shamanism is evil. Along with that has come a very seductive message that if these people join our culture they will make money, they will get all kinds of material goods, medical facilities, teachers, and so on.

At the same time, in our own culture over the past several hundred years, we have seen an increasing acceptance of science—often at the price of spirituality. Many historians surmise that this started, or at least got a lot of impetus, during the Black Plague, during what we call the Dark Ages, because people's prayers were not answered. The plague wiped out one-third of Europe's population—twenty-five *million* people—and prayers didn't get them anywhere. Finally, it was science that discovered that fleas were spreading the plague, and in the end, it was science that eradicated it.

I believe the Vietnam War was a very critical event in terms of bringing us full circle, because the United States held out that this was a war of the all-knowing, scientific, rational culture versus the superstitious communist. The belief was that of course we would win this war, because we had superior technology to the Vietnamese. In the end, Vietnam was a fiasco. The great scientific power was defeated. From that point on, I think we have much more welcomed the idea that there is something beyond science. That the heart is important, not just the mind.

Right now we are at a very unique point in history where, while we have incredible science and technology and amazing methods of communication, we still have a desire to integrate shamanic culture.

True, the indigenous shamans are disappearing fast, but I think that's starting to reverse itself as we all become much more interested and welcome the shamanic views into our lives.

HSW: In fact, there seems to be a merging of science and spirituality starting to happen. Just over the past sixty years or so, the works of quantum physicists such as J. S. Bell and David Bohm have begun to reflect what shamans have known for thousands of years: that everything and everyone are connected in a very intimate and immediate way. And yet, despite this scientific "proof" of our interconnectedness, we still continue on this path of destruction—both of the environment and ourselves. Are we going to be able to reverse this pattern before it's too late?

JP: Well, that depends on people like you and me and how committed we want to be to this. We know that in order to accomplish anything, we first have to have the dream. We have to have the vision. Before I can physically pick up a pencil, I have to visualize myself picking it up before my muscles can make that happen.

Right now we have the vision of a better world. Five years ago, people were questioning if there really was climate change or not. Today I don't think anybody questions that—except maybe a few scientists who are paid by big corporations to dispute the facts. At this point, all legitimate scientists and even the U.S. government agree that climate change is happening. But it's only been in the last few years that we've admitted to that. All of us—from the highest corporate executive to the most far-out New Age thinker—realize that there's a crisis and that we need to do something to change it.

Shamanism is a great approach to that, because shamanism teaches us that if we give energy to our vision, the result will be a remarkable change. A shape-shift. And so the work that a lot of people are doing is about channeling energy into that vision so that the actions will follow and the change will occur on the physical level of reality.

HSW: Because you can't solve a problem with the same mind-set that created it, can you?

JP: Right! As a culture, we've developed some very bad habits. And habits are hard to break, but it's not impossible to break

17

them. Cultures have broken habits many, many times throughout history. It was not easy for those people back in the 1770s to go up against England. Not just because of the military might, but because there was a real habit there of the way the whole British government was set up. But they did break that habit, and we can break our habits, too. I think most of us really want to. Most of us would really rather not have a car if we could just see our way around it. The challenge is to figure out how to make that happen. Because if we want it to happen and we apply energy to it, it will happen.

HSW: How soon do you think this shift can take place?

JP: We are beginning to see it manifest right now. A third grade class in Newton, Massachusetts, is teaching shamanic journeying to kids in that school from kindergarten to fifth grade. When things like that happen, we have a very, very good prospect of seeing a shape-shift occur within the next generation.

HSW: Earlier you talked about creating a "shape-shift." This is a term that comes up frequently throughout your books and workshops, but it's not a concept that most people are really familiar with.

JP: Shape-shifting is a process of transformation. It can happen on a cellular level, where we can shape-shift the body to get rid of cancer and other diseases. It can happen on a personal level, where we change our personalities to, say, become more proficient as writers or artists or to drop addictions. A shape-shift can also happen institutionally by changing the way we govern ourselves and the way we run our lives.

Again, in each of those cases, it's having the vision first and then applying energy to it. That energy creates action to then bring about the transformation. Shamanism teaches us to look at the vision and decide if it is something that we really do want to have manifest, and then gives us some wonderful approaches for applying energy in order to create the shape-shift.

A lot of people think of shamans as healers. And while most of them do perform healings, not all of them do. But all shamans are shape-shifters. For many of them, shape-shifting involves changing the way one community relates to another community, relates to a river that it is starting to pollute, relates to the weather cycles or the crop cycles.

The ancient Mayans appeared to be a great microcosm because they built up this incredible civilization and then they abandoned it. Nobody really knows for sure why they did that, but one of the most predominant theories is that, while it seemed like they had all these technological advancements, they realized that their way of life really wasn't working. They had great architecture, great mathematics, great engineering, and yet they were finding it increasingly difficult to feed themselves. Eventually they rejected all that and went back into the forest.

Today we as a whole planet are discovering something very similar. We've created an amazing culture and technology, but the way we're using it is making it very difficult for us to live satisfied, fulfilled lives and to look at a future for our children.

HSW: Dave Foreman, the cofounder of Earth First!, has said that the defense of the Earth is not "Lord Man protecting something less that himself. Rather, it is a humble joining with Earth, becoming the rain forest, the desert, the mountains, the wilderness in defense of itself." Sounds like shape-shifting to me!

JP: Yes. That's the crux. Where did we ever get this idea that God has singled us out as the only species that can ignore the laws of nature and keep procreating, keep destroying the resources, keep destroying all the other species around us and still be taken care of? We act as if God said, "The lions aren't allowed to destroy all of their prey and all of their prey's offspring and keep on living. The birds aren't allowed to eat all of the grain, including all of the seed grain. But you people, you can destroy everything around you and I'm still going to hold you dear to my heart and let you continue." Whoever came up with that idea?

HSW: It does seem pretty egotistical.

JP: It's egotistical and it's outrageous. And totally irrational, but it still exists.

HSW: When we do shape-shift the collective dream, what do you think that the world is going to look like? Are we all going to ditch our cell phones and go into the jungle and live in yerts?

JP: Well, what I'm about to say is not very popular. One of the most important things that has to happen is that we have to recognize that the Earth's resources are limited; that space is limited, and that we human beings have to take responsibility for that. We have to recognize that we are the *only* species on this planet with no natural enemies, and therefore, we have to do something to control our own population. We cannot continue to create medicines that prolong life, that eradicate illnesses, that cut back on infant mortality rate, and not do something that will balance that out. I don't know what that "something else" is, and I know that people don't want to face that fact. The reality is that we live on a limited piece of real estate and we're not going to be happy if we continue to have to destroy all other life-forms in order to make room for ourselves. Seeing trees cut, seeing animals destroyed, seeing species going extinct is not a healthy thing for us to experience. We don't like it. It affects us deeply in our subconscious.

If we're going to succeed on this route, then we are going to have to take responsibility for our population. That's going to have a major effect on everything else that we do—our transportation systems, our housing, et cetera.

And we don't have to do away with technology to do this, either. Technology in itself is not bad—it's the way that it is used that's important. At the turn of the last century, there was a huge environmental crisis in this country in our major cities. The cities were literally swimming in horse manure. You can read reports about how incredibly deep the horse manure was in places like Boston, New York, Chicago. There were tremendous diseases coming out of this and there were huge arguments about whether the land outside the cities should be used to raise food for people or for horses.

The horse was a huge problem. Not that a horse in itself was a problem, it's just that there were too many of them. And so the car was looked at as a wonderful environmental solution. It didn't kick anybody, it didn't create manure, and it didn't seem to pollute—at least not in the way that people thought of pollution at that point in time. The car seemed to be this incredible solution. And it was, for a time. Now, however, we have too many of them. There's nothing wrong with a car per se—it's just the way it's used. And that's true for all of technology.

HSW: Let's talk about physical shape-shifting. In your books you write about witnessing a Javanese man transform into a bush, and a Shuar shaman shape-shift into a bat. If this kind of physical transformation is so common in indigenous cultures, why do we in the Western world have such a hard time believing it?

JP: Because it isn't part of our cultural thinking. At least, it's not part of our *modern* cultural thinking. When we talk about things like werewolves or Dracula, we make it sound as though it's totally absurd and ridiculous. We tell ourselves that because shape-shifting is always portrayed in a very evil way.

I think a lot of that came out of the Christian movement with the Catholic Church wanting to debunk all the old shamanic beliefs, so they made all this stuff seem very scary. The fact is that our ancestors knew very well that they could transform into bats and wolves, just as the Shuar today know they can do it. We all come from cultures that could do that. Not until very recently did we begin changing that.

You know the story of Saint Patrick chasing the snakes out of Ireland? Well, Saint Patrick was a real person, but there were no native snakes in Ireland at that time. The "snakes" were really the Druids. Not only was the snake the symbol of the Druids, but the Druids could shape-shift into snakes. Saint Patrick knew that in order to bring in the Catholic Church and all that it represents, he had to get rid of the Druids—people who could transform themselves into snakes.

The ability to shift our energy into another form is part of our own culture, but we've chased it away and we've convinced ourselves that it doesn't really happen. And yet, some of our greatest thinkers are embracing the idea. Look at a guy like Carl Sagan. Energy transference is what the book *Contact* is all about. What Sagan is saying there is that we're not going to get to other worlds and other planets by firing ourselves off in a spaceship that can go faster than the speed of sound. That isn't realistic. What we *can* do is put ourselves in a capsule that transforms our energy and shape-shift through time and space. I think it's really, really significant that one of the greatest scientific minds of our century came up with the concept that we're not going to accomplish space travel using machines; that we can only do it by transforming the energy within ourselves.

HSW: You mention in your books that one of the things that holds people back from physical shape-shifting is fear. Specifically, the fear that they won't be able to return. How would one overcome this?

JP: In *Shapeshifting*, I talk about how I shape-shifted into a chair playing hide-and-seek with my daughter. In those days, I was struggling with the fear that one could get stuck in that other realm. Since then, I've done a lot more work on shape-shifting and talked to a lot of shamans about this. The conclusion I've come to is that each life form has a certain role to play, and we manifest into that form for a reason. And one of the roles that human beings play is that we have a tremendous impact on everything else in the world. Not because we're sitting at the top of some hierarchical pyramid, but because it's part of what a human being is in the same way that a bird has a huge impact by eating seeds and then depositing them someplace so that they can grow into trees.

We as human beings have a huge impact on a very wide assortment of life around us, and we come into this life in this form because we have a mission that involves that. We know this as we enter our lives, but in our culture we are taught to forget it. In shamanic communities a lot of time is devoted to recalling that mission and to realizing it—such as a calling of the shaman, for example. And the shamans have told me that you cannot shape-shift out of being a human being for any significant length of time until you've accomplished that mission.

HSW: So how do we determine what that mission is?

JP: We all know someplace in our hearts what our purpose is, even though a lot of energy and effort have gone into helping us forget that. One of the things that Dream Change Coalition does at the workshops is help people to journey to their mission. A lot of that discovery can be done by going deep into our hearts; by feeling our connection with ourselves, with the elements and with everything around us. We just have to break down those barriers and open ourselves to our hearts, to what the message of the universe is for us.

HSW: You've traveled around the world and met with shamans from many different cultures. How would you compare the role of the indigenous shaman and the shaman of the Western, industrialized world?

JP: I think that there is no basic difference between the shamans in our culture and the shamans in any culture. By my definition, a shaman is a person who journeys to other worlds and uses the energy and wisdom and power of those worlds to effect change in this one. A shaman is an agent of change. We all have the potential of being shamans. If you journey to other worlds and use what you get from those other worlds to effect change, then you are a shaman. I think that at this point in time it is very important that we honor all the agents of change in our culture, and that we recognize our own powers and our own abilities as agents of change.

The role of the industrial shaman is the same role as it always has been. It's shape-shifting. It's leading the people into the next shape. It's helping the culture as a whole to visualize the next dream and to apply the energy that is necessary to have that dream manifest.

We as shamans have to really look at what it is we want to create out there for the next generation. And by that I mean not just the next generation of human beings, but the next generation of everything that's out there: fish, flowers, cats, dogs, rivers, rocks. All the entities.

Rabbi Gershon Winkler

What all these teachings are trying to get across is that there is no such thing as ordinary. Everything we have, every red and white blood corpuscle in our body, is part of the mystery. You don't have to go looking for it in so-called mysticism. It's in the ordinary, but it's concealed. That's why in Hebrew, the word for the physical universe is *olam*, which literally means "concealed." The Creator is concealed within Creation. It wants to play hide-and-go-seek, and you're "it"!

—Rabbi Gershon Winkler

24

The son and grandson of ultra-Orthodox rabbis, Rabbi Gershon Winkler grew up in a world of shul and yeshiva, spending years intensely studying the Jewish faith. After completing his rabbinical training in Jerusalem, Winkler moved to New York City and began working with outreach programs as a way of bringing nonaffiliated Jews back to their faith. The more deeply he got involved with explaining the Jewish tradition to others, however, the more he began to question the way he was presenting his faith.

"About 1981 a volcano began to erupt inside of me," Winkler says. "As I was struggling to find answers for the people that I was teaching—who were challenging me with questions I had never dealt with—I began to re-examine the original sources to make sure I was not just giving them party-line answers to their questions."

Feeling the need to go back to the roots of his faith, Winkler abandoned urban life and retreated into the woods, where he revisited the scriptural teachings of the T'nakh (Hebrew scriptures), as well as the postscriptural teachings of the Talmud and the Kabbalah. What he uncovered was an intensely mystical and Earth-honoring tradition that was lost when the Jews were driven from their homeland seventeen hundred years ago.

Over the past two decades, Winkler has been conducting workshops on Judaic shamanism—a tradition filled with its own ancient techniques of healing and ecstatic journeying. The unique blend of humor and compassion that he brings to these teachings has earned him the nickname of "Rabbinic Trickster." He is the author of ten books on Jewish philosophy, mysticism, and folklore, including The Magic of the Ordinary: Recovering the Shamanic in Judaism. *Winkler is the founder of Walking Stick Foundation and Retreat Center in New Mexico, which endeavors to recover and share the wisdom and ceremonies of aboriginal Judaism and other Earth-honoring traditions.*

Hillary S. Webb: You had been a rabbi for many years when you experienced a kind of "crisis of faith" that started you on your quest to retrace Judaic thought to its original, indigenous roots. What did you find at the source?

Gershon Winkler: When I was living out in the woods, I suddenly became aware that the natural world was the word of God in a much more vivid way than any of the books of the prophets. It was there in nature that I began to see what the ancient teachings were really all about.

In both the Kabbalah and in the nonmystical ancient teachings of Judaism, just about every teaching has to do with the Earth. Over two hundred and forty of the six hundred and thirteen laws in our scriptures have to do with the land. There are teachings throughout the Torah about how the land will vomit you out if you don't live on her responsibly. All the festivals that we celebrate today were originally connected to the land and to the seasons. For example, Passover is called *Chag Ha'aviv,* which means "Festival of Spring." Go to any Orthodox community on Sukot and you'll see everybody holding palm branches with myrtle leaves and willow branches and shaking them to the four directions, to the sky, and to the Earth without a clue of what they're doing. It's just tradition. But when you look for its origins in the mystical teachings, you'll see it's a prayer to the four winds, to the sky, and to the Earth to bring blessings during the coming "dead" winter season.

If you look at the ancient Hebrew names for the four directions, you'll see that they don't describe a latitude, they describe an attribute. For example, the word for North in Hebrew is *t'safon,* which means "hidden." North is the place of mystery. The name for West is *ma'arav,* which means "from the place of blending," as in day blending into night, life into death. The South is called either *neggev,* meaning "cleansing," or *da'rom,* the "place of rising." In the East you have *meez'rach,* which means "from the place of shining," or *kedem,* meaning "beginning."

In my workshops, I share teachings straight from the text of the Talmud and the Kabbalah concerning the organic nature and consciousness of all of Creation. I talk about the different powers and attributes of the spirits of the stones and trees and wildlife and people. But before I go into all the mystical stuff, I first give them a background of basic teachings of the Talmud and the scriptures that talk about the Earth and Creation being "All Soul." "All Soul" meaning that everything has a soul—that the human being is not the center of the universe. As chapter twelve in the Book of Job says, "Ask now the beasts and they shall tell you. Ask the birds in the sky and they shall guide you. The Earth, she shall teach you. The fishes in the sea, they shall direct you." The Talmud teaches that God makes it rain not just for people, but for the sake of a blade of grass in some far-off land as well.

HSW: This is interesting, because the idea of spirits seems to go against the basic Jewish tenet that says, "God is One."

GW: Well, it's true that we believe in one God, but that does not in any way preclude spirits. Actually, Judaism is very pantheistic. However, where we draw the line in our pantheism is that, while we believe that all beings—from stones to stars to trees to people—are being spiraled into existence by their own individual spirits, we do not believe that these spirits are *the* source. Instead, they are empowered by Elohim, which is the name we have for God. Literally, "Elohim" means "Source of Powers." Everything else, all other spirits, are just manifestations of that source in the physical world.

Say I want to apply a certain herb for medicinal purposes. The first thing I would do is pray to the Source of All Powers and ask for access to the channels that flow from the Creator to the Creation, so that the spirit of this plant will be able to help the patient.

HSW: In the Talmud there are a lot of teachings and writings about "shamanic" healings—people healing by touch, people resurrecting the dead. What kind of healing rituals specific to Jewish shamanism survive today?

GW: In our tradition, we believe that most diseases are a "plumbing problem"—meaning that our health is dependent upon how open the channels of our body are. What the shaman does is conduct a ceremony to open up the channels and find out what part of the person is being clogged or is out of balance. The ceremony includes eight phases of movement to shake the blockage loose.

To prepare the space for the healing, the first thing you do is take a stick and draw on the Earth the six-pointed star called *magen*, or "the shield." This symbol is also known as the Star of David. It symbolizes the four winds, sky, and Earth.

The *magen* is designed to guard both the healer and the patient against the *Sit'ra Ach'ra*, which means "the other side" or "that which is behind us and that which is after us." The *Sit'ra Ach'ra* is the black hole of the universe—the force that seeks to swallow up Creation into the oneness of the Godhead again. In fact, the universe is swallowing itself into a big black hole all the time. This manifests in different ways: through people—as in the case of genocide—and through what we call natural occurrences, such as earthquakes and tornadoes. In itself, the *Sit'ra Ach'ra* is not evil. It is the part of the Creator that seeks to swallow everything whole, just as there's a part of the Creator that wants everyone to be themselves.

This same desire is a part of every one of us as well. If you think about it in terms of a relationship, a part of me would love to swallow my wife whole and make her completely what *I* envision, what *I* want. But then there's the other part of me that is called *t'zimt'zum*, which means "stepping back." We step back to allow the other to be itself. It's a dance.

In terms of the healing, the *magen* is designed to keep that force back, so that neither the patient nor the healer gets swallowed up by it, because when someone is sick, they are that much closer to death; to being swallowed. This in turn attracts the black hole force of the *Sit'ra Ach'ra*.

The first of the eight movements of the healing is called *S'michah*, which means "leaning." As the healer, you would face North and lean with all your weight on the person long enough to meditate your presence into harmony with theirs, so that their buffer zone is relaxed and welcoming to you.

When that is done, you put a stone in each of the patient's hands—one heavier than the other. Which hand gets which stone depends on what part of the patient needs balancing. The right side is symbolic of the universe's desire to swallow. It manifests in a feeling of lack of control. The left side represents the stepping back, allowing for a piecing together.

The second movement is called *Ta'nufah*, or "swaying." Here, you face the East, gently grab the person, and move them back and forth in a circular motion in order to shake loose the energy that you want to work with.

The third movement is called *Hagashah*, or "bringing near." Facing West, you now escort the patient into sacred space; into the center of the shield. At this point, you would face the person in the direction that addresses whatever kind of healing they need. If they have a block in their ability to start something new in life, you would face them to the East, the place of beginning. If they have an issue regarding self-image, you would face them to the South, the place of cleansing. If it's a problem with relationship—which necessitates blending and merging—or with facing death, which is also has to do with blending and merging, you face them to the West. If they have a problem with mystery—say they have just come out of a seminar and are totally boggled—you face them to the North, the place of mystery.

The fourth movement is called *K'mitzah*, "grabbing." Here you would face South and move your hands in an upwards motion around their field without touching them, grabbing their energy—the *diyuk'na*. *Diyuk'na* is the Aramaic word for the astral body. You grab the astral body and seize the energy that is around the person, starting from the Earth and moving up. Then you grab a handful of Earth or flour or, really, anything that is of the Earth that has not been processed, and sprinkle it all over the person. This is done as a way of bringing the energy of the Earth to the patient.

The fifth movement is *Haza'ah*, "sprinkling." This time it is done with water or, preferably, flower and plant oils. You take some on your index fingers of both hands, and thrust the index fingers at them. You don't direct where it lands, because at that point, it's not in your hands anymore. It just lands where it is supposed to land.

The sixth is *Hak'tarah*, "smoking." Here, you smudge the patient with leaves that you have gathered. You also light a three-wicked candle and, as the smoke is rising, you move the fire back and forth in front of their eyes, which are closed. This brings the spirit aspect of the self to the forefront, so that it can connect with the smoke—the smoke representing the return of matter to spirit. The three wicks of the flame represent the three ways in which the soul manifests in the person: physically, emotionally, and intellectually.

At this point you take a ram's horn, called a *shofar*, and have the patient blow their breath into the wider opening of the horn. You then cup your hand over it and blow the sound of the horn in a bunch of short successive notes. When used properly, the *shofar* has the power to shatter the physical, spiritual, and emotional constitution of the person so that the healer can then realign the patient where they have been out of balance.

The seventh movement is called *M'likah*, "squeezing." You embrace the person tightly and squeeze out the negativity or the obstruction that is causing their sickness. You cradle them in your intention to heal them. After you release them from the squeezing, you take the rocks from each of their hands and throw them in opposite directions from one another in order to split up the absorbed negativity. Each stone needs a separate space to do its transformative work. If they land near one another, it invites confusion into the patient.

The eighth and final phase is called *Hak'balah*, "receiving." If there are friends around, when you release them from the embrace, you let them drop into their friends. If there is no one else there, then you allow the person to drop into the elements, such as onto the Earth or against a tree.

The person that does the healing then needs to walk away and not come back, so that the patient isn't distracted by your presence, thereby stepping out of the moment and the experience. It is also important to do this so that the power behind the healing is not attributed to you.

During these eight phases, the healer remains in a meditative state. However, the difference between Jewish shamanism and many other shamanic traditions is that during the journey the shaman doesn't do anything in the person. The ancient teachers warned against intruding. They believed that it was disruptive and violating to the person rather than healing. Instead, the healer journeys into the realm that is called "Beyond the Pargod." The Pargod is the veil of illusion, and to do a healing, one must go beyond the illusory veil that appears to separate spirit from matter.

HSW: How would one get "Beyond the Pargod"?

GW: Look out the window.

HSW: Okay.

GW: Can you see a tree from where you are sitting right now?

HSW: Yes.

GW: Well, that tree is the Pargod. Why? Because it is veiling mystery. While that tree in itself is mystery, the mystery is concealed within it.

What all these teachings are trying to get across is that there is no such thing as ordinary. Everything we have, every red and white blood corpuscle in our body, is part of the mystery. You don't have to go looking for it in so-called mysticism. It's in the ordinary, but it's concealed. That's why in Hebrew, the word for the physical universe is *olam*, which literally means "concealed." The Creator is concealed within Creation. It wants to play hide-and-go-seek, and you're "it"!

Unfortunately, most of us ignore that. Instead, we buy books and go to seminars in an attempt to decode the universe. In reality, the entire mystery that we are seeking is within everything in Creation that we think we have to transcend in order to find the parallel universe. In fact, everything in Creation *contains* the parallel universe, but it is so well disguised that we take it for granted.

If I were to be asked to state the fundamental credence of Jewish shamanism, I would say that it is about seeking out the magic of the ordinary. When I ask shamans from other cultures what it really means to be a shaman, they say that a shaman is one who trains oneself to step back from the ordinary and to see the magic in it. In fact, the more you step back from trying to figure out the mystery, the more the mystery reveals itself to you.

HSW: What do people gain from going back to their indigenous roots, as you did?

GW: What people gain from this is a response to a very deep quest. A sadness. A lot of the people who come to my workshops are Jews who had been looking for this same stuff in other traditions, since they were quite positive that it didn't exist in their own. They grew up thinking that Judaism was just another religion that was empty and spiritless for them, so they went to India or South America or wherever. What I've been doing is demonstrating that the spirituality they have been looking for in the other traditions is also a part of our tradition. Through these teachings, they can reconnect with their spiritual roots. They can resurrect an old passion that they once had for their people and their ways. Because now they see that the teachings and practices that they've been looking for across the seven seas are in their own backyard.

On a more global scale, I see these teachings as an essential ingredient in helping Israelis and Palestinians live together more peacefully in their common homeland by learning about each other's indigenous ways. I went to Israel three times last year and did retreats with more than two hundred people from that area. The retreats drew both Israelis and Palestinians, including a Palestinian holy man Sheikh Ali Selah Muhammed Hussein, who came all the way from his village on the West Bank to join us. It was here that we dialogued, did ceremonies, and prayed together at a place where we could meet—at our common tribal roots.

It is at our indigenous roots that we will find our fellowship—our sisterhood, our brotherhood. In ancient times, we lived very peacefully and nonchalantly with the tribes around us. The more we go back to those old prepolitical ways, the more we can learn how to reconnect with our old tribal neighbors.

HSW: Because such a division would seem ridiculous to someone who sees the oneness in everything.

GW: Exactly. The Palestinian holy man agreed with that philosophy. He thought that at the core, this political stuff doesn't exist. The problem in Israel is that the Jews that came back to their ancient homeland in 1947 didn't come back with their aboriginal Jewish mind-set. They came back marinated in Europeanism. Had they come back in the way that they left, they would have been able to live there in peace with the tribes, sharing the land, not claiming the whole place as their own.

The way to peace is not through politics. If more of us, no matter what tradition we come from, recover our indigenous roots, whether we are Celtic or Siberian, or Native American or Jewish, then that is the first step to healing Mother Earth and ourselves. It takes a generation of people to teach or birth future generations that will have this kind of consciousness. The Earth is not a toolbox. We are not in charge of it. It is going to go with us or without us. But it would be a lot more fun if we would learn how to go with it.

Alex Stark

When we talk about these worlds, we are just talking about vibration—an energetic level of intensity. And then, of course, because we need to understand it, at that point words kick in. So we talk about good and evil—good being the higher level of vibration and evil being the lower level of vibration, although strictly speaking, in the cosmos there is no good or evil, only energy in differing levels of vibration.

—Alex Stark

Alex Stark's journey down the path of the shaman began early in life when, at age eight, he found himself "looking through people's bodies and studying their bone structure." At age forty, after studying with such teachers as Michael Harner and Barbara Ann Brennan, Stark began to feel the need to clarify his life's purpose.

Following the example of many seekers before him, he embarked on a vision quest to pray for a sign that would further his growth. In the middle of his second night on the quest, Stark decided to take a walk through the forest. At about three o'clock in the morning, as he entered a small glen, he was struck by a sudden burst of lightning. The impact left him dazed but, incredibly, completely unharmed.

Realization of the significance was slow to come.

"It took me five years to realized what had happened," Stark says with a laugh. "I kept on praying the rest of the day. What an idiot!"

Stark later discovered that in the Andean shamanic system—practiced by the tribal people of his native Peru—initiation by lightning is considered the first level of power, and is associated with both initiation and teaching.

As it turned out, no other induction into shamanism could have been more appropriate. In the ten years since, Stark has been working as a counselor and adviser on issues of shamanic transformation and healing, as well as guiding people through their own initiation processes. Stark's shamanic practice is an eclectic mix that includes South American curanderismo, Oriental geomancy, and Celtic mysticism. He teaches workshops on the Path of Love and Power, an apprenticeship in practical spirituality utilizing knowledge from these different traditions.

Hillary S. Webb: In your practice you blend techniques from several different cultures—South American, Chinese, European, African. What is gained and what is lost when combining a number of different traditions?

Alex Stark: I think it's dangerous to mix and match unless you go back to the original principles. By going back to basic principles, it is possible to see how different traditions are connected to each other at the energetic level. After all, we are moving more and more towards a homogenization of world culture, and this implies that shamanic practice will have to adapt accordingly. For example, all cultures are going to deal one way or another with the directions of the compass. All cultures are going to deal one way or another with the Upper, Middle, and Lower Worlds. All cultures are going to have to deal with the concept of will, of intent, power, love, and evil. You have to. There's no getting around that because those are just constituents of human life and of reality as a whole. Similarly, all cultures are going to have to deal with issues of perception and of mind. What's the difference between consciousness, mind, and perception? How do they connect? How do they relate to each other? Techniques are going to develop in all cultures to understand it.

It's wonderful to explore a number of traditions, but one of the great losses of our time is that because we are exposed to so many, we can never learn them completely. The level of in-depth penetration that was handed down over many centuries of work that contains the rituals, principles, practices, and so on of a given culture will be lost as societies become more homogeneous and world exposure becomes greater.

This is also a reflection of the degradation of the natural world. We're losing biodiversity; we're losing our knowledge and our connection to that whole level of activity. And it's very worrisome, because that loss of knowledge results in tremendous amounts of disconnection with the land.

HSW: In indigenous cultures, people have that intimate connection with the natural world. They relate to rocks and trees as their brothers and sisters. How can we in the industrialized world begin to cultivate this kind of deep relationship with the Spirit-in-all-things?

AS: The lesson is in children. Children will give their doll a name and believe that the doll is animate. I know a lot of people who give their cars names. Firefighters give their trucks names because they know at an intuitive level that the fire truck is not only important because it's their tool, but that it has an essence of its own that can be recognized and given a name. Name giving is a very important tradition that we in the West have lost. Children will do this automatically because they are in greater connection with the natural world and with supernatural phenomena.

You don't have to go look for fairies in the woods. All you have to do is spend five minutes of silence in your bedroom and you'll realize that every single object in that room is imbued with Spirit and partakes of the Great Spirit that unites everything. You can do shamanism in a prison cell.

HSW: So, when does someone actually "become" a shaman? How do you know when you're ready to begin working with others?

AS: You become a shaman when you start working. When you start actually using your talents on behalf of somebody else. That's true about any occupation. Of course, you always need to train more in order to move up along the category. It's unfortunate in our society right now that people do a little training and feel they are qualified to practice shamanism. That's very dangerous.

How you know when you are ready to work also depends on what you're going to do. You certainly don't have to work at the highest level. You can work at the family level. You can work on the community level. It's the level of energy of your system and the frequency of vibration that you can handle that determines how many people you can carry. Individuals who are responsible for lots of people obviously have more power. What happens to a lot of people, though, is that they overextend themselves. They start becoming responsible for too many people and then they crash. This happens a lot to spiritual leaders. If the vibrational frequency is too high for the person's body, they have to lower the vibration in order to compensate. But because they are out of balance, they go all the way to the bottom. Then the Lower World steps up and the person gets involved in a sex scandal or a scam or just crashes physically.

If you keep your mind and your intuition open, the level of work will come to you at the right pace. As you learn more, the case will come in to feed that knowledge. As long as your ego is not attached to the power of that assignment or of that client or of that particular problem, you will be handed the work in increasing order of complexity.

HSW: How do you know if your ego truly is out of the way? How can those of us doing this work trust that our motives are completely altruistic?

AS: The main way you can know that your ego is out of the way is if you're not attached to the outcome. If your ego is somehow connected, you're going to want the outcome to be a certain way. You are going to expect something to happen. To me, that is the most important clue. If you do your work according to the dictates of your heart, not your mind, you should be able to detach from the outcome.

HSW: So the shaman shouldn't be trying to create change for his or her own purposes. Because they're too invested.

AS: Yes, although at the highest level of shamanic practice it becomes very obvious that no matter what or who you are working with, fundamentally what you are trying to do is harmonize yourself.

There is a beautiful story told by Carl Jung about a rainmaker who was asked to come and make rain for this village. No other rainmaker had been successful, and the village was basically at the edge of starvation. The first thing the rainmaker did was ask to be given a hut, in which he secluded himself for four days and four nights. After that time, the rains came.

Of course, the villagers wanted to know how he had done this. Finally, the rainmaker said, "When I came into the village I noticed that the villagers were out of harmony with Heaven and Earth. All I did was make myself in harmony with Heaven and Earth."

You cannot work on the client. That's an illusion. You can only work on yourself. If you are aware of that, there is no need to worry about the ego, because you're dealing with it. Every client that has been put in front of you is a lesson not about the client necessarily, but about you. As long as you can recognize that, you're doing the work. And it works much faster that way.

HSW: It seems this would make the process a little easier, too.

AS: Well, sometimes. But sometimes you're being asked to look at stuff that you'd rather not look at.

HSW: In an essay on shamanism you wrote, "Once mastery is achieved, the shaman becomes a hollow vessel for the mystical forces of Nature to act through." This sounds beautiful and frightening all at once. Could you explain this statement further?

AS: Fundamentally, everybody is at the center of his or her singular reality. For you, I am basically a reflection of yourself. For me, you are a mirror that reflects my existence. And this is both frightening and empowering. You can use that knowledge to change the world, simply because the world that surrounds you is really just a creation of your consciousness. Not in a metaphorical sense, but in a *real* sense.

You know, you could make this world vanish. You could literally drop this world. In shamanic cultures, that is known as "changing the assemblage point." This process is at the core of the meditational moment. Once you can stop reality, you can access the infinite.

This is a very interesting phenomenon, because it allows you to understand that the world that surrounds us is simply put there by our own consciousness as a way to help us through the process of life. Think of the power of that. If you are the center of all existence, then you contain the power of the cosmos. You contain the power of all the suns. In fact, you are the sun. And you are capable of channeling that energy. That is what is referred to in all traditions as love. As a practitioner, you can use that quality of existence in order to help somebody else who's having an issue in his or her own consciousness. The giant paradox is that at the same time that we are fundamentally single, we are fundamentally connected. It's by holding those two truths within yourself that you can help the other.

The Hindus have a beautiful way of describing this when they talk about the Bodhisattva. The Bodhisattva is a being who has reached liberation from delusion but chooses to return to this plane—the Plane of Illusion—in order to help others on their path of liberation. And that, fundamentally, is what you're doing as a shamanic practitioner. On the one hand, you are holding the reality that you have achieved the infinite, and on the other, you're holding the reality that there is a temporal limited existence that we know as the world. And you are in both at the same time.

Now, to train for that, what you do is you visualize the Center Pillar. The Center Pillar is the "All"—your innermost essence, the point of all beginnings, the center of the world, eternity. It is nowhere, the void, the "unmanifest." It is the ladder that connects you with the other worlds; the smoke hole through which both you and spirit journey. It is the crown of your head and your spine through which your soul enters and leaves the body. All shamanic training involves opening up the crown and becoming the Center Pillar. It's fundamental to any shamanic practice. If you don't practice that exercise, you will never achieve anything.

Actually, I should qualify that. It *can* happen spontaneously, depending on the level of your soul's preparedness for this journey.

HSW: Earlier you talked about the Upper, Middle, and Lower Worlds as a basic tenet of all shamanic practice. What exactly are you talking about when you refer to these worlds?

AS: Well, the Middle, Lower, and Upper Worlds are ways of expressing the fact that there are three vibrational levels within that Center Pillar. Actually, there are infinite levels of vibration, but for practical purposes, you can discern three broad categories. One category, the Middle World, is the one that we are attuned to when we are awake. The Upper World is the vibrational level of light and, of course, of love. Then there is a vibrational level that is lower than both of those—one that is associated to the darker impulses. That is the Lower World.

Really, when we talk about these worlds, we are just talking about vibration—an energetic level of intensity. And then, of course, because we need to understand it, at that point words kick in. So we talk about good and evil—good being the higher level of vibration and evil being the lower level of vibration—although strictly speaking, in the cosmos there is no good or evil, only energy in differing levels of vibration. And it is possible to transmute lower levels of energy into higher ones. In any case, different cultures have developed different words to refer to this. When I talk to beginning students about shamanism, I refer to the Middle, Lower, and Upper Worlds because that's the easiest way to connect to it. It's all talk, really, but it's wonderful talk because through the ritualistic process you are now engaging in a dialogue with those energies.

HSW: In what way does ritual act as a dialogue?

AS: Ritual is the language of the sacred. You cannot approach the sacred without ritual. The sacred is continuously interacting with us. It warns us by making us fall on our butt. It rewards us by giving us our daily bread. There is continuous interaction, and if you want to learn to manage that interaction, you have to use ritual. So for practitioners who are interacting with the forces of the cosmos daily, ritual is essential. You cannot do this work without it.

HSW: Here's another quote from your same essay: "To maintain this stature is arduous work, as the rules and norms of conduct of society and Cosmos must be faithfully adhered to. Failure to do so creates great danger. The shaman, however, cannot turn back, as his life carries him or her on into deeper and deeper layers of the cosmic vision he is now embodying."

AS: The whole journey of life is fundamentally an attempt to remember that, at the most intimate personal level, we are the center of the world. We are the center of the cosmos. We are the light. We are love. We are God. It takes time to remember, because after the initial period of childhood, you forget it.

The other problem is that your ego—ego being attached to the material world, to the manifestation on the physical plane of that light—wants that process to stop, because remembering requires that you abandon all of your attachments. But once that door has opened and you see that light, baby, let me tell you, you can not go back! Because that's what you came here to do in the first place.

Students often misunderstand that one. They think that there's some force that's not going to let them go back. But that force is *you*. There's no going back. You just can't. Because you've already turned that corner. Other people may live their entire life without any glimmers of what we are talking about. They'll have to wait for another incarnation.

Now, on the *other* hand, in order for you to be successful at seeing the human condition or the world condition as it really is—as an illusion—you have to be fully committed to your life on this plane. Which means that you have to be committed to your principles, you have to be committed to your society, and you have to live according to the rules that you agreed to when you entered this world. Which means you can't lie, you can't steal, you can't kill—the Ten Commandments, in other words. Moses went to the mountain and had a conversation with fire. In fact, the burning bush represents the Center Pillar of the World.

What this means is that you have to live your life in a particular way if you expect to see God. A lot of people think that once they have discovered a little bit of this and a little bit of that, they can forget the rules of this world because there's a bigger world somewhere else. Think again. There is no other world, remember? You're it!

HSW: Okay, so say I've seen the light. I've studied with all kinds of teachers and I've acquired a bunch of shamanic wisdom. How do I incorporate it into this world?

AS: There's a story about three rabbis who were taken by an archangel to witness the Wheel of Ezekiel, which is at the highest order of reality. And at that level they were shown the seventh vault of the seventh heaven—the abode of God himself. They became participants in the great mysteries and then were brought back to Earth. One of the rabbis couldn't handle it and went mad. The second rabbi didn't know what to do with that information, and he became a cynic. He attributed the whole thing to his imagination. The third rabbi did nothing with the information at first, but in the days and months that followed, he wrote songs, which he then sang to his wife and daughter.

That story captures the essence of this work in terms of its relation to daily life. You have to make it useful in the daily world. You can't hold it. Seeking to hold this knowledge—not to turn it into art, dance, music, poetry, philosophy, healing, whatever your inclination might be—is tantamount to suicide.

HSW: What do you mean "suicide"?

AS: You would become lost. You would lose your path. You would stop enjoying the world. That's why in a lot of the Andean teachings they recommend that as soon as you gain knowledge, you share it. Because knowledge is meant to be shared. Power is meant to be applied as work. Riches are meant to be given back. There's always a recycling through the basic principle of reciprocity. "Reciprocity" being the fundamental karmic rule of existence.

HSW: What's the best way for someone to begin incorporating shamanic practice into their lives?

AS: Fundamentally, all shamanic teaching is a reevaluation of your perceptual apparatus. You have to learn to perceive the world in a different way. We're at a huge disadvantage in this society because we have to reprogram ourselves to understand reality in a different way. In order to do that, you have to have gobs of discipline. You have to be steady on your practice. You have to be willing to accept that ritual is going to become a part of your life. You have to have an admiration for the mystery that you behold continuously, a willingness to take chances and a willingness to be ready to face the unknown at any moment. To look at reality with beginner's mind, with innocence, takes a while to discover.

For a lot of people, shamanism is something that fuels their ego side, something that fulfills certain lacks, certain needs that are partly ego, maybe karmic as well. And that's fine, because whatever gets you to where you're going is what gets you to where you're going!

HSW: And the ego part of it, the parts that aren't quite "pure," will be adjusted accordingly?

AS: Yeah, eventually you start to realize that the mechanism of existence includes making mistakes. It includes going into it for the wrong reasons. Because at the initial stages of your discovery of this thing, you're just a moron like everybody else.

I started studying feng shui as a way to pay bills, I had no idea at that point that what I was getting involved with was of a whole other caliber of experience. That it really was about me, and not about paying bills or finding some sort of financial power.

Everybody's route is going to be a little different. Everybody's path is going to be original. It's always your very own path.

Geo Trevarthen, Ph.D.

I always tell people that the shamanic way is experience, not faith. Blind faith is to make you satisfied with not seeing.

—Geo Trevarthen, Ph.D.

Dr. Geo Trevarthen is a hereditary Druid shaman. Tradition traces her family back to the Uí Néill Kings of Ireland, their ancestors the Milesians, and according to some of the myths, to the Tuatha Dé, a band of pre-Celtic shaman-priests known for their great skills of magic. Although persecution from outside influences during the seventeenth century forced her ancestors to go underground with their spiritual practices, they managed to preserve the essential matrix of their spiritual tradition and visionary techniques, passing them down from generation to generation within the family.

"We never called it 'shamanism,' of course, since the term 'shaman' is a Siberian word," Trevarthen says. "But in my family, the spirit world was never separate from the physical. In fact, my family has always seen the physical as the densest level of Spirit. It wasn't that unusual for my mother to come downstairs and say she had been talking to my great-grandfather that night, and he has this, that, and the other to say."

Growing up, Trevarthen read everything she could on primal spirituality, trying to find the counterpart to what her family did. It wasn't until Trevarthen read Michael Harner's book, Way of the Shaman, *that she was able to give a name to the "family business." She studied with Harner for six years, and also studied Gestalt therapy and subtle energy work with Dr. Rudolph Bauer. Finally, at the spirits' prompting, she began teaching her own workshops on Celtic techniques for connecting to the sacred. Her Ph.D. dissertation was examined in Celtic studies and anthropology at Edinburgh University. It was the first study to academically demonstrate the existence of Celtic shamanism, and explore some of its deeper layers of meaning from a scholarly perspective. An expert on Celtic shamanism, Trevarthen has taught for fifteen years at centers such as Omega, Esalen, and Findhorn. She currently teaches Pagan Celtic Religion at Edinburgh University.*

Hillary S. Webb: In Celtic folklore, the Tuatha Dé are sometimes referred to as the Tuatha Dé Danu, the "Cocreative People of God." In what way is this idea of human beings as cocreators of the universe fundamental to the Celtic visionary philosophy?

Geo Trevarthen: In the Celtic tradition, the belief is that God created the universe out of him/her/itself. God *is* the stuff of which the universe is made, because there wasn't anything else for God to make it out of. So if God is in all matter, then we ourselves are facets of God. The idea, then, is that God is becoming an ever more complex and evolved being through this whole experience of manifesting into form. Creation then becomes a mutual process between God and us. He's creating us, she's creating us, we are creating him/her/it. I wish we had a non-gender-specific pronoun!

Essentially, the goal of Celtic spiritual practice is not to remove our individuality, but to purify ourselves and to remove all the things that are extraneous so that we can come into total alignment with our highest selves. If we dissolve the self, as some spiritual practices suggest, then in a sense we are dissolving Creation because we are stripping away the things that God created us to be. I'm certainly not saying that it is not appropriate for people who are on different paths to try to dissolve the self—to do as Krishnamurti said and "walk like a salt doll into the ocean of God," because God's got plenty to learn from everything. But the Celtic path is much more about "Let's purify the self, but let's keep it." It's a little bit like what Joseph Campbell is saying when he talks about following your bliss. It's like following the truth of your being, because it is on the way to this truth that you are going to find that perfect relationship with God and become who you most truly are.

HSW: But what is purification? What is perfection?

GT: Well, literally, perfection means, "through doing" or "to do thoroughly," *per facere*. Perfection is not flawless, but it *is* thorough. I see perfection as striving to be as connected to Spirit as we possibly can, and being as true to the Divine Truth within us as we can be. One of the wonderful things about the Celtic myths is that even the Dagda, the great All-Father, appears as a buffoon at times. One of the ideas being hammered home is that even if you go out and make a total dork of yourself, you are still divine.

HSW: It's amazing to contrast that with the dictionary definition of perfection being something that is "flawless." When we aim for perfection using that mind-set, we end up chasing a goal that is impossible to attain. And when we fail to achieve this impossible goal, we pick apart ourselves and each other. "I haven't worked hard enough," "I'm not attractive enough." We get caught up in a cycle of scarcity, with nothing and no one ever being good enough.

GT: The thing to remember when you get in that cycle is that even if you're just sitting in a room eating popcorn and watching TV, you're still giving God another window on the world. That is an experience that you and the Creator are sharing together. In that sense, whatever you do, you've absolutely fulfilled your purpose for being here. You've done what you were made for. On the other hand, you've got to bear in mind the *quality* of the experiences you're giving God. It's important to ask yourself, "Am I showing God a good time?" Because, honestly, how many millions of times does God really need to watch that episode of *Friends*?

HSW: So that's the meaning of life? To show God a good time? I love it!

GT: Absolutely, why not? Why would God want to have a *bad* time?

HSW: If we go at our lives with that in mind, that the Creator is experiencing life through us, we get totally different criteria for what our experiences in the world should be. I can see how, suddenly, the quality of the experience becomes the most important thing. Then, even the most mundane of activities becomes a spiritual experience.

GT: The other thing is that everyone at one time or another has been at a place in their lives where they've felt very poorly about themselves and therefore let themselves be ill-used by other people because they thought they deserved it. This perspective says, "Okay, even if I feel like *I* deserve it, does the Creator deserve it?"

HSW: An insult to yourself becomes an insult to God.

GT: Precisely. The other thing that is important to remember about the cosmology of the Celtic tradition is that we don't have a God-god and a devil-god, again, because of the idea that there is nothing that can exist outside of God. There is no force of evil that can overthrow Creation because it is all a part of it. In Celtic tradition, the polarities are much more like "chaos" and "order" than they are "good" and "evil." Yes, there are entities that do manifest as evil, but not on the level that could overthrow the cosmic order, because even the most malefic, evil entity in the universe is still part of God. There is nothing that can exist outside of that.

HSW: So then, would the shaman's response to an evil act be to shrug it off and accept it as a necessary part of God's will?

GT: Well, no. Evil may be an integral part of the whole, but that doesn't mean that if you see someone doing something that is evil, that you don't stand against it.

HSW: I guess the next question would then be, "How do you define evil?" It seems so subjective. What seems evil to me may not seem so for you.

GT: I see evil as something that causes suffering that is not necessary to Creation. For example, death itself isn't evil because everybody needs to die. On the other hand, it is *not* necessary that anyone be tortured to death. It might be necessary for a relationship to end, but it is not necessary that it end in a way that is cruel and vicious. So essentially, evil is that suffering which is inessential to the fulfillment of Creation. The greatest triumph of evil is when it takes something good and beautiful and wonderful and divine and turns it into something vile. To take sexual love and make it perversion, dissipation, and rape. Or to take aggression, that warrior power that is good and protective and enables us to be active in the world, and turn it into genocide.

HSW: Are we able to really differentiate what is essential to Creation and what is not? Can we see that clearly?

GT: That's when we have to hook up with Spirit as best we can. I think there are areas that we can generally agree on. If someone is hacked to death by a mad ax murderer who has just done it for the hell of it, we might hazard a guess that it wasn't essential for that person to die that way. Then again, of course, God can choose to have whatever experience God wants.

There's free will in there, too. As I said, we are cocreators with God in this reality. We can choose our experiences. I've chosen things in my own life that I don't think were part of Divine will. Still, I think that even in those situations, Spirit is always going to try to bring a lesson out of that, even if it was an evil thing that we chose to do. Because it's not just a lesson for us, it is a lesson for God. So when we have terrible experiences in the world, when the gut punches come, we must try to focus on turning the negativity into whatever good we can.

HSW: The greatest triumph of good, then, being the ability to take something ugly and to make it beautiful.

GT: Exactly. And I really believe that the only true suffering that we ever experience is separation from God. Although what is in the world can hurt us, if we are really in union with God, it cannot *harm* us. If you can hold that state of spiritual awareness in the moment of trauma, however impossible that may seem at the time, then it never gets you where you live. And it will not separate you from the communion that it is perfectly possible for all of us to have with God.

HSW: I'd like to switch directions a little here. You teach a women-only workshop called "The Wolf's Trajectory," that—and I am reading from the course description here—shows women "how to constructively use longing for a soul mate as a directional focus in life." You say, "We allow the hunt for the beloved to become the magnetic north that points us to our bliss on many levels."

Tell me more about this.

GT: Most of the books and workshops that are out there for women are about one of two things. The first kind says, "Catch a man and everything will be fine." Well, we all know that *that's* not true. The other kind is one that says, "All right, women, make the most of yourselves. You don't need a man!" Personal development is essential, but it is totally unnatural to tell a woman, "Don't hunt," when everything in her body is screaming at the top if its lungs, "Hunt! Hunt!"

The idea behind this workshop is that this desire for partnership is not a bad thing. In Old Irish, the word for desire is *rún*—just like the Norse runes. *Rún* means "mystery," it means "desire," it means "beloved." When you say *mo rún*—which literally means "my beloved"—it is also saying that this person is the mystery, that they are desire. And desire was the motivating force in Creation. It was mystery and desire that caused God to create the universe in the beginning. It was God's desire to be more than what he/she/it is. Desire is not bad. Desire is essential.

The workshop essentially teaches women to use what they desire in a man as the magnetic north that is going to direct them both to the kind of man that they really want and to the life path they'll meet him on. It's saying, "Follow the wolf's trajectory." I remember watching my dog chase after a herd of deer once. She aimed directly at the back of the herd. So the only kinds of deer that dog was going to catch were the very young, the very old, the sick, or the crippled. A wolf doesn't chase the butt of the deer, a wolf aims ahead and cuts the deer off at an intercept point. She gets the young, healthy buck. That's what we want. We don't want the too old, the too young, the sick, and the crippled—we want the twelve-point buck.

The first thing I ask the women in the workshops is what they really want in a man. Even if it is the wildest, most unreasonable thing, there is a kernel of truth in there. So if they say, "I want to marry Indiana Jones," first they have to realize that they are going to be much more likely to meet an Indiana Jones type on a dig in Egypt than they are in a pub in Iowa. The other point is that what they want is also what they want to be. If they want to marry Indiana Jones, chances are they don't just want to be sitting there looking at him; they want to be the perfect female counterpart of that.

HSW: Joseph Campbell said the two questions in life are "Where am I going?" and "Who will go with me." And God help you if you get them in the wrong order.

GT: Right. If you don't truly know yourself, you are not going to catch an appropriate man, even if he is handsome and rich and whatever else.

HSW: So where does shamanism come in to this process?

GT: Emotionally and spiritually there is this sense that we want to be part of a dyad. We know on a certain level that the "enlightened couple" is one of the most powerful things in the universe. When that dyad comes together in perfect harmony, we know it. When a couple really has that, you can see that the total is much more than the sum of the parts.

One of the things we do in the workshop is work with the concept of the spirit mate. That is, connecting with the spiritual aspect of the beloved who is always there, even if you don't have it in the physical. I connected with David, my fiancé, in spirit for probably twenty years before meeting him in physical form.

The thing about connecting with the energy of the beloved on the spirit level is that it gives you a model for right relationship. It gives you an energetic sense of what that feels like, and gives you ways to recognize and to choose. Experiencing that energy in spirit can draw it to you in the physical. Because with love, like attracts like. Love doesn't come from lack; it comes from the fact that you are radiating this energy of union. I often found that people were most attracted to me at times when I was experiencing the most profound connection to my spirit mate. I got together with David at one of those times.

HSW: So why is this a women-only workshop? Aren't men looking for this kind of spirit union as well?

GT: Well, sure. I think that more men, especially men on the spiritual path, are feeling that way. I mean, look at Thomas Moore's book, *Soulmates*. He's writing about his longing for that as well. Doug, at the Rowe Conference Center where I'm going to be teaching, asked if the workshop could be open to men as well. And I said, first of all, I don't think most men have this problem yet. Second of all, I think it should always be a single-sex workshop. After all, if it were open to men as well, there would be fifty women and two men and those two men would die of female persecution! Doug realized later that perhaps that would be a poor idea.

HSW: One thing I've always wondered is if a spirit mate will always manifest as a romantic partner. What if our spirit mate turns out to be a child, a parent, or a best friend?

GT: When I talk about the Divine Beloved in general workshops, I generally say, think of the Divine Beloved as God in whatever way you can feel the most affection for. Ask for a manifestation of the sacred in the way that you can feel most profoundly connected to and in the way that you can most intensely feel love. The people who come to this workshop tend to be the people who are longing for that romantic love, but the spirit marriage can take any form. It can be any manifestation of God that you particularly feel love for. It doesn't have to be a sexual manifestation at all. Some people aren't terribly oriented towards the romantic love scenario. If the deepest love they feel is for the Great Mother, it may manifest in that way. For others it could manifest as a best friend or a child or a brother. The possibilities are endless in terms of the ways that God can manifest to us.

HSW: Are we ever denied meeting the spirit mate in physical form?

GT: Well, there are no guarantees, but I also don't believe God plays nasty tricks. I don't think that the desire for the beloved, for the other half of the dyad, is ever put there just to torture us. It's there for a reason. I'd gotten to the point myself where I had pretty much given up on finding my spirit mate in physical form. I had gotten to the point of absolute release; to a place where I could be totally in the void and release everything, including the physical union with my spirit mate. At that point I accepted that the reason for my desire might have been to bring me to that place, not for me to meet my counterpart.

HSW: Surrender.

GT: Yeah, surrender. There's a wonderful Cherokee shaman, Gitonda, that I spoke with recently. She said that on this path, the foundation gets ripped away time and again until the abyss becomes the foundation. That's exactly what it felt like. It was this perfect sensation of just soaring in formless spaciousness. I'd gone through the lowest point of my life. Everything was ripped away, and I was so grateful that it had all been taken. Suddenly, there was perfect freedom of action and perfect clarity. I was fully in the sacrificial posture. It was within six weeks of that happening that I met David.

I think that even if I had never met David, I wouldn't have felt as hideously deprived as many people do in the world, because I would have had the connection to him in spirit. But I also recognize at this point that there are things that you can only do in the dyad.

HSW: Such as creation, I suppose.

GT: Well, yes, certainly the physical creation of a child is one. But the way I describe the whole experience of being together in physical form is that you become like two networked computers. All of a sudden you are twice what you were. Actually, you are more than twice what you were because there's the point in-between. One *and* one is more than two. There's the *and*. It is the infinity loop. It is this generator circuit that goes higher and higher forever. It's the Trinitarian structure of the universe. When God divided into polarities, force and source, male and female, God became three as well as two, because God was still one even though divided. God, Goddess, and Creator. It's no wonder we feel this tremendous energy when we unite with the other half of our dyad. We're participating more fully in the creative dynamic of the universe.

I know that if I'd hit on "The Wolf's Trajectory" earlier on in life, I probably would have met my mate sooner. However, the fact that I didn't and went through years and years of mad frustration and misery has made me really able to appreciate how focused many women are on this—and focused in a way that's not going to be useful. Not focused in a way that is going to inspire, but focused in a way that's going to basically get them wrapped around the axle. You know, the Ally McBeal thing.

HSW: Our current role model for dysfunctional relationship issues.

GT: That show tortures me. My whole energy shifts watching it. In this culture, you start out with the "across the crowded room" thing—with emotional affect. That usually leads to some kind of energetic manifestation, whether that is spiritual energy or sexual energy. Most of the time people get the two of them mixed together, because most of the time people don't experience spiritual energy clearly, except maybe during orgasm or sexual interchange with somebody else. So it goes from affect to energy and never gets to the higher levels of Divine will and angelic intellect.

I think the ideal way for a relationship to manifest is exactly in the opposite direction. The first thing should be Divine will—what God wants for us, which is also the desire of our own highest self. Divine will should never be thought of purely as an external. Second is the "angelic intellect," the higher mind connection. Third would then be the sexual, spiritual energy. Do you make each other more energetic? Is the total more than the sum of the parts? Finally, fourth, emotional affect should come in. Emotional affect should be like the cherry on top of the sundae, but we've filled the whole glass with maraschino cherries, which, anyone can tell you, will make you sick! We've made sentiment our be-all and end-all. That doesn't get us anywhere. True love is love under the will of our angelic intellect.

HSW: What exactly are you talking about when you say we have to get in touch with our "angelic intellect"?

GT: What I mean is to examine things from a place of spiritual awareness. When you get in touch with the higher mind, you are getting the view from above, essentially seeing everything like the angels see it. It is the work of saying, "Okay, am I desiring what the Creator desires through me, or is this my own stuff going on?" Distinguishing between the two is something that really takes practice. It is possible to journey in the wrong state and project a bunch of fears or whatever is going on for you at the time. It is only through journeying repeatedly and practicing over time that you really get that feeling of the "truth tingle," where you know exactly when it is coming through and when it is not. I've gotten to the point now where I can usually tell when I am out of that divine harmony because I can feel the dissonance—like hearing someone sing off-key. After doing this work awhile, you'll find you no longer have to make the effort of telling yourself, "I will not want this delicious, unattainable object that is so bad for me. I will not want to drink a bucket of liquor or go back to my vile, philandering boyfriend." It gets to the point where you literally do not want them because it is throwing you out of harmony with the sacred; causing you to suffer separation from God. You get to the place where external morality or external will isn't stopping you doing things that are out of harmony; it's your own feelings.

I always tell people that the shamanic way is experience, not faith. Blind faith is to make you satisfied with not seeing. Essentially the only measure of value that you can have for this process is to ask yourself, does this process make you better here and now? Does it make you feel better? Are you more available to your friends and your family? Are you a more effective person?

For me, the answer is yes. I've felt more love and bliss on this path than many people will ever experience, and that has moved me to try to make the methods of this path available to others. The methods are neutral, and applicable to any religion, or none. The central point is, as the Creator's children, it's our birthright to know our parent, and share in the joy of cocreation.

Serge Kahili King, Ph.D.

© Thierry Pfay

Shamans are essentially change artists. So while the mystic practitioner traditionally is trying to get beyond this world, the whole point of shamanism—at least the adventurer shaman—is to turn it into a party. The essence of shamanism is changing reality, and the essence of changing reality is changing beliefs.

—Serge Kahili King, Ph.D.

In the early 1900s, Harry Leland Loring King, a messenger for the king of England, was sent to Hawaii as a diplomatic courier. There he met Joseph Kahili, a native kahuna, who took King in and trained him in Huna philosophy—the system of teachings behind Hawaiian shamanism said to have its roots in the lost continents of Mu and Atlantis. When his son, Serge, was fourteen years old, the elder King began to pass the teachings of Hawaiian shamanism on to him as well, initiating him into the order of kahunas.

In his book, Mastering Your Hidden Self, *Serge King recalls his training:*

"My father was my toughest teacher. Before I understood what kahuna training was all about, I harbored a lot of resentment toward him for certain things he did. . . . For the kahunas, self-development means that responsibility for your development lies with yourself. There is no limit as to how far you can go, and there will be a guide of some kind at every stage. But each person has to get there on his or her two feet. There is no one to push you or pull you, coax or cajole you, force you or lead you along. And that's why it is tough."

When his father died three years after his initiation, King was hanai'd *(adopted) by the Kahilis—the family of the man who had initially trained his father. While it was not a legal adoption, King was accepted into the Kahili family as one of their own, and continued to train with them in the ways of Hawaiian shamanism.*

In addition to his years of studying with the Kahili family, Dr. King spent seven years in West Africa being trained in African shamanic traditions, and has made in-depth studies of other such traditions around the world. He is currently the executive director of Aloha International, a worldwide network of healers that promotes the Hawaiian healing tradition. He has written numerous books on Hawaiian shamanism, including Mastering Your Hidden Self, Kahuna Healing, *and* Urban Shaman.

Hillary S. Webb: What distinguishes the Hawaiian shamanic tradition from other forms of shamanism?

Serge Kahili King: Hawaiian shamanism is different from other forms because it follows what we call the "Way of the Adventurer," while most shamanic traditions in the world follow the "Way of the Warrior." There are a few other traditions that follow the adventurer tradition, but it is the minority. In very simple terms, while all shamans are healers, the warrior shaman treats illness as an enemy and then seeks allies in the spirit world and battles the illness as an entity. In adventurer shamanism, the basic premise is that evil and illness are behaviors, that there is nothing to fight. The process of healing is one of changing behavior.

HSW: It sounds like this form of shamanism is more psychologically oriented than the "warrior" traditions, in that it is more about working directly on yourself than with some external source.

SKK: Well, you know, all of it is about working on yourself. Even when we are doing something that looks like we are working with something external from yourself, you know it is not. By working with the external, you are changing yourself. It all relates to that, no matter which approach you use. Both paths have to do with changing beliefs; it's just the way they go about it.

HSW: So how would the "adventurer" shaman go about it?

SKK: Well, there are numerous kinds of techniques that we use to help somebody change their behavior. The basic idea behind this tradition is that all illness and all problems essentially come from reactions to stress. It's the tension that causes the problem. So all of the healing methods that we deal with are designed to relieve that tension. When the tension is relieved, the body heals itself, the mind makes the decisions, and Spirit can be heard. All the techniques begin with that.

After that, it is just a matter of working with the particular belief patterns of whomever you are helping. As a healer, you have these fundamental ideas behind you, but you have to help the person you are treating within the context of that person's own particular belief system. There are four major techniques that we work with, depending on the beliefs of the person we are working on. These are just words, of course, but we classify each of these techniques, which are really ways of thinking, as the scientific, the psychic, the shamanic, and the mystic.

HSW: Please explain.

SKK: Basically, the first level, the scientific level, is based on the idea that everything is separate. If a person has a first-level relationship with their body—which means that they perceive their body as something separate from them—then you are going to be better off teaching them some of the more physical ways of changing such as exercise, diet, and herbs. In terms of altering things that are producing stress in the body, you would work with them to reinterpret events that caused the stress. You are not trying to change the events and not trying to pretend they don't exist. Instead, it is about looking at what happened that created the stress and making a different interpretation of it. That can relieve a *tremendous* amount of tension. All those kinds of treatments are very physical, common ways of doing things that are understandable by most people that are in a first-level relationship.

HSW: In your book, Urban Shaman, *you talk about a healing technique called "repatterning." The concept behind repatterning being that the body lives only in the present moment and does not distinguish between vivid imagination and an actual physical experience. You write that by changing the ending of an event in your imagination, you give the body a new memory of it, causing the body to adjust itself accordingly. As an example of this, you tell the story of a woman who had received a bad burn on her leg from a motorcycle exhaust pipe. Several weeks later the burn hadn't even begun to heal, and so the woman decided to re-create the accident in her mind. In her visualization, she changed the ending so that her leg stayed clear of the pipe and was never burned. The wound healed three days later.*

Does this mean that we can, in a sense, go back in time and change past events just by altering and adjusting the memory of it in our minds?

SKK: Something like that. Now is the moment of power, and here is where you change them. It doesn't matter what the past is, because you are not dealing with the past—only with present memories of the past. So you can change it.

HSW: How far could someone go with that idea?

SKK: As far as one dares.

HSW: Okay, let's explore this. Say, someone contracts AIDS from a one-night stand. Would it be possible to do some kind of journey into the past and change the memory of the events so that the sexual encounter never took place?

SKK: It is possible, yes. But just because it *can* be changed doesn't mean that it is *easy* to change. What has to happen here is an actual change in the belief of what occurred. For a change to take place in the body requires a complete focus in the present moment and a total change of mind about what happened. So, for certain kinds of things, especially the more emotional things, one has more difficulty in changing them. It is possible, yes, certainly. But that doesn't mean it is going to be easy to do or even feasible for certain people.

HSW: Okay, and how about the second level?

SKK: With the second level, the psychic level, we are dealing with telepathy, clairvoyance, spirits, reincarnation, and all the sets of beliefs that are in that area. Let's say that same person has some deep emotional problems with a sibling, and they feel that there is an emotional bond there. This is really a second-level relationship. Here we might have the person send healing and love, examine past life relationships with that person, and heal those in the present moment by using combinations of telepathy or clairvoyance. We might even have them do some Hawaiian forms of feng shui work in order to change the energy flows between them, working with what we call the *aka threads.*

The third level, the shamanic level, is the area where we do the journeys, working with dreams and perceptions of life as a dream. Let's say this person wants to increase his or her prosperity—because when we talk about shamanic healing we are talking about body, mind, *and* circumstance—and that they see this as a very symbolic thing. Well, we might take them on a journey into a place called "The Garden." There we might either plant symbols of prosperity or find a symbol of their prosperity that already exists within their consciousness and work with changing that symbol. For example, you might find a broken fountain in the garden. In that case you might help them to repair that fountain.

HSW: Why does that work? How does a symbolic act such as fixing a fountain translate into prosperity in the physical world?

SKK: It translates in a lot of different ways, but one simple way of looking at it is that symbols are a language. A lot of people think that if they don't have the words that it is not real or it is not language. But symbols are a much deeper, broader language than words. So when you change the symbols in your subconscious, you are, in a sense, giving a different message to yourself about how things are, and your own subconscious responds quite profoundly. The beauty of it is that it bypasses the conscious mind so that you don't even have to know what the symbols mean or how they relate to your particular situation. You seek one, one comes up, and that's what you work with. It is a language of its own.

HSW: And the fourth level?

SKK: The mystical level is basically the beliefs of oneness. Everybody, no matter what their spiritual tradition, has these to some degree; it's just a matter of finding the things that people identify their oneness with—their children, their property, their country. Whatever it is, that's the level of relationship. Let's say this same person that we have been dealing with is having a problem with a child. This person identifies very strongly with that child—not as an emotional bond, but in a way in which there is hardly any sense of differentiation between the two of them. There are a lot of possibilities for treating this one, but one thing we might do is have that person imagine themselves as being that child and then, as the child, changing habits or changing patterns or changing behaviors.

HSW: Hmm . . . a kind of emotional shape-shift?

SKK: Right. We call this grokking. What happens in such a case is that when a person perceives that other person as himself, there is a communication that takes place. When you change one side of a relationship, both sides change.

We use this technique on things like storms as well. If there is a big storm coming towards us that we know will be very destructive, we would identify deeply with the storm. As the storm, we become aware of the storm's potential, the ways it could go, and then pick a direction that is least destructive. It's the same thing with a person. You can identify with that person, become aware of the potentials for change in that person, and then pick one that is less destructive, more productive, or whatever the goal is.

HSW: Isn't this manipulation?

SKK: No, because it doesn't work if you try that. What happens if you try to manipulate is that you are no longer identifying with the person and so you pop out of the grok. It only works if you can find something that the person is willing or desires to do. Because what you are doing is giving strength and energy to something that they already want. But, for instance, if you think somebody should stop smoking because *you* think it's bad, and you go in and try to get that person to stop, you'll be fooling yourself. If they don't want to stop, it will have no effect. You can't force anybody to do it.

HSW: How does one become proficient in doing things like grokking, dream changing, et cetera? What is the best way to train to do this kind of work?

SKK: The main tool in shaman training is working with the conscious imagination, also called "active imagination." Yes, it is important to learn how to use energy, but that energy is shaped and directed through the shaman's imagination. Most of this work is about using one's imagination. That doesn't mean that it's not real. It means you are using your mind to go beyond the appearances that you have learned. I have taught many people how to change the effects of fluorescent lights on their body by having them imagine themselves surrounded by a light that harmonizes the energy around them. Use your imagination with the belief that your subconscious can be talked to, that trees can listen and hear you and give you information back.

HSW: You said in one of your books that Westerners have an advantage over indigenous people in terms of the training we get in developing our imaginations. You say that our access to books, radio, television, and films means that we have been training ourselves for this kind of work all along.

This is a unique—and wonderful—perspective. Many people argue that these things, television especially, deadens our brains, giving us a disadvantage in doing this work.

SKK: It's not a disadvantage at all! The longest part of a shaman's training in indigenous cultures has to do with the development of the imagination. Because, really, there's not a lot that usually happens in a traditional indigenous culture. The elder who is doing the teaching has to take the apprentice and break down their bridge of perception about the way things are and get them to look beyond the patterns of things that they have become familiar with.

We in the modern world have so much that we take for granted: reading, writing, movies, television, books. It's awesome the amount of material that we absorb each day. These things give us such a rich source of material to work with. We have all of that stuff, all of those different ways of thinking, different types of behaviors, different peoples, different kinds of experiences in our memory bank to call upon, to combine and use in very creative ways. Typically, a person without those types of resources like we have in the modern world finds that a great struggle.

HSW: It's nice to know that all our technological toys have a spiritual function as well.

SKK: Now, look, I don't in any way want to put down an indigenous culture, okay? But it's important that we do take a look at what human beings in a technological culture are doing. Everybody looks at the bad side. Yes, there is a bad side and we have to heal that, no doubt about it. But, my gosh, look at the good side! People in the world today are able to help other people all the way on the other side of the world because of the communication methods we have developed. One of the things that has impressed me the most profoundly was when some country—I think it was Armenia—had a terrible earthquake. People from the United States pitched in and sent supplies over. Then when San Francisco had an earthquake a few years later, the people of Armenia sent food and clothing. Neither would ever have known about the other without our modern means of communication.

Of course, this also allows people to argue on a larger scale as well, but the benefits are just so fantastic in terms of bringing people together. More than ever before there is an awareness of the rest of the world that most individuals have never had before. There is an awful lot of good happening. It is important to remember that, even while you are aware of the old familiar bad. Because this work is not about ignoring the bad, but healing it.

HSW: Let's get back to imagination. Now, just developing a good imagination is only part of mastering these techniques, right? In your teachings you talk about motivation and confidence as two of the most important things for the shaman to learn.

SKK: Well, confidence in particular. That's behind all of it. You can use imagination and visualization until you are blue in the face, but until you actually have a confident expectation of creating a change, nothing is going to happen. The power is there when you accept it as a truth. And that's all about confidence.

Now, motivation has to do with energized intent. English is a difficult language because so many different words have such subtle connotations. So when we speak our intent, it's not really enough because there has to be energy behind it. There's has to be a strong desire to change something. This is what distinguishes shamanism from mysticism.

HSW: How so?

SKK: As individuals, mystics and shamans cannot be classified, of course, but as it is classically defined, "mysticism" is an acceptance of what is and, in some cases, a recognition or assumption that this world is an illusion and that it is therefore unimportant. The mystic doesn't try to change the world, only to get past and move on to something else.

Shamans, on the other hand, are the original artists of the world. And the whole point of art is change, to reinterpret, to modify, to create. Shamans are essentially change artists. So while the mystic practitioner traditionally is trying to get beyond this world, the whole point of shamanism—at least the adventurer shaman—is to turn it into a party. The essence of shamanism is changing reality, and the essence of changing reality is changing beliefs.

The other most important thing is what's behind all shamanic work, regardless of the form that you practice. What's behind all this is what we in Hawaii call the "Spirit of Aloha." That is, love. Love is why people heal; it is why the body immediately begins to heal itself when there is a problem. This is why people help each other. Wherever you find a situation where people are not filled with fear, and a crisis occurs, the first thing they do is help each other. Always. It's spontaneous, because that love is there fundamentally. It's why people leap into rivers and run into burning buildings. Human beings even help nonhumans. They help trees and rocks. Someday they will probably try to help stars in the sky! That love is so powerful, and that's why this stuff works. It's why shamanism exists, why all forms of spirituality exist, and why people move and develop and bring other people with them. That's far more powerful than all the fear-based anger. Whatever we can do to strengthen that fundamental love is going to help all of us.

Gabrielle Roth

Courtesy of Gabrielle Roth

Movement is the nature of the universe. For me, God is the dance. It's the motion of being. The energy of that is infinite, it just keeps going. There's no dogma in the dance. All you have to do is surrender yourself to the dance and let it reinvent and rearrange you.

—Gabrielle Roth

In shamanic societies, there has always been the dance. Dance was a sacred act, the sine qua non of most rituals. Tribal people would dance for hours, churning themselves into ecstasy in order to free their souls and communicate with their gods. Unlike our ancestors, our spiritual worship in the West has to a great extent become a sedentary activity, with meditation and prayer most often done in complete stillness. Rarely does the body get in on the act, and few spiritual teachers ever demand of us that we do any differently.

And then there is Gabrielle Roth. For the past thirty-five years, Roth has taken thousands of people on a shaman's journey through the rhythms of their bodies and into the rhythms of their souls. Her books, workshops, and music recordings provide a context in which the spirit and flesh come together as one and dance like lovers upon a stage. Through the 5Rythms, her self-styled form of ecstatic trance dance, Roth uses movement to reignite shamanic ecstasy in a culture and people that have become trapped in a kind of physical and emotional inertia. Roth guides her students on an adventure into the often unexplored, sometimes daunting, region of their own psyches, and brings them back into alignment with the rhythm of their own souls.

Several years ago, I attended one of Roth's workshops. Over the course of the weekend, the boundaries between our bodies, our egos, and our souls became more and more diffuse. I watched myself and my fellow students move from self-consciousness to selflessness; from the agony of excruciatingly uncomfortable movement patterns that we had never cultivated within ourselves—or worse, had been taught to repress—to the ecstasy of rhythmic liberation.

"Put your psyche in motion," Roth says, "and it will heal itself."

Gabrielle Roth is the author of Maps to Ecstasy, Sweat Your Prayers, *and her latest book,* Connections. *She is the artistic director of her dance/theater/music company, The Mirrors; and through her recording company Raven Records (cofounded with her husband, Robert Ansell) has produced more than twenty music compilations, considered to be on the cutting edge of shamanic trance dance music.*

Hillary S. Webb: When I first asked you to be a part of this project, you said that the timing was perfect because, as you said, "We need a new vision for the shaman." What did you mean by that?

Gabrielle Roth: We need to bring the shamanic model into the twenty-first century. People today are still very reliant upon indigenous cultures, indigenous models, indigenous pictures of what a shaman is. Although the work of a shaman is timeless, the form of it, the theater of it, the energy of it will have to change because shamanism is indigenous to its time and place. It uses the symbols, moves to the rhythms, celebrates the blessings, and addresses the wounds of a particular culture at a particular time. I love the Deer Dance, but I'm much more likely to be deeply touched and catalyzed by experiencing a Sam Shepherd play, reading a Patti Smith poem, or dancing my brains out to a U2 song. In my own contemplation of shamanism, I have found it useful to define it as the transformation of cultural and personal neurosis into creative form.

And the word "shaman" is heavy. One of the things that really disturbed me about the word in the beginning of my investigations was that, if you had shamanic energy, it was either so special that no mere mortal *could* be it, or so weird that no one would *want to* be it. And those two poles defined shamanism in Western culture, or at least in *puritanical*, Christian Western cultures. In the West, it has to be whipped up into some really fancy Carlos Castaneda hallucinogenic trip for people to be interested. Otherwise, there is a lot of mystery about it, and people don't like mystery. People like *People* magazine. They like glossy.

HSW: The last dictionary I looked in gave the definition of "shaman" as someone who is a fraud.

GR: Oh God, that is even worse.

HSW: I have a dictionary on hand, so let's see what it says. Okay, this is from the American Heritage Dictionary. *Shaman: "A member of certain tribal societies who mediates between the visible and spirit worlds for purposes of healing, divination, and control over natural events." Well, hey, that's not too bad!*

GR: That's very cool.

HSW: That's certainly the best one I have ever seen. This is a new diction-

ary, too. Perhaps that is a sign of the times, a sign that we in this culture are reexamining who or what a shaman is.

GR: If I were to add something to that definition, I would say that shamanism is the ordinary act of being extraordinary.

HSW: While at the same time letting go of the expectation of wanting or needing some Big Vision every day to feel connected, and just allowing life in its simplicity to move you.

GR: Yes. In functional terms, a shaman is the center of the tribal ceremonies, the keeper of the tribal secrets, and the healer of the tribal wounds. Underneath that, I think that the work of the shaman has always been the work of the spirit and the work of the soul. It's about not dividing one's own spiritual self from other parts of oneself. You know, dividing things into "This is my spirit and this is my work." Or "This is my religion and this is real life." "This" is all bullshit! All of it is one possibility. It's one inhale and one exhale. It's one dance. We have to reclaim spiritual practice in our ordinary lives. Everything is spiritual practice when you have your head on right. You can't say, "This is spiritual practice, that isn't." It's all spiritual practice.

HSW: What are your feelings about the word "shaman" at this point? Do you have resistance to talking about your work in those terms?

GR: None at all. At least, not for myself. But you do want to talk to whomever you are with. For a while there, I was feeling like I had to constantly educate audiences about shamanism, and meanwhile, I had a lot of work to do, and I could do it without even mentioning the word "shamanism." Because of that, I just kept it Zen, kept it down to its bare bones. But shamanism is rooted in movement and rhythm, and so anyone who really understands the shamanic paradigm will see it right away in the work that I do. I've never compromised any of the energies of the work. It was just a matter of lifting the veil of language.

We are much more wounded than we were in the beginning. Or maybe our egos are just bigger. We need to shift our identification from our ego concerns to the needs and nourishment of the soul.

Traveling between the Worlds

Nowadays we live in a divided world with less awe, less wonder, less harmony. In the beginning, shamans were probably very busy dealing with the bigger picture, trying to understand their place in the world from a place of innocence and awe and sacredness. We've even lost our place within ourselves. Not only are we dismembered from the world, from the universe, but our bodies are disconnected from our hearts and our minds, leaving us in a state of dismemberment and dysfunction.

HSW: You have talked about movement as "the medicine that heals the split between our minds and hearts, bodies, and soul."

GR: Movement is the nature of the universe. For me, God is the dance. It's the motion of being. The energy of that is infinite, it just keeps going. There's no dogma in the dance. All you have to do is surrender yourself to the dance and let it reinvent and rearrange you.

HSW: Going within to take us without?

GR: In my point of view, in shamanic trance work, we are not going "out there." We are going "in there." We are going deeper and deeper into the spirit of all things. The body is the door, the gateway through which we can move into these other dimensions. When you are dancing in trance, you are not going "Somewhere Else." "Somewhere Else" is already inside you. You are just arriving somewhere inside the big "Somewhere Else." And if you keep going inside, then eventually inside becomes outside. We are turning ourselves inside out. That is a shamanic journey.

I think part of my mission has been to create the maps that allow people to go from the surface of themselves to the deeper inner core in a way that they could document their journey in their own voice, with their own gifts.

HSW: Instead of trying to force ourselves into some kind of model that we think we should be.

GR: There is nowhere to go when you are trying to be something that you are not. In my practice, there is no right and wrong. You use whatever you are feeling. Say you are having a very bad day and you are feeling frustrated. Why try to bypass the frustration? Frustration is energy. Instead, you can take that frustration and embody it, turn it into a dance. By really going inside of it and letting it move you, it becomes the vehicle that takes you to the next space. If you deny your frustration, it becomes a part of a lie. And the body can't lie; it can only tell the truth. If you don't allow it to tell the truth, then the lies goes deeper and deeper and deeper inside until we no longer know what the truth is.

HSW: And a lie that is repressed . . .

GR: It becomes depression on some level, because you have depressed your own responses to life. Throughout life, we keep evolving and growing. But to deny who you are is almost a "de-volution," a regression. You can't go forward if you are dragging the heaviness of that lie with you. That is why movement is so profound. It carries you directly to the core of your own self and into what is real for you.

HSW: Is that why many people in our culture are so afraid of their bodies? We are afraid of the deeply hidden truth that we might find out about ourselves?

GR: The body is Pandora's box. It holds all the things that we have been denying. People are afraid to tap into that because there is a possibility that your ego will be very unhappy with what you find out. Because whatever it is geared to do—to please, to perform, whatever its operational instructions have been—if you are true to restoring your soul, it will fuck with your ego and that will cause distress.

HSW: So instead of facing that potential distress, the ego takes charge of the body and, as you also say, "egos don't dance."

GR: No, egos don't dance. They strut. They perform.

HSW: They are self-conscious.

GR: Actually, the ego does dance, but its dance is completely repetitive. It is never original. It is always either about being seen or not being seen. It is fully self-conscious in one way or the other. It doesn't just give itself up to the dance.

HSW: It puts up a barrier between ourselves and the spirit that moves us— from which we access our own individuality and power.

GR: The deeper we dance, the deeper we breathe; the deeper we breathe, the deeper we live. It's all just so simple.

HSW: Though maybe easier to say than to do.

GR: Self-consciousness around the dance seems to be particularly Western. In many cultures it is part of the actual cultural paradigm. Like in Africa, or Indonesia, or India. Those are cultures that are still dancing as a response to everything. They grieve, they dance. They celebrate, they dance. Whatever it is, they dance. Dance is the embodiment of history. But anyone who has been Westernized, that is where you will find the self-consciousness because of the split between spirit and flesh that has occurred. We have created a world of shadow dancers.

HSW: Meaning what?

GR: Dark and light are one. It's an amazing place of beauty to be in the dark or in the light. Then there is the shadow, which is that edgy world that separates those two things. That's the ego place. The shadow dance is a very different one from the dance that happens when we go within and allow the dance to take us without, where we are constantly dissolving the contraries, dissolving that field of duality and just giving it all up to our truth.

HSW: In Maps to Ecstasy *you talk about the goal of movement as getting us to the "still point." Is that where this state of nonduality can occur?*

GR: That's right. When I dance, there is this place that I get to where I, Gabrielle, disappear. In that place there is no effort. I am tuned in to everything. That place is the rhythm of stillness, where you are inside the movement. This is the place where all the contraries dissolve, and movement and stillness become one energy. That still point is a place of deep inner peace, but where everything is in motion—just moving at a different speed. It's a paradox, of course, but in everything is the seed of its apparent opposite. When you get to that place, you've moved into that transitional world where all polarities disappear.

HSW: All duality is dissolved.

GR: All duality is dissolved. I read a sign recently that said, "If you are not living on your edge, you are taking up too much space."

HSW: Is the shaman someone who lives on that edge at all times?

GR: I don't think anybody is anything at all times, but a shaman knows how to get there and back. That's why they create maps to help other people do the same.

HSW: That is a key idea that I would like to point out, because it is what makes shamanism so profound for me. That is, it is about putting the power back in the hands of the individual. That's a pretty radical idea for a lot of people. One of the things that I see so much, that I find particularly discouraging, is that most people don't see that sacredness within themselves. Instead, we try to put it onto someone else who we deem to be more "holy" than we are. People have lost touch with the power of their own souls.

GR: Yes. Everything is holy, and everyone is holy. Anything other than that is a duality, and in that duality is a very painful dance. It is a dance of separation, of deep and profound disconnection from what is so and from what is true.

HSW: As you talk about all of this—rhythm, motion, stillness—I think of an experience that I had several years ago. I was on a ship and we were sailing through some pretty rough seas. It was stormy and the waves were really tossing us around. I happened to be standing by this one little girl who was seasick. She was really miserable. One of the crewmen came up to her and said, "Don't fight the waves. That will only make you feel worse. Dance with them."

I take what that crewman said as a metaphor for life in general. If we try to control everything that is happening around us, if we are

fighting against whatever rhythms the world is throwing at us, we will
be miserable. We will get sick. If we just let the rhythm of the world lead
us like a dance partner who we trust knows the steps better than we do,
we can achieve grace.

GR: That is a beautiful story. I totally agree. I had a workshop at
Esalen Institute many years ago when there was a severe, six-point
earthquake. We were dancing Chaos at the time the earthquake
took place, and none of us felt it. When we went out on the deck
afterwards, all the other people were clinging to their seats, clinging
to the deck, they were all white and shaky. We hadn't experienced
it because we had been inside of it.

HSW: *Like being inside the eye of a hurricane. Another stillpoint.*

GR: We were the same energy as the earthquake, dancing in that
chaotic pattern.

HSW: *And then it becomes fun. Easy.*

GR: It was. Of course, afterwards you think, "Oh God, that was a
fucking earthquake!" But to go with things is so much easier than
to try to prevent them from happening.

HSW: *Many spiritual traditions are based—to varying degrees—on the*
idea that the universe is made up of various vibrations, a kind of
vibrational stew. The same belief is a basis of a lot of theories of quan-
tum physics. The rhythms you talk about fall into that metaphor very
neatly.

GR: Absolutely. All movement is patterns and waves and cycles. It's
all vibrations, really. That's why you aim to reach the fixed points
around which everything is fluid. In shamanic work, we are looking
for how to adapt ourselves to the laws that govern these vibrations,
how to become them, how to get inside them. Those principles govern the motion of the dance, and we can use those as markers on the
way to a magical, whimsical emptiness.

All healing boils down to loving yourself enough to care for
yourself. We need to ask, "Am I worthy of my own attention?" My
work has become a search for how to heal these broken pieces, how

to heal this dismemberment, how to weave together the parts of the soul, the self. For me, the soul is not an elusive energy. It exists fully when the body, the heart, and the mind are unified. When all that becomes one unified field, then we are soulful. The only way to be a holy person is to be a whole person. And that's the goal of any true shamanic work.

Brant Secunda

Courtesy of Brant Secunda

The role of the human being is to maintain the balance between Earth and sky. To pray for the rain so that it does rain. To pray for the Sun so that the Sun returns each morning. People in the modern world have forgotten this. That is why we have polluted rivers, and why we can't breathe the air that we were given. We are here to make ceremonies, to pray for the Earth, to pray for the gods.

—Brant Secunda

In 1970, the day after his high school graduation, Brant Secunda left his parents' house in Brooklyn, New York, and made his way down to Ixtlan, Mexico, on a quest to find don Juan, the shaman made famous by the books of Carlos Castaneda. Once in Ixtlan, he learned of a village a five-day walk away, where he was told he could meet and study with a shaman.

On the third day of his walk into the jungle mountains, Secunda wandered down a deer trail and become lost and disorientated, eventually passing out from dehydration and sun exposure.

"The next thing I knew, I was having these visions of circles of light surrounding me," Secunda says. "Inside the circles were all kinds of birds and animals—tigers, pumas, like that. In the very center was a deer. I was dying, and all the animal powers were there to help me feel my connection to Creation."

Not long after, he was awakened by a group of Indians standing over him, sprinkling water on his face.

"They asked me why was I lying there like some drunk," Secunda says with a laugh.

As it turned out, the Indians were Huichols, part of a small tribe said to be the last people in North America to have maintained their pre-Columbian traditions. Eventually Secunda became the apprentice to don Jose Matsuwa, one of the tribe's most well respected shamans. For the next twelve years, Secunda immersed himself in the teachings of Huichol shamanism, a tradition famous for its miraculous healing and ceremonial practices.

Today Brant Secunda is a shamanic healer and ceremonial leader in the Huichol Indian tradition. The founder of the Dance of the Deer Foundation Center, Secunda teaches ongoing, in-depth study groups on Huichol shamanism and leads pilgrimages to sacred sites around the world.

Brant Secunda: The main focus of Huichol shamanism is health and healing. In their own language, the Huichol are called *Virarca*, which means "the healing people."

In the Huichol tradition there are two types of shaman: singing shamans and healing shamans. The healing shamans are doctors. The Huichols heal by going into a mild trance, during which they travel into the *Nierika*—the doorway that connects our heart to all of

Creation. There the shaman would talk to the deer spirit and ask for guidance as to what to do for the person. The shaman then might brush grass or a feather, or something like that, over the patient. This acts like an X-ray machine so that the shaman can look inside the body. Ideally, the patient should look clear, like a crystal. Where the energy is not clear—where there's darkness—is where the illness is. Once the location of the illness is identified, the shaman will send the spirit of the deer inside the patient. It is the deer that really performs the healing for the shaman. In the Huichol tradition, the deer is used as the intermediary because it understands the language of the gods. Also, the deer is the animal most suited to be a human being's ally. A wolf, for example, is too wild for a human being to work with, but a human being and a deer have the same energy

Once the deer spirit has done the healing, the shaman will suck the illness out of the patient's body. Often the sickness will come out of the body in the form of a stone or a bone or a worm or blood— something that would defy our model of reality. The shaman will spit that out and immediately give it to the Earth or to the fire to be purified.

Hillary S. Webb: Can any illness be healed in this way?

BS: The Huichols say that nothing is impossible for the gods to heal. Don José once healed a man who had slashed his Achilles tendon with a machete. Normally, the man would never walk again, but within a month after the healing he was back walking out in his cornfield with only a very slight limp. I met my wife when she came to me for a healing. She had a fatal form of hepatitis and because she couldn't eat, she weighed about seventy-seven pounds. After the healing, she gained thirty pounds in two weeks. Then there was another case that I worked on that is the only documented case of pancreatic cancer reversing itself.

It's important to realize that, to the Huichols, the idea of healing includes not only personal healing, but planetary healing as well. The Huichols see themselves as responsible for the well-being of the Earth, for maintaining a balance between Earth and sky. Performing ceremonies throughout the year helps maintain this balance—ceremonies for the crops, for planting the corn, for harvesting the corn. That's why the singing shamans are the most revered in the Huichol tradition. Because through chants, through ceremonies, through drums, through dance, they are singing the balance of the world and continuing the well-being of Mother Earth and all her relations.

HSW: How does rattling, drumming, and so on help continue the well-being of the Earth?

BS: The role of the human being is to maintain the balance between Earth and sky. To pray for the rain so that it does rain. To pray for the Sun so that the Sun returns each morning. People in the modern world have forgotten this. That is why we have polluted rivers, and why we can't breathe the air that we were given. We are here to make ceremonies, to pray for the Earth, to pray for the gods.

People say, "What difference does it make if we pray and make ceremonies?" It makes all the difference in the world! Our prayers help to nourish the spirits. Ceremonies empower the Earth. Don José used to say, "As long as people do their ceremonies, the world will continue. People will be able to continue. If we stop ceremonies, the world will go on maybe, but without human beings."

HSW: This is something that I've never quite understood. Doesn't the Earth need us as much as we need it?

BS: Well, it's true that for the world to continue as it is, we all need each other. But when you think about it, people have only been on the planet a few million years. Human beings are really Johnny-come-latelies on the scene. The world existed before us, and it could very well go on without us. The Earth would just have to find other ways to get power.

HSW: In your workshops you teach that there are four "powers" that must be achieved in order for someone to become effective as a shaman.

BS: The Huichols speak about the four important powers: love, which is the foundation of all four; physical power; psychic power; and intelligence. According to this tradition, for a person to be a truly powerful human being, he or she must develop these four powers equally. Being a shaman is not just about having visions and psychic powers. If someone has strong vision, but is not acting right in their everyday life, then they are not considered as powerful as someone who is also considered a kind, loving person. Mastery of these four powers is what makes a great shaman truly great.

HSW: Let's go through each one. You said the foundation of all power is love. So tell me, what is love?

BS: Love is the nurturing power that keeps the universe and our own existence together. The Great Spirit created the universe with the power of love, and that love nurtures our bodies and our hearts and our spirits. It makes us whole. Love is the nourishing power that sustains us. Without that love, none of us would live, and we couldn't give back to the Earth in return.

Of course, love is also the special feeling of the heart that brings ecstasy to our existence. This ecstasy—the feeling that a human being gets when he or she is connected to the sky and to the Earth and the animals and flowers and the colors of the sunrise and sunset—is the power of love.

HSW: If love is such an important and natural part of our being, then why is it that so many of us have such a hard time giving and receiving love? This increasing tendency towards addictions, genocide, environmental degradation indicates a real lack of love in our culture, for ourselves, for each other, and for the natural world.

BS: Nobody really knows. Whenever I asked don José that question, he used to say that nobody really understands—that the gods and goddesses work very mysteriously. In a mixed-up way, I think it helps instill in a human being the idea of faith. The idea of faith is a hard point to grasp, especially for people who don't believe in a higher power. I know a lot of people who say, "How can there be a God? Look at all the sickness and cancer and religious wars that have happened." There is no real answer for that, really. You just have to believe it in your heart and experience for yourself the power and the joy and the love of the Creation Spirits.

HSW: I think that was what Kierkegaard was getting at when he said, "If I am capable of grasping God objectively I do not believe. But precisely because I cannot do that, I must believe."

BS: That's a good one. And faith also helps us to believe in the natural world. Having faith in the spiritual powers of nature helps to instill love in our hearts. Seeing colors helps us be more in love with the world around us. It creates a special feeling of love and harmony. Bliss, basically. Because if you look at a beautiful flower, you feel beautiful.

HSW: Is this what is meant by seeing with one's heart?

BS: Yes. The Huichol path is also known as "The Way of the Heart," which means learning to experience the world with your heart. It means seeing with the heart, hearing with the heart, feeling with the heart, speaking through the heart. In this tradition we translate that even further and say that since the deer is the symbol for the heart, then we are speaking through the deer. If the deer, who is the messenger of the gods, is speaking through us, then the gods are speaking to us through the deer. It's very profound, when you think about it.

HSW: Living from the heart is a real challenge for those of us brought up in Western society. We are taught from a very early age to think in terms of what is "reasonable" or "rational." How do those of us who have to exist and function in this mind-dominant world still keep our hearts open and connected to Spirit?

BS: Just do it. Just live through your heart. The idea is not to think in an intellectual, analytical way, but to try to experience our world through feelings and emotions, which are the mediums of the heart. We should try to experience our world more objectively and not subjectively analyze everything that comes before us. If you see an eagle, it is an eagle. Don't think, "What does that eagle mean?" Just experience the world as it is. Be in it and just be quiet. Stop the mind. Stop the internal dialogue and just be. And that's what really amazed me about the Huichols. They are much quieter internally than we are. In the modern world, there is so much going on that we don't always quiet our minds.

HSW: And the Nierika? *Earlier you referred to it as a doorway from the heart to the Spirit and an essential part of the Huichol shaman's healing process.*

BS: The *Nierika* is the doorway, a portal that connects our heart and our spirit to the four directions and to the Upper World. In the Huichol cosmology there are five directions—the fifth direction being the *Nierika*—the sacred center that connects us to the other four. Don José explained the *Nierika* to me as the sacred face of the Divine; a mirror reflecting back the knowledge of the ancient ones. When you go into the *Nierika*, you connect this world to a hidden world, a place that allows a human being to speak to the gods. A lot of the work that I do with people, especially in the on-going groups, is teaching them how to travel into the *Nierika*.

HSW: The second of the four powers you say is physical power.

BS: Physical power is pretty evident. It simply means making our bodies as strong as possible. The Huichols are very physical people. They live outdoors, so they naturally have a physical strength. They consider it normal to be physically strong.

Making our bodies strong also helps us develop a relationship to the Earth. By feeling your body connected to Mother Earth, one becomes naturally empowered. In the Huichol villages, there's no running water. They have to go down to a spring, put the water in gourds, and carry the gourds up on their heads. And they love it. Going to gather water, making their bodies strong, is an important part of their life. It is part of what it means to be a Huichol. The whole act combines spirituality with secular life.

HSW: And how about the third—psychic power? In your workshops, you talk about how during your apprenticeship don José had you eat nothing but fruit for fourteen months as a way of developing your psychic abilities.

BS: Taking on a special diet is one way to develop psychic powers. Another way is to fast for long periods of time. Another way is to give up sexual contact. That way you are focusing all your energy on spiritual endeavors so that you are able to learn to see and feel and listen to the gods. Another way to develop psychic powers is by learning to find harmony; by doing exercises to give away negativity—such as fear or jealousy. Once you are rid of this, you are able to hear the gods. Because if you are so focused on, say, anger, how can you hear what the gods have to tell you?

HSW: Of course, we should mention that the Huichols are well known for their worship and use of the peyote cactus as a means of gaining access to the spirit realm. This is an important part of their tradition.

BS: The Huichols go once a year to the land of peyote known as Wirikuta. There we ingest peyote in order to learn from the gods and learn to communicate with the spirit world. The peyote opens us up to visions.

I do want to emphasize, however, that that is only *one* way. A lot of anthropologists focus on the peyote part of Huichol shamanism, but that is only one part of the whole picture. Things like rattling, drumming, chanting, and dancing produce a similar shift in consciousness by bringing out our good spirit, our good self, and help to make us whole people.

HSW: What do you mean by our "good self"?

BS: It's who we truly are. We are happy, powerful human beings. All this other stuff—anger, fear, jealousy—is not really who we are. This is totally different from the Christian cosmological perspective that says we are born with sin; that we are really bad. In Huichol shamanism, we believe that human beings are powerful. That we all have part of the gods living inside of us. That's what I mean when I say that we are trying to become as perfect as possible, and that's why we do exercises to purify ourselves. We try to purify ourselves in order to become purer, more powerful human beings.

One of the objectives or goals of having ceremonies is to get into that "perfect" ecstatic state—to be able to leave your imperfections behind, at least for the duration of the ceremony. The Huichols say that it is important to act in a good way, and that trying hard is the most important thing. But shamans are just normal people. They make mistakes like everyone else. The difference is that there's no

Heaven or Hell in the Huichol cosmology. If a Huichol does something wrong, he or she can absolve themselves of it through doing a ceremony to help them to start anew.

HSW: The last of the four powers you describe as the power of intelligence.

BS: In the tradition of Huichol shamanism, "intelligence" means living your life in the right way. The Huichol put it in very simple terms: If someone is hungry, you feed them. If someone needs help, you have compassion. A lot of what intelligence is about is being a compassionate person.

Right action in your life is so important, because it keeps a check on power. If you live right, if you don't abuse power, your work will create positive energy for the Earth and our environment. That is the main difference between a shaman and a sorcerer. The sorcerer is only concerned with his or her own power, and works in a very egotistical and harmful way. The shaman, on the other hand, uses his or her power to bring rain, to bring the sun, to bring balance to the community.

When you act in a good way with your power, the gods will give you more. That is why the most powerful shamans are always more powerful than the most powerful sorcerers.

HSW: As part of your work, you lead trips to places of power around the world. What can be gained by going to a place of power that someone cannot get at home?

BS: We say that these places of power are dreaming gods or dreaming goddesses who have taken on another form. These places of power, especially the strongest ones, are living beings, living spirits. They can empower. So we return to them in order to receive their blessings, their wisdom, their essence. We also go to receive *kupuri*, their energy or life force. *Kupuri* is the Huichol word for what we in this culture might call "God." It is from this energy that all the forms of God come from.

HSW: We talked a little bit before about combining spirituality and secular life through physical power. In what other ways can we bring our connection to the sacred into our daily lives?

BS: It is important to remember that shamanism is not just something that you do once in a while, it's something that you live by every day. I try to live my life in a sacred way. I tell my dreams to the fire every morning. I do a lot of exercises of giving away negativity and bringing in the positive. I do many healings on people every day. With every breath that I take, I try to remember the Eagle Goddess bringing in the breath of life. All day I try to think of the gods all around me, of my grandmother the ocean, and of the fire living inside of me. I try to make my life a ceremony.

Ipupiara Makunaiman

When a person gets into this work they begin to see amazing things happen—things that from a Western world perspective are too much to be true and too much to believe. But if you really change your way of thinking and just allow yourself to be a tool in Mother Earth's hands, you can do miracles.

—Ipupiara Makunaiman

Ipupiara Makunaiman was born into the Ureu-eu-wau-wau, a remote Brazilian tribe whose name translates into "people from the stars." According to legend, his people originally came from a planet near the Pleiades. A prophet among them predicted that the inhabitants of a distant planet named Earth were doomed—destined to consume themselves into extinction. As the story goes, the emissaries traveled to Earth, materializing into human form in the Amazon, where they would await the time when they were to spread their message of salvation.

Ipupiara, whose name means "freshwater dolphin," is one of the last few members of this once well-populated tribe. By 1997 only forty-three of the Ureu-eu-wau-wau people survived—decimated by the encroachment of the logging industry. When he was a young man, Ipupiara's mother insisted that he help his people by going to the white man's school. Once at the university, however, he found himself growing more and more ashamed of his indigenous heritage.

During his last year at the university, Ipupiara fell seriously ill. Despite seeing numerous doctors, he was unable to be cured using modern means. Although his mother begged him to see the local healer, Ipupiara refused, insisting that if the white doctors couldn't fix him, a shaman never could. His illness got worse, until he was unable to move or speak. Realizing he was dying, Ipupiara finally agreed to be treated by the shaman.

"When I saw the old man dancing and chanting around me, I said to myself, 'Ipupiara, you are done for,'" Ipupiara recalls. "The old man opened up my mouth and poured a bowl of bitter, greenish stuff down my throat. I felt a warmth going through my body, and then I fell asleep. When I woke up, I was hungry. In one week I was walking and talking."

From that point on, Ipupiara became a dedicated student, learning the ways of his people's shamanic tradition. Today he and his wife, Cleicha, also a skilled healer, travel the country giving lectures and workshops on indigenous wisdom.

Hillary S. Webb: The Western world is so attracted to the wisdom of the indigenous world. As someone who has lived and taught in both worlds, do you think that it is really possible for those of us brought up in this culture to fully comprehend the spiritual teachings of native people?

Ipupiara Makunaiman: What you must know is that this wisdom is universal. It doesn't belong just to the indigenous world. It belongs to all of us. Maybe when I talk to you, you can hear my accent, but the teachings that I hand down to you have no accent. They are yours. They are universal. We are all shamans. It doesn't matter where you come from. You can come from the lowlands in Brazil or China or Austria or Jamaica or Russia. You don't need to be born in the jungle or wear a bone through your nose. Even with a bow necktie a man can be a shaman.

HSW: When you say, "We are all shamans," how exactly do you mean this? Do you mean we are all "potential shamans"?

IM: No. We are all shamans. Right now. When the Creator created us, he put in our DNA, in our cellular makeup, all the information that we need. We are like a hard drive in a computer. I remember the first time I had a computer in front of me. I knew that the computer had some programs in there, but where were they? I had no idea how to access those files until someone showed me.

When we are born, we are born with all that data stored inside of us. When we wake up, when we have that awakening to work with the spirits and to work with these teachings, the first thing we have to learn is how to retrieve that data. What people have to do is to discover their particular skills. Experiment until you find the right way for you.

HSW: Because every shaman has his or her own technique.

IM: The word that stands for shaman in my language is the person who travels into different dimensions to seek for knowledge that he can bring back in order to make a change in this reality. We all can do this in different ways. Some shamans do beautiful work with fire. Personally, I know my healing power resides in stones. My wife, Cleicha, can do a lot of different healings, but the best healing you can get out of her is when she uses eggs.

And you don't have to do shamanic healings to be a shaman. There are so many different kinds of healings. As a writer, you are doing shamanic work by collecting this knowledge and putting it in a book so you can help other people. There are many different powerful skills. There are people who just talk. If they talk, they heal people.

HSW: Last year I went to a seminar that you gave on shamanic healing techniques. You were scheduled to do individual healings on people before the workshop started, but your luggage—including the sacred stones you use in your healings—had been lost at the airport. You decided to postpone the healings until you got them back. This got me wondering, what makes a sacred object sacred? What makes those particular stones that you use different from any other stone you might find?

IM: All stones for me are powerful, but the stones that I have collected and dedicated for healing purpose are the most powerful because they are part of my *mesa* [sacred medicine bundle]. Imagine that your wedding ring gets lost. If you get another one, I think it will be always be just a replacement for the one that you lost, because the first one has a lot of meaning for you. I know my stones and they know me. For years and years they have been with me, and I can get the right response from them when I work. If I were to use new stones, I would have to collect them and I would have to do a ceremony to consecrate them to my *mesa*. Any stone that you pick up is a powerful stone, but it is not your *huaca* [power object] until you dedicate it to your *mesa*. When you get that stone integrated into your sacred *mesa*, that stone is also sacred.

HSW: In other words, a relationship has to be created with that stone before a working partnership can be established. In a way, it's like the idea that anybody you see walking down the street is a potential friend, but you have get to know them, establish a connection with them, before you can really consider them a friend.

IM: Sure. Isn't that what you do? You can walk down the street and meet somebody, but that doesn't mean that that person is going to be your friend. But if your energy is in tune with that person's energy and you are compatible, then you can start to become really good friends and not just acquaintances. It is the same thing with stones.

HSW: What makes stones in general so powerful in a healing?

IM: Stones are here to heal Mother Earth—to get Mother Earth stable. In the same way, stones work very powerfully to suck up negative energy from people. In our daily life we come across so many issues that can really disturb our positive energy. When you do a healing on a person who is emotionally disturbed, if you rub the stones over the person, the stones will pick up all that emotion that is not good for that person and the person will feel okay. That negative energy stays in the surface of the stone, and if you leave the stone alone, it will destroy that negative energy. These days if you go to many psychiatrist offices, in the waiting room they will have a big bowl with pebbles. If people who are nervous or disturbed touch those stones while they wait, when they go in the office they are really in better shape. If you look around, you can see how many stones I have. A big one here, a basketful there. I need stones around me to feel right.

HSW: While you are doing a healing on someone, are you telling your stones and huacas *how you would like them to work, or are they informing you how best to use them?*

IM: That is the crucial part. When a shaman is working, he or she is just a vessel. Just recently I had a woman come to me who had cancer. I asked her "Why did you come here to see me?" She said, "Oh, because I learned from other people that you are powerful." I told her, "I am not powerful. Mother Earth is the one that is powerful. I am just the switch that will connect you with Mother Earth."

I am not the one doing the healing. You are not the one doing the healing. It is Mother Earth doing the healing. That is why, as a healer, you have to learn how to interact with the spirits. As soon as you know how to interact with spirits, it is easy for you to do healings. If I know that you are coming for a healing, I will call upon the spirit that protects me, helps me, the one that resides inside of me. I will ask them to be around me and to guide me, because I'll be just a channel. That's the reason why some traditions use hallucinogenic substances. They use hallucinogenic stuff to get disconnected from this realm. If you can block yourself to this realm here, then you can fully connect to that dimension and to the spirits. This is the best way to do a healing. The moment you get disconnected, things work. If you allow the spirits to work through you, you can do things that will surprise you.

When a person gets into this work they begin to see amazing things happen—things that from a Western world perspective are too much to be true and too much to believe. But if you really change your way of thinking and just allow yourself to be a tool in Mother Earth's hands, you can do miracles.

HSW: So I guess that makes the shaman the huaca *of Mother Earth!*

IM: Yes. That is perfect. That's really perfect.

HSW: What about faith? How much does a person's basic belief system play into the effectiveness of a healing?

IM: There is no healing possible if the person that comes for the healing has no faith. You have to come with an open heart. I don't know of any healer or shaman that can do healings on a person who is closed to it.

HSW: Total faith? No doubt whatsoever?

IM: It doesn't need to be one hundred percent faith. As long as that person accepts the *possibility* of a healing, even just a little bit, then there is a tiny space open. And through that tiny opening, a healing can occur. The other way around, no healing is possible.

HSW: There are stories about how Jesus Christ was unable to heal anyone from the town in which he was born because the people did not believe that a carpenter's son could be so powerful.

IM: That's right! Jesus was one of the great shamans that I know of, and he could only do miracles because people really believed that he could. There is a passage in the Bible where Jesus brings his best friend Lazarus back to life. Jesus was away doing his preaching, when Lazarus's sisters, Marta and Maria, sent a message telling Jesus that Lazarus was sick. Jesus didn't pay attention and Lazarus got worse. Marta and Maria sent another message, but still Jesus didn't pay attention. Four days later, Jesus finally decided to return to the city where Lazarus was living. Marta and Maria saw Jesus coming and they ran over to him and said, "Oh Master, why have you delayed so long? Lazarus, your best friend, passed away four days ago. If you were here, he would be healed." Jesus said, "Take me to where Lazarus is buried." In that time, they buried people in big caves and would roll a big stone in front of the opening. Jesus told Marta and Maria, "Remove the stone." They said, "No Master, Lazarus has been buried there for four days. His body is rotting. Millions of maggots are eating Lazarus's body right now!" Jesus repeated again, "Remove the stone." They said, "Master, don't you understand? He has been dead four days. His body is stinking." Jesus said, "Please, remove the stone." This time, Marta and Maria called people to remove the stone. When the stone was removed, Jesus went up to the main entrance of the cave and said, "Lazarus, stand up, walk out, and give me a hug." And Lazarus did.

Now, if Jesus could operate the miracle of bringing Lazarus back to life, why didn't he just say "abracadabra" or something like that and make that stone disappear? He just told Marta and Maria, "Remove that stone." That stone was the lack of faith. As soon as they had faith that he could do this, they removed the stone. With that little tiny bit of faith, Jesus could operate that miracle of bringing Lazarus back to life.

This is what happens. If you don't believe that you can be healed, don't go to a healer because he won't do anything to help you. But if you have the commitment and you put all your guts to reverse whatever you have, you'll be healed. It doesn't matter if it is cancer, an ulcer, AIDS, whatever it is. If you open your heart and allow Mother Earth to perform a healing using a shaman as a channel, you'll get healed.

HSW: If through shamanism we can cure any illness, do we need modern medicine at all?

IM: We do need medicine. But you know, our mind is the most powerful medicine of all. We can create that same chemotherapy to reverse cancer using our mind, because now even doctors know that cancer is caused by negative energy. Did you know that we don't have cancer in the rain forest? And why? Is it that we are special people? No! Western world people are just like people from the rain forest. They are made of the same ingredients, the same molecules. The problem is the negative energy created here through daily life by people living with stressful schedules, turmoil, jealousy, hate, not enjoying life—all of this. These things create distortions in your positive energy, and this can lead you to an illness.

The other day a friend of mine felt he was getting fat and decided to go on a very strict diet. He cut down on all his food and he lost a huge amount of weight. Then he got concerned that he was losing too much weight, so he decided to eat more, but he kept losing weight. Unfortunately, he looked at a book on symptoms that suggested that rapid weight loss could be caused by stomach cancer.

At the moment he thought, "I have cancer in my stomach," he created energy for generating a cancer in his stomach. When he came to me, the first thing I told him was, "Don't think negatively. Try to reverse that thinking." He went to the doctor and the doctor said that he had no cancer.

HSW: Do you think that that is a problem with the way medicine is practiced here in the West? That the doctors tend to focus on the strength of the disease instead of the ability of the person to heal themselves?

IM: The mainstream doctors are very powerful, very knowledgeable. But when they don't find a way to heal a person, they just give up. If a person comes to a doctor with a cancer, the first thing they do is say, "You have cancer. You have just two months to live." I did some healings on a woman whose doctor told her that she has only two weeks to live. When I saw this woman I knew she was going to live a long time. And she has cancer! She said to me, "Ipu, this cancer will not defeat me. I am going to be the winner." I told her, "The way you are thinking, you are reversing your cancer." Now she is feeling much better. She will probably live twenty or thirty years more, even though the doctor told her till he was blue in the face that she would not live more than two weeks.

HSW: Most people would believe that and, lo and behold, live only two weeks.

IM: Oh, yeah. They would start counting down the days! That's what happens when it is what you believe.

HSW: Having lived and worked in both worlds, do you find it more difficult to work with the spirits of a big city as opposed to the spirits of the jungle?

IM: There is no distinction. The energy in the rain forest is exactly the same that we have here. In a concrete jungle there are also healing powers. Touch the walls of this building and you can feel the power because every single molecule in this building is full of it. If you go to a wall and you put your hands on it, you can feel the energy of all those molecules. Even living in a big metropolis like

Washington, D.C., surrounded by computers and all those gadgets, we are surrounded by positive energy. What happens in the big cities, though, is that we don't really get in touch with that energy. We only get in touch with the negative energy. It's like we worship that negative energy.

Some people may say, "Ipu is wise." If that is so, I think that my wisdom comes from that I take what Mother Earth wants to give me. For instance, I don't see anything wrong with using technology. In the rain forest we have the *samauma* tree to communicate. I'll tell my friends, "There is an American woman on her way. Let me know when you see her coming." When they see you, they are going to knock on the tree and I can interpret the sounds as, "Oh, she is just about to cross the river." That's the way we have of communicating in the rain forest. Here you call me on the phone to say, "Ipu, I am on my way." It is just a different way of doing the same thing. In that same way, we can honor Mother Earth wherever we are and in whatever way we do.

Hank Wesselman, Ph.D.

© Jill Kuykendall

We're living in a time of great change. Increasing numbers of young people, midlifers, and elders are discovering that there are higher functions coded into the personal mind-body matrix. These can remain dormant throughout life, but once they are awakened they can transform us utterly.

—Hank Wesselman, Ph.D.

95

Anthropologist Hank Wesselman has been described by his peers as possessing "the sober objectivity of the trained scientist with the mystic's passionate search for the deeper understanding." As is evidenced by Wesselman's writings and teachings, when these two polarities unite, amazing things have a way of unfolding. When asked, Wesselman himself maintains that "when these two sides of myself began to come together, my whole life changed a great deal."

Hank Wesselman's introduction to the spiritual traditions of the indigenous peoples began as a Peace Corps volunteer, during which time he lived and worked among the Yoruba tribe in Nigeria, West Africa. In the 1970s, while doing anthropological research in southern Ethiopia, Wesselman began to experience spontaneous and dramatic expanded states of awareness that defied any scientific explanation. In order to understand these experiences, Wesselman began to investigate the time-tested methodology of traditional shamans. After moving to Hawaii with his family, Wesselman underwent a series of spontaneous altered states in which his consciousness merged with a man existing in an alternate world. Further exploration revealed that the man, named Nainoa, is one of Wesselman's descendants, living five thousand years in the future. His experiences with Nainoa are described in his books, Spiritwalker: Messages from the Future, Medicinemaker: Mystic Encounters on the Shaman's Path, *and* Visionseeker: Shared Wisdom from the Place of Refuge.

In the introduction to Spiritwalker, *the first of the series, Wesselman writes: "Scientists tend to focus on their goals within an exclusively scientific, intellectual view of the world. I am no exception. I mention this to show that I was in no way preprogrammed for what was to occur. In fact, my scientific training and prejudices would seem to have preprogrammed me against having such an experience."*

Because of this, Wesselman, like many in what he calls the "transformational community," suspects that most of us are born with a kind of "spiritual program" on our genetic code—our DNA. What we need to do, he says, is learn to "double click" that program to access states that can take each of us beyond the realm of ordinary consciousness. Wesselman now offers experiential seminars and workshops in shamanism at places such as the Esalen Institute in California and Omega Institute in New York State. His newest book is The Journey to the Sacred Garden: A Guide to Traveling in the Spiritual Realms.

Hillary S. Webb: You have said that you consider yourself to be a part of the current "transformational community." Explain what you mean by a "transformational community."

Hank Wesselman: I think of us as the transformational community because we are the people who are acting as a bridge between what *was* and what *is coming into being*. Spirituality, like everything else, is changing. My work in evolutionary biology, my research, and my meetings with remarkable people in the transformational community over the past thirty years have led me to suspect that there are countless numbers of evolutionary sleepers out there in the mainstream of humanity. These people may contain within themselves an extraordinary biological energetic program on their "inner hard drive," which, once "double clicked," can reveal who and what we can all become as the human species continues its ascent towards the culmination of our evolution.

Evolution simply means *change*. And we're living in a time of great change. Increasing numbers of young people, midlifers, and elders are discovering that there are higher functions coded into the personal mind-body matrix. These can remain dormant throughout life, but once they are awakened they can transform us utterly. The inner fieldwork of the Eastern mystic suggests that these timing mechanisms involve the ductless glands, the brain, and the heart; and once these centers are activated, they can enlighten the whole body, which in turn often undergoes striking changes. Current research has revealed that the actual physical structure of the brain, the cerebrum, can be changed in as little as fifteen minutes in response to a powerful altered state experience. Which means that the old adage that the brain is fully formed by the time you're three years old and it's "all downhill from there" is a myth.

The indigenous people have developed families of techniques for altering consciousness in specific ways. These techniques constitute a form of technology. We could call it the "technology of transcendence," "technology of transformation," or a "technology of the sacred."

At this particular time, the human species as a whole has not experienced the triggering of these higher functions. There are those rare individuals out there in the mainstream who stand before us as signposts, as prototypes of what humankind may become when the whole population awakens and crosses an evolutionary threshold to become a new species.

This is not fantasy on my part, but rather a very real phenomenon, which is known to students of evolution as "speciation." When it happens quickly, it is called "punctuated equilibrium." It may be that we are currently on a threshold where we could make that jump.

HSW: Will we recognize this evolutionary leap when it happens? Has evolution speeded up so much that we will be able to step back and really see where we were compared to where we are now? Evolution is usually such a slow process.

HW: Well, you know this is a time of ever-increasing change and transition. The millennium change has given us a certain perspective hasn't it? When we went from the second millennium into the third, a lot of people took stock of who they are, where they're at, what's not working in their lives, where they'd like to be, what's coming up, and so forth and so on. And this is encouraging change.

In the late eighties an anonymous Gallup Poll revealed that as many as one out of every two of us has had an involuntary paranormal experience at some point in our lives. This indicates that as the population awakens from the consensus slumber of culture at large—in which everyone is anesthetized by television and hypnotized by the glitter of our gadgets—our life experiences can change dramatically. It is then that we can begin to manifest a true hero's journey, one that can lead us into direct experience of Spirit. And as most of us discover, this experience becomes possible only through the doorway of the heart, through the experience of compassion.

HSW: Looking at our current world situation, it's hard to imagine that we have really come closer to that kind of universal compassion and understanding that you are talking about.

HW: More and more people are becoming aware of Paul Ray and Sherry Anderson's book called the *Cultural Creatives: How Fifty Million People Are Changing the World*. Fifty million people represents more than twenty-five percent of the population. These people hold a very different system of beliefs and values than those out there in the mainstream. These are people who know that there are alternate realities. These are people who know that it is possible for individuals to learn how to go into these alternate realities to accomplish various things, initially on behalf of themselves, and increasingly on behalf of other people. These are folks that believe in the existence of the spirit helpers and spirit teachers that indigenous people know so much about. Curiously, although most of them are streaming away from our organized religions in droves, they all express beliefs in some kind of cosmic consciousness or godlike being. In addition, Jesus of Nazareth is viewed as an important spiritual teacher whether or not the believer is psychologically Christian.

These are folks who believe in the existence of a field of power. In anthropology it is called "animatism"—an animating force that fills and enlivens everything with a force that is very highly dispersed throughout the universe, but very densely concentrated in living beings as life force. This is the *mana* of the Polynesians, the *chi* or the *qi* of the Chinese, Korean, and Japanese traditions. I believe part of the reason that the *Star Wars* trilogy was so popular is that we all knew that The Force was real.

Now, this perception of an animating force that is found within everything everywhere leads to a very strong conviction that everything is connected to everything else. This in turn leads to an almost ritual comprehension and understanding of Nature—"Nature" has a capital "N" in our book. Virtually all of us in the transformational community are deeply concerned with stopping corporate polluters, finding the limits to short-term gain so that we can discover the long-term ecological sustainability on which the future of our civilization and species depends, et cetera, et cetera, et cetera. We are very environmentally savvy.

HSW: You'd have to be. If one acknowledges that there is no distinction between Nature and us, that all is one, then one must also accept that what we do to the natural world we likewise do to ourselves.

HW: And of course this brings up the whole arena of relationship. Relationships are more important than material gain for members of the transformational community. There is no question about this. They have a deeply humanistic perspective. They are deeply concerned with the issues of women and children, the issues of minorities, the issues of the elderly. Members of the transformational community are deeply concerned with the well-being of everyone everywhere on all levels of society. They watch what is going on in our current world situation and are aghast at what is happening. They are aware that what we've really got on our hands is a crisis of leadership at every level of the world corporate system and in our political leadership as well.

HSW: Tell me, do you think that this modern mystical movement is signaling an end to "rationalism"?

HW: You've asked a big question. I read an interesting book written by a historian named Richard Sellin called *The Spiritual Gyre*. He has proposed that the idea that Western civilization has developed in a linear fashion is an erroneous one. He believes instead that civilization develops in cycles that tend to repeat themselves every two thousand years. The first great cycle took place during the Neolithic period—a cycle that came to an end with the emergence of the first city-states among the Sumerians. This gave rise to the next cycle, which was dominated by the Akkadian Empire—the Babylonians, the Hittites, and the Assyrians, the Egyptians to the south, and so forth.

That cycle essentially ended with the collapse of the Roman Empire two thousand years ago. Which means that we are coming to the end of another cycle right now. What is interesting is that at the end of the last cycle, a new religion came into being: Christianity. And this became the dominant religion in the West for the next two thousand years. Sellin describes the first phase of our current two-thousand-year cycle as a "Theocratic Phase." During this second,

"Secular Phase," truth was determined by divine direction from God, then interpreted through a politicized and beaurocracized priesthood. This phase lasted about fourteen hundred years, coming to an end with the Renaissance. That's when scientific rationalism—the rise of science, the rise of intellectualism—first appeared. During this phase, religion was generally discredited and truth was redefined within a new mythology: science. This phase has lasted for about three hundred years. The current spiritual reawakening suggests that it has come to a close, and we have moved into the third and final phase of the two-thousand-year cycle: a "Spiritual Phase" in which science and spirituality will be woven together in an attempt to transcend both previous phases.

HSW: And then?

HW: I think that it is highly probable that all of the world religions are going to cease to function within the next two to three hundred years, and that a new kind of religion is going to take form—one that will most likely become the dominant world religion for the next two-thousand-year cycle. That's why what you are doing and what I am doing is so interesting. We are spreading the seeds, so to speak, seeds that may take form as the next religion. And this next religion will not be about organized *anything*. If there is one thing that the people in the transformational community don't like, it is organized religion! What they want is the direct transformative experience of the sacred that defines the mystic. It is no longer about belief. It's no longer about faith. It's about direct experience.

HSW: When you explain it like that, I can really see how science and spirituality come together. Up to this point we have had to be content with basing our spiritual beliefs on faith, while "rationalism" and science demand empirical evidence. To bring those two together is tremendous.

HW: Ken Wilber has proposed that the four levels of spiritual unfolding are belief, faith, direct experience, and personal transformation. The work that you and I are doing is really about the third and fourth levels, because we have gone beyond belief and faith. You can have mythic beliefs, magical beliefs, scientific beliefs, and rational beliefs, but beliefs usually fail to transform us in the end. They fail to carry us. After ten or fifteen years, nothing changes. That is where faith steps in. Faith soldiers on when belief fails to compel us anymore. And faith can take us in one of two different directions. In one, it can spiral us back down into belief. That is fundamentalism, the dark side of religion, in my opinion. In the other direction, faith takes you to the third stage of spiritual unfolding: direct experience. And when you have had direct experience of Spirit, it moves you immediately into the fourth and final stage: personal transformation. And *that* is the goal. Once people have been brought into direct connection with their inner sources of wisdom and power, they change considerably because they experience authentic initiation.

HSW: You write that the goal of the spiritual quest is "not about clearing up the mystery, it's about making the mystery clear." It's a wonderful line. What exactly does it mean?

HW: I got it from a Zen master named Robert Aitken Roshi. He said, "Our job is not to clear up the mystery, it is to make the mystery clear." You see, it is all a mystery. The entire thing. The universe, the galaxy, you, me, talking over the telephone—it's all a part of an incredible mystery. And this is what intrigues us. This is what draws us. This is what fires us up to continue on the quest.

HSW: But what exactly is the difference between "clearing up the mystery" and "making the mystery clear"?

HW: Let me put it this way. When I go to conferences, there are individuals who love to get up on stage and wow people with their PowerPoint presentations. What they are trying to do is to "clear up the mystery." They like to get inside people's heads and move things around. They've become today's evangelists, in a sense. I don't try to move things around in people's heads. What I want to do is double click that program on their inner hard drive and get them involved personally in the mystery. That's what it is all about. When we experience the mystery directly, we make it our own.

HSW: Are we are at a level of consciousness where we can "make the mystery clear"? I mean, are we really able to comprehend the true nature of reality and our place within that framework? Doesn't it usually end up being an individual projection, as if we are looking into a deep, dark pool and seeing only the reflection of ourselves on the surface?

HW: Yes, we can comprehend it. As we've said, we are living in a time of ever-escalating change. This change is being facilitated by a worldwide communication system, and a high technology the likes of which has never been seen before. I think the possibility of transformation is absolutely enormous. It is happening on a societal scale. Once a critical mass is achieved, everything will begin to shift in new directions.

When people dwell overly on the negative and start saying, "Woe is us," I like to tell them: "Look, all this negative stuff that you read about in the newspapers every day and see on the news programs every night—all the embezzling and stealing and raping and pillaging and plundering and murdering and molesting—is being generated by only two percent of the world's population. Ninety-eight percent of the world is not involved in this. Ninety-eight percent just wants to have a good life, raise their children, have enough to eat, have enough possessions so that they have what they need." And so forth and so on. It's the two percent that seems to be duking it out, with all the rest of us paying the price. The awareness of what is going on is surfacing, and this is going to move things. There is just no way it's not going to.

HSW: You place a high importance on this idea of awareness. In one of your books—I can't remember which one right now—you even say that existence itself is defined by the patterned flowing of three elements: matter, energy, and awareness. Why is awareness so important?

HW: That's a big question, one that I have attempted to address near the end of my first book *Spiritwalker*. At the Big Bang, the creation, the primordial source essence expressed itself into the manifested world in three forms: matter, energy, and the awareness that each had of the other. That's how the universe as we know it came into being. It reveals that consciousness is a field of existence, just like matter and energy. The important question to ask is, how will society change when the awareness takes hold that consciousness, not matter, is the primary ground of all being?

This awareness, this idea, is inextricably interwoven with spiritual experience. When we as individuals personally experience connection with the unlimited power and a mysterious godlike mind, these higher evolutionary functions are triggered within us and some sort of predetermined schedule is set into motion. I don't believe this schedule can be given to us by any outside agency. No holy books, no secret ceremonies and rituals, no leaders or gurus of faiths can do this for us. This is because each one of us already has it.

HSW: Which takes us back to the beginning of this conversation, doesn't it? Talk about cycles!

HW: By using the shamanic method, each person is gifted with their freedom, their sovereignty, and their right to develop spiritually. In doing so, each of us becomes our own teacher, our own priestess or priest, our own prophet, enabling us to receive spiritual revelations directly from the highest sources.

This is an appealing proposition to Westerners, and virtually everyone in the transformational community knows that it is possible to connect with realities in which all the mysteries, great and small, become known.

Ken Eagle Feather

Courtesy of Ken Eagle Feather

Don Juan would appear in front of me, clear out of the blue. The first several times I saw him materialize, I could not perceive of him just stepping out of thin air. That was way beyond my scope, so at first I would just see him walking towards me like you'd see anybody walking towards you. Once my body was able to process that kind of data, I would literally see him step out of thin air.

—Ken Eagle Feather

105

Like many young men in the early seventies, Ken Eagle Feather went off to fight in Vietnam and returned home downhearted, his life stripped of all meaning it had had before the war.

Not long after, Eagle Feather was given a copy of Carlos Castaneda's now-famous book Journey to Ixtlan. *He immediately began practicing the shamanic techniques described in its pages and, as his practice continued, he not only found himself able to access the emotions that he had been forced to shut down during the war, but he experienced tremendous leaps in his intuitive abilities. So inspired, Eagle Feather moved to Arizona with the intention of finding a teacher like don Juan Matus, the Indian seer described in Castaneda's books. It never occurred to him that he might actually meet don Juan himself.*

One day, while walking down a main avenue in Tucson, Eagle Feather saw an old Indian man walking towards him, staring with what looked like recognition. Late for class at the local university, Eagle Feather continued on his way. Once settled into class, he says, a wave of energy broke through him, and at that moment, he knew he had just seen don Juan, the famous nagual himself.

"A couple days passed and I saw him again, this time standing near a small market on the outskirts of town," Eagle Feather writes in A Toltec Path. *"I approached him and held a very short conversation; I was too intimidated to remain long in his presence."*

Over the next few years, their paths crossed many times. Thus began his apprenticeship with don Juan in the ways of the Toltec Path, a shamanic tradition whose roots stem from ancient Mexico.

Don Juan later set him to writing books that would elaborate on the material presented by Castaneda. Ken Eagle Feather is author of four Toltec-shamanism books, including Traveling with Power *and* A Toltec Path. *He has been on staff for the Association for Research and Enlightenment, The Monroe Institute, and Hampton Roads Publishing Company. A reflection of his transition to a new level of study and learning, Ken recently changed his name to Kenneth Smith.*

Hillary S. Webb: You have been described as an "Urban Toltec." People, especially other Toltecs, see you as a renegade because you have parted

*with the old ways of working with nature as shamanism has tradition-
ally been described, and have embraced technology as a way of accel-
erating the process of learning to enhance perception.*

Ken Eagle Feather: I have never parted ways with nature. However,
my work has shown me that technology accelerates shamanic types
of learning tremendously. I've been on staff and gone through a
number of programs at The Monroe Institute, an organization that
uses audiofrequencies to facilitate balancing the electrical activity of
both hemispheres of the brain. When the brain is synchronized, you
automatically enter heightened states of awareness, often known as
"dreaming awake."

I have also had interesting success using float tanks, which also
help produce meditative states. In a float tank, you are suspended
in an environment where your musculature does not have to
respond to gravity. It requires energy to go exploring consciousness
and exploring reality. Since relaxation and concentration are the two
principal features of psychic functioning, when you no longer have
to offset gravity and no longer have to deal with distractions, you can
take that energy and pay attention to other things. A person could
think they were doing wonderful things by ignoring technology and
not get anywhere. Whereas, if they had listened to their heart when
it said to try technology one time, it would accelerate their psychic
growth by five years and all of a sudden they are on their way into
where they want to go.

*HSW: Do you think that technology could one day replace nature in this
work?*

KEF: The sentimental side of me believes that nature can never
be replaced. It has a fundamental role. But technology is also an
aspect of our natural selves. It's a projection of what is inside of
us. We couldn't have designed airplanes if we didn't have the
ability for teleportation within ourselves. We have projected these
things into an external environment that reflects the internal abilities. And so technology, if you just look at it from the human perspective, is very natural within that human frame of reference. I
think the universe is consciousness, no matter what form it takes.

I think it is just different kinds of consciousness with different roles.

I definitely see the value of interacting with nature. What I'm doing is saying, hey folks, we've got a new world here, we ought to reexamine the place technology has made for itself in this work. I'm not saying I'm right or wrong. I'm saying that if you can use technology, if it works for you, then cool.

HSW: One of the most prevalent arguments I have heard against the use of technology in this work is that there is the danger of it being used as a crutch. For example, if someone learns to get into a meditative state using a float tank, they may not be able to get to that place on their own.

KEF: Yes, there is the danger of becoming stuck in technology, but this is true for any metaphysical system. Robert Monroe, the founder of The Monroe Institute, considered his technology to be like training wheels—that it was designed to do away with itself in the end. I've seen it happen that the new neural pathways have been grown to such an extent that people then command that capacity without the use of technology.

And it is important to remember that using technology does not mean leaving the fundamentals of learning behind. Your learning fundamentals are going to remain constant whether you are out in nature or whether you are dealing with technology. The basics are still there. It's meditating and remaining open, trying to gain a sense of competence without thinking you are a know-it-all, being respectful, trying to make sense of it without making *too* much sense of it.

HSW: In A Toltec Path *you write, "The Toltecs have created a land where the inhabitant's primary concern is the development of perception." How do you define "perception," and why is the development of it so important on this path?*

KEF: Perception is your means of acquiring data. It could be visual, auditory, kinesthetic, intuitive, or instinctual. Perception is important because that's how we figure out and relate to the world around us, even if we are in a dark room.

As a species, we are developing and increasing our perception all the time. Anthropologists have suggested that in the time of the caveman, humans' eyes weren't quite as developed as they are now and our vision therefore had an absence of color. While color was in the world, we could not perceive it. In the future, I think we are going to see an eighth color of the rainbow. It's already there, but our physical eyes haven't evolved to the point where they can resonate with that particular frequency, and therefore we cannot perceive it.

HSW: It's been said that when the early European explorers sailed to this country, the Native Americans were unable to see the ships they came on. Such things were beyond their perception. In fact, the natives had to physically touch the ship before they could see it.

KEF: I refer to this as "closure." If you are reading a paragraph and there's been a word deleted so that there's just a blank space, most people will unconsciously insert the word and then tell you it was there all the time. That is "closure." This also pertains to what you were just talking about—where things get so far beyond you that you have no relation to them and you complete the picture with what you know to be true. Your body can't process the information, and as a result, your mind fills in the dots so that you perceive a situation the way you were trained to perceive it. Which is really scary, because then you are at the mercy of your training. That's why I have gotten more and more interested in what I call "freedom-based education." The essence of freedom-based education is learning how to have integrity of perception, while at the same time knowing that at any moment you may have to let your model of reality go in order to entertain something new. Because there is no way we can really come to terms with the magic and the mystery around us. As soon as you start to describe it, you have taken the pie and made it into one slice. You can gradually expand that slice of pie, but you can never perceive the entirety of it.

HSW: Then why get involved in any spiritual system if, in the end, all you know is that you don't know anything?

KEF: There is a beauty in this kind of not knowing. It's intelligent "not-knowing," and is not ignorance. By the time you get to the point where you are comfortable with the idea of knowing nothing, you have educated yourself enough that you find that it's actually fun not to know, because it keeps you open to expanding your perception even more. That is the dance of remaining solid and remaining open at the same time. It's a really interesting dance because it's a skill. Anybody can learn the skill, but it's a very hard skill to learn because it is so contrary to the way we are normally taught.

You have to know that you don't know anything and be comfortable with that. In that way, you are always leaving yourself open to the mystery. To my mind, that's what any good spiritual path should teach.

HSW: The challenge, then, is finding the right path.

KEF: I don't think there is necessarily a "right" way. It is up to the individual. I really like to see people experimenting and having fun with a variety of different systems at first, because in the beginning stages it is very much trial and error. Jump into it like a smorgasbord. Read some Zen books and try some Zen exercises; read some yoga books and try some yoga exercises; read some Toltec books, try some Toltec exercises. Same for Taoism, same for Christianity.

Of course, based on my own personal experience, if someone wants to progress past a certain point in this work, there comes a time when they have to commit to a specific discipline. The commitment to a path is an acknowledgment that you are awakening to your own nature. And it's important to have the daily consistency that a single discipline provides. That is the only way you are going to have the power and the focus to really move energy even more. So allow yourself to experiment, allow yourself to be open, and then ask your heart which system is the right one to follow as your main path.

That said, I think that there are two things that are always found in a good system. The first is that it be nonexclusive. Even though you've done experimenting with a variety of different paths, when you commit to one, that path should not tell you to stop flirting with other ways of looking at the world. Indeed, it should encourage it.

HSW: Otherwise, you've found yourself a cult.

KEF: Precisely. The second thing is that, as we were talking about with technology, the path should have within it the seeds of its own destruction. This means that while you are learning the path in and out, you are also learning that it is temporary. Because a stage of development occurs where you discover that the path itself is just one single exercise to get you to that place where you are totally nourished by God; where your will and God's will have been unified and you are surrendered to Divine order. To me, that is Christ consciousness. To me, that is awakening the entire kundalini track. To me, that is what every system is at its core, whether it is Taoism, Toltec, Christian, or whatever. The best of the best are all very clear that what they're giving you is a way to get to somewhere else.

HSW: How important is it to have a teacher to guide you down the path? Could someone conceivably learn this on their own?

KEF: That's a great question. I see it from a number of different angles. Don Juan says that the role of the teacher is simply to show you the possibilities, and then give you the tools to enable you to do the work yourself. That's learning from mastery; that's learning for self-empowerment. And then you are totally responsible—the teacher is not. So there always comes a time where no matter what stage you're in, you have to get off your butt and do the work yourself.

In my particular life, though, I have never seen anyone get on too far without a teacher or without adhering strictly to a particular path, given the things I mentioned before. But having said that, it is also very conceivable to me that we have now gotten to a level of indoctrination as a species where we are open to a new order of spirit where maybe teachers aren't as necessary as they were before. I don't know. I think it's one of those questions that's better if you don't try to answer, because then it makes everyone wonder. As soon as they start wondering, they remain open. And as soon as they remain open, things can happen.

HSW: Is this "freedom-based education" the way you were taught by don Juan?

KEF: Yes. What he would do is throw me out of whack to the point where I would emotionally and physically lose my orientation to the world. I would have a loss of meaning. I'd be out for a walk and, in my typical days of connecting with the world, I'd be totally not paying attention to anything. Don Juan would appear in front of me, clear out of the blue. The first several times I saw him materialize, I could not perceive of him just stepping out of thin air. That was way beyond my scope, so at first I would just see him walking towards me like you'd see anybody walking towards you. Once my body was able to process that kind of data, I would literally see him step out of thin air. In this particular manner of his teaching, he was continually throwing me off-balance. I would spend the next couple months putting myself back together, and as soon as I regained any degree of balance and became comfortable with the world as I thought it was, he would show up and throw me totally out of balance again.

HSW: What did this accomplish?

KEF: The more I had to get myself into balance, the better I could withstand this continual shattering of my reality. In doing that, my abilities of perception increased.

HSW: What's the connection between being in balance and increasing one's abilities of perception?

KEF: When you are out of balance with yourself, you are not connected to the world. When you are not connected to the world, you're just connected to yourself, and the perceptions that you *do* have are going to occur as a state of projection. This is what don Juan called "self-importance."

It is the inherent nature of humans to have this thing called self-reflection. Reality itself is just a mass amount of self-reflection. When we define our world, we are really just reflecting and then producing from that reflection.

Don Juan's Toltec teachings aren't to get a person to become a Toltec, per se—although for some people that might be the case—they are about minimizing self-reflection. They are about becoming a person of knowledge, which means that you are merged so much with the world that you are no longer reflecting on yourself; instead you are purely a complete part of the world. Once you are connected with the world—which means stopping the internal dialogue—you start getting fed a whole new line of data. You're no longer in a cassette tape loop that's stuck on automatic reverse, playing the same thing over and over again.

HSW: You say that the teachings of the Toltec path are to minimize self-reflection, and yet, in your books, you stress the importance of grooming one's individuality. Is it possible to do both at the same time? The two seem contradictory.

KEF: The individuality I am speaking of in terms of the Toltec path is actually found by getting rid of self-importance. By getting out of your own way to such an extent that you become exactly as God created you; the way God has designs for you. To do that, you have to let all of your self-reflection go. Otherwise, you are always defining who you *think* you are, rather than discovering *who you truly are.*

Making yourself merge with God's will gives you the gift of your complete individuality. One of the benefits to that is that within the nature of God's order, we don't have to uphold our world. I think that's what leads to aging, and why when most people get to old age they are depleted. They have spent their entire lives upholding the world because they think that if they let go, God's going to let go of them. If we just let go and let God play out how God wants it all to play out, we'd be continuously replenishing our energy.

Don Juan is the only person I have ever met who was one hundred percent of an individual and, at the same time, not even here. He was so connected with the world, so blended with the universe, that he became a *function* of the universe. He had gotten to that point of blending by discovering who exactly he was the way God created him, rather than the way society created him. As a result of that, he was his own person. That process—the journey of getting to that evolutionary connection with the world—is the work of the Toltec. Or, for that matter, the work of the Taoist, the Zen, whatever.

HSW: Practically speaking, how does one achieve this state and become a "function of the universe"?

KEF: First you have to blast yourself out of complacency and realize that you are going to die. I don't care if you believe in reincarnation or not—you are going to die. Then you take that power and decide how you are going to use your death to bring yourself to life. This is what don Juan taught as "Using Death as Your Advisor." You ask yourself, "If I am going to die today, what is it that I want to be doing?" At that point, you start examining everything all over again, and all of a sudden going out and partying, getting high, getting drunk, doesn't make it anymore. That's not worth dying for. As soon as you start asking yourself, "What do I have to do?" you allow yourself to become quiet. As soon as you allow yourself to become quiet, you start hearing outrageous things. Good stuff! Crazy stuff! Stuff that awakens your heart and makes you feel connected with the world.

It's not an easy process. A lot of times this transition from the old style to the new style of being can be miserable. You get to a place where nothing makes sense anymore, and you go through a dark night of the soul. And then, just at the last moment when you think all the lights are going to go out, you'll make a connection that keeps you going. At that point, things start making sense. Then all of a sudden you know how to connect with the world automatically—how to feel it, rather than think about it. And when you start feeling that connection, you start opening up. And when you start opening up, you *really* begin awakening the heart. And then your world is no longer like you thought it was before.

Now, the danger with *that* is that then you think you now have found the *real* new world and you become a New Age fundamentalist.

HSW: What's wrong with New Age fundamentalism?

KEF: Because then you are in a huge bag of self-reflection, rather than in a tiny bag of self-reflection. You think you have found it all, but you're still not really connected with the world. What you've found is just another logic, another sense of the world. And as we discussed earlier, that is an impediment to the rest of your growth. And so you give that up once again and you go through a transitory process where you have to look the fool again while you are redefining your paradigms once more. This happens over and over. Pretty soon you realize you could be a professional fool.

Don Juan would say that we can't explain the world; it's a total mystery. You have to get comfortable not knowing anything. And that is one hundred and eighty degrees different from the way we're trained. But the bottom line is that there is no describing what we are in the midst of. It's an amazing adventure.

Christina Pratt

Our soul's purpose will always bring us back into community, back into balance, and back into contributing to the world. It's pretty much the only thing that is guaranteed to bring you back into right relationship with everything else.

—Christina Pratt

As in so many stories told by shamans about their initiations to the path, Christina Pratt was, and perhaps still is, a reluctant shaman. She herself admits that she stepped onto the path kicking and screaming, knowing that it meant abandoning her lifelong dream of becoming a professional dancer.

"I did not ever want to be a shaman or really even choose to know about it," says Pratt. "I was living in New York and dancing when I had an initiatory experience that was provoked primarily by a depression." During this calling, Pratt underwent a classical shamanic initiation, a terrifying ordeal in which, as she describes, "everything is backwards. All that was dark is light, all that was light is dark, crazy people seem sane, normal people seem crazy, animate objects stop moving and speaking, and inanimate objects writhe and communicate. The trial time during which I was tested was terrifying and lasted three days. Ultimately, I failed and experienced my death. From the death came a rebirth of a woman who could pass the test and ultimately free herself from the backward, inside-out experience."

She says, "At first, I didn't understand in the larger context what had happened. All I knew was that it had completely changed me, my life, and my perspective on everything. I saw absolutely everything differently. As I learned more about shamanism, I was able to reframe my whole life. It allowed me to understand this and all the profound experiences that I had had. Up to that point, all they had added up to was proof that I was probably crazy."

Even after these experiences, as well as a deep sense of having discovered her soul's purpose as a healer, Pratt had to wrestle with abandoning her old self, and step fully into her new role of shaman.

Today Pratt runs the Last Mask Center for Shamanic Healing, which offers a wide variety of individual, one-on-one healings, and community shamanic healing experiences, workshops, and classes. Her shamanic work is a synthesis of studies with Ecuadorian, Tibetan, Tamang, and African shamans, the Foundation for Shamanic Studies, the Center for Intuitive Energy Processing, and personal shamanic experiences. Besides producing workshops through the Last Mask Center, Pratt is on the faculties of the Omega Institute, Rowe Center, Hollyhock, Breitenbush Hot Springs, and Sleeping Lady Retreat Center. She is a frequent speaker for the American

Holistic Medical Association. She is also the author of An Encyclopedia of Shamanism, *a one-thousand-page, two-volume book that contains more than 750 in-depth entries on the concepts of shamanism and the practices of shamanic people.*

Hillary S. Webb: Tell me, why the "Last Mask"?

Christina Pratt: As I was learning about shamanism, I learned that shamanic cultures use masks to embody spirits and to bring out aspects of themselves. It is about showing your power and showing who you really are at your best. In this culture when we talk about "masks," we are always talking about hiding and about all these "false selves" that we wear to get through the day. You know, the good worker, the good mother, the good husband. For us, the mask has taken on the opposite function. It is still a powerful thing, but we use it to hide our power instead of to emerge as powerful beings. The idea behind the name is that your human body is the last mask that you are wearing to cover up the power of your soul. The focus of the workshop cycle that I teach is on stripping away all these masks so that you are just wearing this last mask of your own authentic self and thus living out your soul's purpose.

Really, the teachings that I do are not so much examples of being a shaman, but are more examples of one endeavoring to be a spiritual grown-up. That is really what I teach people. Everybody needs to be a spiritual adult in order for us to fully manifest our soul's purpose. This was the point of shamanic cultures. Shamanic cultures focused on the idea that every individual has a soul's purpose and it was the community's responsibility to do all that it could do to support that person in growing into that. These skills learned through shamanism give us what we need to be spiritual grown-ups. Until we have these skills, we are not actually adults.

I believe that shamanism is a path of mastery and, particularly, a path of balance. The shaman's job has always been one of course correction. From a shamanic point of view, the greatest gift of our humanity is our ability to make a mess of things. Meaning, from the spirit world's perspective, humans are the lowest beings on the consciousness totem pole. We learn through the messes that we make, which is why the spirit world is so available to help us—because we need so much help!

HSW: That's certainly humbling!

CP: So the spiritual adults of the community are there to communicate with the spirits to try to "course correct" for themselves and their family. The shaman steps in when things get so off course that we need to make a bigger correction as a community and as individuals within that community.

A whole lot of spiritual principles come into play when you are doing that role well. One of the main aspects of being a shaman is being able to dump your own stuff. You have to be a hollow bone. And this is the piece that I think is missing in the training that people think they are getting. That psycho-emotional piece needs to happen. For contemporary people, that takes some time to learn. That's one of the fundamental things about shamanism. If you are being a good shaman, there are no illusions; it is not about you. When shamanism came into my life, I really saw how when I was sitting with a client, I was a better version of myself than when I wasn't. I saw that when I had to take on the role of "shaman," I did a really good job of having boundaries, of not taking on people's stuff, of staying grounded, of getting out of the way and letting Spirit guide me, of staying balanced and in the moment. As much as I resisted and hated it, and as scary as it was, all of those things made for a better version of Christina.

HSW: The dissolution of the ego. Dropping the "I" to become more of who you truly are.

CP: That's the piece that I think a lot of people don't get. Those people get into shamanism because it is about power. And where they take that path of power is the difference between shamans and sorcerers. In shamanism, everything is based on that initiation experience that involves utter humility. You die. The ego that has got all that stuff wrapped around it dies. So as situations come to me that would stroke or enhance my ego, I think, "Man, don't let this become a high horse because it hurts so bad when the spirit world knocks you off of it."

HSW: Which it invariably does.

CP: Yes, it does. And if you are being a good shaman, it will again and again and again. Because you can't be a good shaman unless you stay humble. And if you are not doing that, then the other option is to be a sorcerer. Then you don't have to worry about all of that. And that is a choice.

HSW: The sorcerer, then, by that definition, is a shaman without humility?

CP: The difference is that shamans are responding to the needs of others. They are drawn into their healing work by the needs of others. They are called to the work because they are the ones who are able to respond to the needs that are present in the community. Not because they want to, but because they can. It's very much like a spontaneous act of heroism in that you are the person who can jump into the lake to save the kid and so you do. You don't think, "I want to be a hero today—I'll go do this." You do it because you are the one who can. Shamanism is a lot like that. You are responding to the needs that are present. With sorcerers, the training is very similar and they do many of the same things, but they are responding to their own needs. And that makes all the difference in the world.

HSW: And harming people in the process?

CP: There are lots of sorcerers that may never overtly harm anyone. Perhaps they are on a path of personal discovery. They want to know how powerful they can be for themselves, which makes it a very self-serving process. So one needs to be very careful in reading books by Carlos Castaneda, for example. Don Juan was a *brujo*, a sorcerer. He was a sorcerer that was basically written about from the idea of exploring your human potential. But that's not shamanism. Shamanism is not about one's human potential. It is about your potential as a conduit for Spirit in order to help others and keep the community in balance. Which is why I don't believe anyone who says, "I want to be a shaman." Because frankly, it sucks. It is a really hard job. Whenever anyone comes to me and says, "I want to be a shaman," I never take them on as an apprentice. It means that that person is either a fool or wants to do it for the wrong reasons, and I don't want to work with that. Someone else with much more patience and compassion than I might find a way to work them through all that and bring them to a place where they could potentially be good, but I don't think I'm going to live that long! Besides, I really think that one of the aspects of receiving a calling—whatever that calling might be, not just shamanism, but any true calling—is that we say, "No, no, no, I don't want to do that." There's always going to be a certain reluctance in the beginning.

So even though the psychologists and the anthropologists and the people who have written about these things for the last sixty years often use the words "shaman" and "sorcerer" interchangeably—partly thanks to Carlos Castaneda—they are *not* interchangeable, even if it is the same person doing the same thing. An act done with the intention of a shaman has one name, and the same act done with the intention of the sorcerer has a different one. Shamanic cultures that live with this kind of thing all the time know the difference.

Part of the reason we in Western culture insist on remaining blind to this is because we are a culture of sorcerers.

HSW: Wow. That's quite a statement.

CP: We are a culture of abuse of power. Ours is a system of power *over*, not being responsible for the fact that you have rank or privilege or power as a teacher or a parent or a government official. Anyone in power in this culture has something at stake in maintaining the system. Even your basically humble academic is still going to maintain the system, and our system is sorcery, not shamanism. Consequently, the freedom to misunderstand this is propagated in almost every book written about shamanism. And I find that particularly irritating. It is a major soapbox that I have.

HSW: Something you just said touches me on a very personal level. And brings up a concern for my own work on this path. One of the things that I love about this work is that there are very explicit tools for the exploration of human—okay, my own—potential. For me, part of the beauty of this path is learning to break out of the consensual mindset of reality and its limitations and discovering what more exists beyond consensus reality. Is that sorcery, then?

CP: Well, it can be. I've had several conversations with people in this vein lately. For example, this one woman was talking about cultivating this enormously rich life within the astral realms. She had this whole life going on that she had to astral travel to. But at some point she realized, "So what?" That is the thing about the path of self-expression for the sake of self-expression—eventually it becomes a big "so what?"

HSW: Akin to spiritual masturbation?

CP: Something like that. *But* the other way to think about that is that if you decide to fully express your soul's purpose in this lifetime, then exploring those boundaries will be serving a purpose.

We have to trust that the most that we can contribute to this world is to live our soul's purpose. If you spend your life serving others and never live out your soul's purpose, you are going to end life with a great big zero. People think that if they live their soul's purpose, they are going to be a self-centered jerk. What they don't understand is that our soul's purpose will always bring us back into community, back into balance, and back into contributing to the world. It's pretty much the only thing that is guaranteed to bring you back into right relationship with everything else. And the thing about staying in balance is that balance is not a place that you live and buy real estate. It's something you keep coming back to. The beauty of shamanism is that it teaches that you can't be afraid of the chaos, because between the moments of balance are the moments of chaos. You can't get to the next moment of balance without them.

HSW: How does one discover if they are living their soul's purpose?

CP: Did you ever play that game when you were a kid where someone hides something and then you have to try to find it, and all they can say is, "Hotter. Hotter. Colder. Colder"?

HSW: Sure.

CP: Okay. So, in the infinite wisdom of the universe, these people in the physical plane who are so good at making messes are given one mission—to find their soul's purpose. It's like an enormous puzzle to be solved. And I don't mean that you figure out what your purpose is and then you just go do it. I mean that you live life and figure out what it is along the way. It's a big game of hotter-hotter-colder-colder that you play with the universe, only your soul's purpose is the thing that is hidden, and your emotions are the language that Spirit communicates to you through. Your passion is the "hotter-hotter." When you are feeling depressed and passionless, that is the "colder-colder." That's how the universe gives the signal. It's that simple. But if you live in a culture or follow a religion or live in a way that tells you that your passion is *bad*, you're in trouble. Our emotions become so gummed up with all that business that they are not available as the language with which to communicate with the spirit world. Then you have lost the main guide to your soul's purpose. One of the first things in finding your soul's purpose is to get back to feeling passion freely.

HSW: And in order to do that . . .

CP: In order to do that you have to get to the place where you are no longer running for your life, or rather, where you are no longer running from death. You have to start choosing life. And that is the hardest thing for people in terms of living their soul's purpose—because most people only have skills to run from death. But you have to be willing to choose life if you are going to live out your soul's purpose. And that is a whole different skill set. And let me tell you, it is *way* scarier than running from death!

HSW: How so?

CP: Because then everything is just what it is. There are no distractions. Your mom is just who your mom is, your dad is who your dad is, your past is your past, and you are here in the moment. Now what? Every possibility is open to you, so what do you do now? It's the hell of abundance. You have so many choices of what you could be doing. So what do you do now? Well, if you are my student and you have been paying attention at all, you go ask Spirit.

Finding your soul's purpose means combining the openness of the heart with the fierceness of the gut, and reaching out and grabbing life for all that it is worth, while at the same time surrendering to Spirit's plan for your life. That's the thing about shamanism—it is a path of balance, but it is not passive. Since it is active, you have to be very sure that the acts that you are taking are aligned and balanced. Again, because it is really easy to step across the line between shamanism and sorcery. That is why your relationship with Spirit—making sure you are aligned with Spirit—is where every action begins. Then you go wholeheartedly out into the world. It really is an act of spiritual warriorship.

HSW: Says Charles Dubois, "The important thing is this: to be ready at any moment to sacrifice what you are for what you could become."

CP: That is something I turn to again and again and again.

HSW: Is that act of surrender, the willingness or readiness to sacrifice the old comfortable self at any given moment for something "more," also what makes someone a spiritual warrior?

CP: I think that is one of the essential things. That is, not to be so attached to who you are that you are not willing to dump the whole thing for who you could become. A spiritual warrior is someone who understands that we all come here with a purpose that will take our whole life and our fullest potential to manifest. Everybody's life purpose is ultimately a path of mastery. As that quote implies, there's always a better version of Christina. It's not that Christina isn't good enough. It's being able to be in full acceptance and love of who you are in the moment and, at the same time, knowing that you could be more. It's really an interesting balance because it means seeking a path of greatness without caring about the greatness. It's a paradox. But then, I think that most of the things that are true are paradoxes. That's how we know they are true.

HSW: So the focus of the path is on continual transformation, a kind of alchemy of the self, with sacrifice as the means by which that transformation takes place.

CP: The essence of shamanism as I understand it is about being able to transform anything. That's right—you don't just get to keep being more. You have to truly sacrifice something in order to gain

124

something new. I don't think that is a belief that is part of our current mythical paradigm. But I have seen it change people's lives.

HSW: Such as when you finally relented and gave up your dancing career.

CP: That was a sacrifice. In the beginning, I saw the skills of shamanism as the skills of any mature spiritual adult. I felt I needed to learn to do that so I could be a better dancer and get the dance jobs that I wanted. Then over the next several years, my dance life was completely drying up. The whole shamanic thing was really flourishing, but I was ignoring it. I remember there was a point where I was really frustrated about dance because I had gotten so close to what I really wanted to accomplish, and it still wasn't really happening. I could feel that there was resistance—not from within me, but from the outer world towards me. I thought, "Why does it have to be so hard?" Then I got kind of pissy, and I said, "Okay, if this is what I am supposed to do, then prove it to me!" Which, by the way, you usually don't get away with saying. I said to Spirit, "Okay, if I open up my life to seeing clients, you bring the clients." So I didn't do anything to bring in clients, but of course, in six months I had more clients than I could physically see.

HSW: And now? Do you still struggle with that sacrifice?

CP: It's less and less pronounced as I mature. I gave up something that had formed my life for the possibility of a different life. And it's a much better life. I mean it's not that it's not hard, but it was worth the trade-off.

As I was writing the encyclopedia, the more I read, the more I saw that the shaman's job is essentially to keep closing this gap between where people are and where they need to be in order to be in balance. And then I saw how big the gap is now. That brought on a depression. It wasn't a personal depression. It wasn't like I thought I had to save the world. It was more just the realization of how far off course humanity has gone and how we may or may not be able to get back to balance. As a race, we may heal into death. I really got that it is very possible that we won't make it because we are so profoundly out of balance. We don't even know we are out of balance because we don't understand anymore what balance looks like.

That awareness became a burden. I had to learn how to live with this knowing day-to-day. That is not a new challenge for people in humanity—I'm not the first person to come up against that.

HSW: And so how do you live with that burden?

CP: By knowing that I am not alone. This is important—I am not the only person involved in helping to close that gap. There are many others involved in the same thing. But more importantly, I am never alone in my own efforts because Spirit is with me in all things. To live in a shamanic perspective is to know that humans are not alone. It is impossible. Spirit is always here. We can never be alone. I am never alone.

OmeAkaEhekatl (Erick Gonzalez)

© Mary Kaye Bates

Our job as healers, shamans, writers, teachers is to say, "It's okay to trust. It's okay to love. It is time now to remember who we are." Today more than ever, we have to use our true gift, which is free choice and free will to choose the kind of world we want; to choose the evolution that we want to experience. Our message is here to make people aware of what is happening so that they can make good decisions for the well-being of their children. We must secure what is given here and leave it in a better shape than how we found it.

—Erick Gonzalez

When I asked Erick Gonzalez to describe to me the events that led him to the path of Mayan shamanism, he responded in a way that clearly illustrates the Mayan outlook of life and the cosmos.

"First, we must go back more deeply," he told me. "We all come here to the physical plane with a need to learn something, to heal something. As soon as we come in, there are already great challenges and conditions of life set upon us so that we may do the work that is needed for the healing of our spirit, mind, and body. As we grow, we must use these conditions to procreate ourselves back into our higher self, into a more spiritual being."

In Gonzalez's case, the challenge placed in front of him was a crippling disease in his own body. Born in Guatemala, Gonzalez developed polio and was paralyzed by the age of two. For the next seven years he engaged in a constant struggle with his body, undergoing numerous painful surgeries and treatments by Western doctors. Finally, his grandmother brought him to see a healer who worked on him using the traditional Mayan healing techniques. Gonzalez made a full recovery.

"When you start being gifted from Spirit to help you in your healing, you find gratitude and surrender," he says. "And in that search of healing you see more of Spirit. That is when your healing truly begins."

Today, Erick Gonzalez is an Aj Q'ij, *a Mayan "Daykeeper," spiritual guide; and healer. Over the past twenty years, he has worked and studied with Native spiritual elders from Mexico, North America, Colombia, and Guatemala. Gonzalez currently travels around the world doing ceremonies and teaching the Mayan ways. He is also a frequent contributor to the Association for Traditional Studies'* Traditional Studies Journal.

Hillary S. Webb: The teachings of the Maya have been kept secret from outsiders for centuries. It has been only very recently that the Mayan people have begun to speak up and share their knowledge with others. Why now?

Erick Gonzalez: Several reasons. One is because of the condition in which we find our world today—a state of ecological, environmental, spiritual, and social collapse. Even if our people wanted to separate, wanted to stay only with our own ways of life, we would still be affected by the surrounding environment that is changing.

Shamans are warriors. We have to fight not only for ourselves, but for life itself—for the animals, the plants, the ecosystem. We have the ability to make good positive changes. We can reconnect to that which we have lost, and the way we want to do this is through education, through sharing, through continuing doing our ceremonies and showing an example of what communities or society should be like in relation to and in harmony with nature. So that's one reason the decision has been made to now share these teachings with the world, and to heal our wounds by what they call "healing the sacred hoop."

The other reason is that humanity has entered our purification time, the completion of the thirteenth *baktun* that is spoken of in our prophecies.

HSW: What's that?

EG: A *baktun* is the completion of a cycle of time. You see, the Maya were timekeepers of this planet. Our people were very observant; very scientific. We call our belief system a cosmology, because it is not a religion or any other kind of a political-social practice, but an understanding about how the mechanics of the universe work. The Mayans were great astrologers and astronomers and mathematicians, with a deep understanding of time and space. Many things come with this kind of knowledge, such as understanding the dimensions, understanding the vibrations of the universe, understanding the golden mean and the golden ratio, which are the keys to understanding nature itself.

A long time ago the Mayans read the stars and said, "We should hide all this, take care of it." Instructions were given so that this knowledge would be hidden until the time when that knowledge would need to be revealed once again to the world. So that's what we are doing.

HSW: I assume that the end of the thirteenth baktun *corresponds with the Mayan calendar's prophesied "end of the world," which is said to take place on December 12, 2012.*

EG: This date will be the beginning of what we call the "sixth sun." It is a new era, a new beginning for our consciousness, for humanity.

For a hundred years before, and from then on, the vibration of the Earth will be changing. Already we can see that the vibration, the frequency of the Earth has changed, as well as the adaptation of many plants, animals, the climate, and so forth. All are undergoing great change. We humans are also changing. Metabolically, physiologically, spiritually, and psychically we are changing really fast. It is a great step in our spiritual evolution.

HSW: So the "end of the world" is going to be more of an end of our current paradigms, a shift in our response, rather than a mass destruction?

EG: Yes, although when great changes happen, there is also great turmoil. We are entering the purification time where all of our senses, all of our history, all of our psychic abilities, all of our body, mind, and spirit need to go through a purification. We will experience Earth changes, catastrophes. Some will not make it. Lots and lots of the biological aspects of the world will not survive the purification. Those things and people and frequencies that cannot adapt to the changes will be destroyed. Most of humanity has not adapted, but those who do adapt to see and feel things of the higher level have a great opportunity to have a spiritual evolution.

The message that is being brought out in these teachings is that we have not reached the point of no return. That's number one. The second thing is that we have an opportunity right now to truly embrace the great changes for a greater evolution for humanity and for Mother Earth, the planet that we live on. Many things are being revealed to us at this time—who we are, what are we made of, where we are going, what our place is in this web of life. Not so long ago, the Europeans thought that the world was flat. Then they said that we were at the center of the solar system, and then that we were the center of the universe. Look at how things have changed! Today scientists—they call them "cosmologists" now—have been able to detect eleven dimensions beyond our own. These truths the Mayans have been saying all along. Through our observations, we are able to detect where the wormholes or the vortexes exist in time and space. And by doing ceremony, we are able to create these vortexes ourselves.

HSW: You are able to create them yourself?

EG: As Einstein found out with the laws of relativity, as speed increases, the concept of time becomes different. Like the stars, for example. They are in our past. What we see when we look at them is an image from billions of years ago. We don't know what the sky really looks like now, because of the relationship between time and space. Einstein said that if we were to travel at certain speeds, we could reach into the past. Or go into the future.

For the Maya and many other shamans throughout the Americas like the Olmecs, the Zapotecs, the Aztecs, it was not uncommon to travel into different dimensions, different times. All these dimensions, all these worlds, all these realities are parallel universes that are manifesting themselves at the same time. We are in the third-fourth dimensional place, the Earth plane. The Maya call it *Kaj-uleu,* "The Sky-Earth Place." Other dimensions are more like a fluid stage or vibration stage. Because of their knowledge and their integration with the cosmos, the Maya and other indigenous people have been able to know and map these vibrational stages. And so in our ceremonies, we are able to journey through the universe and manifest ourselves in many different aspects of Creation at different times and places.

HSW: There goes the budget for NASA!

EG: Right! You don't need big ships. Just as we can see a different perspective of the universe when we look through the telescopes to see the macrocosm or through the microscopes to see the microcosm, we can also shift our perspective of time and space. If we shift our concept of time and space, the mind becomes the vehicle for interdimensional or intergalactic travel into the different realities. We can do it for healing, for learning, and for growth. That's why our ceremonies and our healings are so powerful. Through use of the elements here in the third-fourth dimension, we are able to open the doors to the other dimensions.

HSW: How does working with the elements make this happen?

EG: We interact with the elements; we talk to them. When you are quiet and you listen, then things are revealed. When someone asks a medicine person, "How did you learn how to mix these plant medicines to create this effect?" we say, "The plants talk to us." When we smoke our pipes, we take the herb that came from the Earth and we smoke it so that it will go into our system and interact with us at a cellular level, at a conscious level, and at a subconscious level. In our lungs we are sharing our oxygen, our carbon dioxide, with the herb. When we exhale into the air, the air takes it and carries our prayers to that force.

It's the same thing with fire. When we talk to the fire, the fire talks back. In our fire ceremonies we don't use firewood, and we see things there that you will not see in any other fire. When we look at the fire, we are looking at it like a movie. The fire reveals pictures to us. In this communication we receive instructions.

HSW: This sounds like a form of divination or scrying.

EG: Yeah. In that way we have a visionary, vibrational conversation with the elements. This is how we learn how to move the energy that is needed to create a condition that we want.

HSW: Such as a healing?

EG: Yeah. One could say that the secret of healing is by using the breath. If we direct it in a conscious way, the breath creates conditions in our mind, in our body, and becomes a vehicle for altered states of mind. Some people call it "shamanic breath work," because through the breath you create that feeling of altered states. The Maya call it the *I'q.*

HSW: I'q?

EG: *I'q* is one of the four elements with which we can integrate. *I'q* is the air, the energy that gives life, and the medium that all the invisible forces travel through. There is something happening through the air that we are able to recognize. It's not only invisible, but it is visible. For example, the exchange of life force from the trees to us. The tree's breath out becomes our breath in, and then, after all of the chemical exchanges in our bodies that change the oxygen into carbon dioxide, our breath out becomes the tree's breath in. That's *I'q* right there. Through the invisible force, something happens and things are exchanged.

And when you start going deeper, *I'q* becomes a doorway into the other realm. If you do thirteen very quick, very powerful breaths in a row, your brain will start to get dizzy and you will have to lie down. If you continue on, an altered state will happen automatically because of natural chemicals in the brain. As you practice that, those breaths become powerful enough to create movement in a spiritual way. Then we start journeying in the visions, and in these visions we deal with our problems, deal with our sickness, deal with what we need to learn and experience. You see the world of true vision.

HSW: So essentially you are talking about using the elements as a way of getting into altered states.

EG: Yeah. We go into altered states of conscious, into higher dimensions, where we can interact with Spirit. In these visions, your mind becomes a radio to listen to the frequencies of the universe. It becomes the telescope to see the macrocosm, and the microscope to see the microcosm. And it's not just in a visual way, like we do now from the third-fourth dimension. You experience the collective consciousness of those elements and of those higher levels of being. You can become, let's say, a molecule of water. Suddenly you know what it is feeling, what it is thinking when it is the morning dew. You become that molecule—you start seeing and hearing and feeling and knowing the collective aspect of the water in all its moments of being, such as when it is falling down from the sky, becoming denser and denser until it freezes into an icicle. In that place, there is no past and no future. There is only now, the being. That's where you're said to find your own song and be who you are. The *I'q* is the door to all that.

HSW: How does becoming a drop of water help us?

EG: One reason is the practical survival thing. Knowing or feeling nature or the elements or different aspects of life is to become one with it; to participate in Creation—not just observe it or try to control and change it, like the modern world has done. The modern world is always fighting it, trying to change it into what we want it

133

to be. We need to adapt to it. We need to understand it. We need to work with it, because like Chief Seattle said, whatever we do to the web of life, we do to ourselves. All things are sacred. All things are a reflection of the Creator himself, herself, and within each of us are the answers to what we need to do. Only when you understand this can you create results. If you are one with the water, then you can communicate with the lightning and the thunder and rain and the clouds and create what you need. It's like with the Aborigine people of Australia. The outside world says, "How can they live in that desolate place? How can they find water?" Well, if you ask them, they say, "The water talks to us." They dream the water. The water's energies are flowing through them.

HSW: It makes me think of the stories about the rainmakers. Is that what they do? Identify with that drop of rain so much that they can manifest it?

EG: Yeah. Or when we do ceremonies, we ask the spirits to allow us a small time for us to do our ceremony. Time and time again we see the blessing where the lightning and the thunder and the storm go around where we are, and then as soon as that ceremony is closed and we move from there, it comes down.

The other reason to feel this oneness with the Earth is that you learn to appreciate it. You start respecting and loving it so that you stop desecrating it, like we do now. They say that we are the most advanced society on the planet, but we've lost our simplicity of respect. We are dirtying the only world we have—desecrating and polluting the water, the air. That is why most of the world is sick. If we could understand what a precious thing water is, air is, we wouldn't be polluting it. As soon as we found out that gasoline, diesel, and all the emissions that come from our power plants were destroying the air and the water, we should have stopped.

HSW: But we don't want to give up our toys, do we?

EG: It's the arrogance of ignorance. We are so arrogant that it creates an ignorance. We think we know the answers and that we have the technology to stop it, when we actually don't. We are so arrogant that we don't see our ignorance about what we are doing and how we are behaving. The aboriginal people of the Earth didn't overfish or over-hunt or dirty the water. There was enough food and clean water for drinking because common sense said you'll get sick or you won't have enough to eat. They learned to ration. They learned to grow enough, to save enough, to plant enough, to leave alone enough, to remain in a balanced way. Now we don't. That's a danger in the planet right now. If we become like the aboriginal people of the Earth, then we'll be back in balance. If we could feel the Earth, be one with it, then we would know ways to resourcefully use it and not deplete it.

HSW: Which is where shamanism comes in, then? To teach us about this one-ness to help us out of this mess?

EG: There have been many great teachers throughout history who have said this. Jesus Christ, Buddha—for us it is Quetzalcoatl. Now again there are many among us trying to do the same. Now, like then, the majority does not listen, though a few do. There is always a small group that listens and survives to move forward to create a golden era. That's how our world is right now. Like the birds stir in the morning, we are also stirring. That is why you are writing this book. That is why many now want to know, "Who are the shamans?" "What are their medicines?" "What is this thing that we have been cheated of?" Our songs are being heard. The drums are starting to be fixed and tightened and played. Like the birds in the morning, we will sing. We will walk into this new dawn. It will take us one or two generations to truly embrace that, but it will happen.

Our job as healers, shamans, writers, teachers is to say, "It's okay to trust. It's okay to love. It is time now to remember who we are." Today more than ever, we have to use our true gift, which is free choice and free will to choose the kind of world we want; to choose the evolution that we want to experience. Our message is here to make people aware of what is happening so that they can make good decisions for the well-being of their children. We must secure what is given here and leave it in a better shape than how we found it.

The beauty of what we are experiencing now on this planet is that we have been given the opportunity by the universe to see our-selves as the spiritual beings that we are. It's the understanding that the Creator wants to realize itself; to finally become one through all that is created. At this very moment, the Creator is experiencing becoming this phone, this vibration, becoming your writing, becoming your book. The message is to maintain that respect; to connect with Spirit and say, "This is a thing we need to share right now." Dedicate it to the trees that keep our *I'q* for us. Dedicate it to the children. Dedicate it to ourselves. With that, we send our love to all people, to all things, and all beings.

Lewis Mehl-Madrona, M.D.

I think that traditional healers have always worked with stories because they have appreciated the role that stories play in Creation. The creation story is the formula by which the world is created. It's not just a metaphor. Your story of yourself is the formula by which you create yourself each day.

—Lewis Mehl-Madrona, M.D.

Why do people get sick? How do they heal themselves in miraculous ways despite conventional medical opinions to the contrary? How do our personal and collective stories play a part in our health? What is our role in the construction (or reconstruction) of the world within which we exist?

These questions flowed naturally throughout the course of my conversation with Dr. Lewis Mehl-Madrona, a Stanford-trained physician who, inspired by his Cherokee grandmother's healing ceremonies, has dedicated his practice to bringing native healing techniques into Western medical consciousness. His argument for the cause: Western medicine, while useful in many ways, is an incomplete system—one that has a very limited attitude towards illness and the recovery of health.

"In medical school I saw that there was a gap in what I was learning," he told me. "Some of the things that I had seen as a child—miraculous healings,

whether by holy rollers or snake handlers or tongue speakers or Cherokee healers—were denied reality in the medical world. But I knew those things existed. . . . Then I went to a lecture given by a world-famous endocrinologist. He started off the lecture by saying that life is a 'relentless progression towards death, disease, and decay,' and that the job of the physician is to slow the rate of decline. I thought, 'There's something wrong with this picture.' It was just one of many things that led me to look beyond what I was learning for something broader."

The story of Mehl-Madrona's experiences straddling the two worlds of Western medicine and native shamanic healing is told in his book, Coyote Medicine: Lessons from Native American Healing. *Currently the coordinator for Integrative Psychiatry and System Medicine at the University of Arizona's College of Medicine, he lectures worldwide.*

Hillary S. Webb: You maintain that in order for someone to be healed, he or she must answer these three questions: "Who are you?" "Where did you come from?" and "Why are you here?" Anyone who can give a clear answer to those three questions has a much better chance of getting well.

Let's look at each question and what it all means in regard to healing.

Lewis Mehl-Madrona: The way I learned it, the "Who are you?" question is really fundamental because it gets to the root of your place in the universe. How do you define yourself? What is your identity? How do you construct yourself? What sense do you make of your existence? How do you make sense of the fact that you are alive?

And then there is "Where do you come from?" The first thing that I think of is "I come from my ancestors," because each of them has contributed something to my DNA. But you could also say, "I come from the stars," because, after all, what is in my body was once part of the Big Bang. So I come from atoms and I come from molecules and I come from meteorites and I come from minerals.

"Why are you here?" Well, the answer to that is what gives us meaning and purpose. It's up to each of us to construct our meaning in life, to invent it. So if you are sick, maybe you want to rethink whatever meaning you have invented for yourself.

I think the most profound story that I know is the Phoebe Snetsinger story. She was a woman with metastatic cancer. She was dying, and at some point she decided to stop all treatment and go bird-watching. That's what was meaningful to her. Bird-watching. She decided that she would try to see every species of bird on the planet before she died. Well, guess what? She lived another ten years. And the ironic thing was that she finally died in Madagascar in a car accident after having seen the last species on Earth.

HSW: *That's incredible.*

LMM: Isn't that amazing? She died the moment she fulfilled her purpose. And not from cancer but from a car wreck!

HSW: *It really is amazing. So then, theoretically, if you answer these three questions, you can be healed. Really?*

LMM: Well, at least you have a much better chance because you've examined your relationship to the universe. These basic questions really invite you to contemplate your relation to the whole of Creation. That's really what I think the intention is. If you are sick, then somehow one needs to examine all of these relationships to Creation and find out where the disturbances and disharmonies lie. The rule of thumb is that if you don't like where you find yourself, then look to how you got there. Look to your relationships. Look to your path. Look to your stories. Look at who you are, why you are here, and where you came from. And then change it.

HSW: *It sounds like by asking those questions, one is examining their personal mythology, writing and rewriting the story of oneself.*
In Coyote Medicine, *you talk about storytelling as being an important part of healing.*

LMM: I think that we construct the world every day through the stories that we tell. You get up and you read the morning paper and you see the stories about the world and participate in the enactment of those stories. You go to funerals and you hear the stories of people's lives. You go to weddings and you hear the family telling stories that convey the rules for membership in the family—what is appropriate and what is not appropriate. I think that traditional healers have always worked with stories because they have appreciated the role that stories play in Creation. The creation story is the formula by which the world is created. It's not just a metaphor. Your story of yourself is the formula by which you create yourself each day.

A really great exercise that I do with students is to get them to talk to somebody that they don't know, assuming a different context, and to see what they tell about their lives. One context could be trying to get a job. Another context could be trying to get a date. We tell such different stories, depending on who we are talking to.

HSW: How true.

LMM: We're trying to create ourselves to be the person that we tell about in the story. That's what we are striving for. I try to get patients to listen to what they say about themselves and see if they live it.

HSW: Or if they are telling the same stories over and over, while ignoring other parts of themselves.

LMM: Right. People get stuck in the same story. Like the victimization story. You can get so stuck in that. If you are stuck in that story, then everything feels like a trauma.

HSW: You have also said that every story has a spirit.

LMM: In a sense, *you* are the spirit of your story. But the cultural stories that are told over and over take on a life of their own. The George Washington "cherry tree" story, for instance. That's a story that has taken on a life of its own. I mean, who knows if he really did it or not? It doesn't matter because it is a story that exists independently of George Washington. Or of cherry trees. It has become an entity. A spirit is a nonphysical entity that has validity, existence and meaning, purpose and structure. The stories that are told over and over, they meet those criteria. They have their own life.

HSW: And depending on the personality of any given story, it can either lift you up or pull you down.

LMM: Exactly. Look at how our families inform our stories about ourselves. How our culture informs our stories about ourselves. All these things go into the creation of ourselves. Sometimes a story embodies sickness. Often they contain things that we think are true and can't be changed.

I have a patient who, when she first came to me, was depressed, anxious, and bulimic. What she couldn't question was her family's view of women. In her family's view of women, appearance was everything. The way that a woman had meaning was by looking good and snagging a high-earning husband. Her parents supported her interest in acting and dance and singing all through grade school and high school. For her it became her meaning in life, but for them, they were just grooming her in skills she needed to snag a high-earning man. Suddenly she was ready to go to college and decided she wanted to go to Juilliard and study singing, dancing, and acting. But her parents wanted her to go to the local private university where there were a lot of eligible, high-earning young men. She was totally confused, because the family's agenda was different from her agenda, and what *she* wanted had no validity. So then bulimia becomes the solution.

Part of our work together was to tease out the family story about women. Who are women? What are women? Where do they come from? Why are they here? What is their purpose? She did not want to be a woman whose purpose was snagging a high-earning guy and having 2.2 kids and living in a really wealthy neighborhood. Well, of course that put her into enormous conflict with her parents, but making that conflict overt relieved her bulimia. It took it out of her body and put it back onto the family. That is what I mean by looking at "Whose story are you living?"

HSW: *How does one go about taking out of oneself whatever "story" we have subscribed to?*

LMM: Ritual is a really important part of that process. Through ritual we learn to expect more of ourselves than we have in the past. We learn that we are capable of more than we thought we were. We learn that there are forces and powers to help us get there that are higher and bigger and greater than we are. It gives us a feeling that we have tools and resources to get where we want to go.

In my client's case, through ritual we connected to her great-grandmother, who was a struggling feminist of the nineteenth century. She could be a resource for her to say, "Stand up to your parents. This is important to all of the women of our family who have ever lived."

HSW: Which brings us back to the importance of answering the question "Where did you come from?" If she didn't know her ancestry, she wouldn't be able to use her great-grandmother as an ally.

LMM: Our ancestors have designs on us. I believe that they have things that they want us to be doing. They have their own agenda that we are supposed to carry out.

HSW: You write, "The shaman specializes in finding meaning by venturing outside of borders into chaos and meaninglessness." Would you say that one must essentially shatter one's own personal mythology in order to enter into a kind of identityless state from which one can re-create one's meaning and purpose?

LMM: Right. Typically, we can't see the contradictions in our stories. We can't see that some of the things that seem important to us are only made up. For instance, with my patient—she grew up with a certain definition of what looking good meant. I got some pictures for her of those African women who put those big things in their lips and said, "Look, in this context having lips that look like this is looking good." And then I got some pictures of some really fat Samoans and said, "Look! In this context, *this* is looking good! You are in a culture that defines looking good in a certain way that you have bought into. It is okay to do that, but it isn't on the stone tablet that God gave to Moses. You have more freedom than you think." I also got her to challenge the notion that thin is happy. I mean, thin people are happy, and fat people are happy. Thin people are miserable, and fat people are miserable. Those things are not actually related, but so many of the bulimics have this culturally derived notion that thin is happy. It's not. It can be unhealthy to be fat, but that doesn't mean it is unhappy by definition.

The shaman steps out of the box and says, "Hey, this is just made up. Some coyote dreamed of this one day and you took it to be reality. But it is only the figment of some coyote's imagination!"

HSW: That's a great way of looking at it. What is reality? Well, it is all a dream of Coyote, the trickster.

LMM: Right.

HSW: So what do we do now that we know that?

LMM: It gives you the freedom to dream your own dream.

HSW: I would imagine that that in-between space in which one goes from one dream to another can be a terrifying place.

LMM: Sure. That's the chaos between the worlds.

HSW: And I'm sure in many cases, the fear of that space stops most people from stepping out of the old dream and into a new one.

LMM: Right. That is a scary in-between place where you realize that nothing is real and everything is a dream. It is both freeing and terrifying.

HSW: Several years ago I went through that place. My relationship had recently broken up, I had changed jobs, I'd moved. Everything that I identified myself with was torn away from me. I felt this sense of complete blankness and identitylessness. I went through several months of feeling like a balloon that was not tied to anything. It was a very scary feeling. One day I was talking to a friend of mine, and I told him, "I don't know who I am anymore. I don't know anything about myself." He looked at me kind of thoughtfully for a moment and then said, very matter-of-factly, "Well, you like scarves." I was wearing this pink scarf that day—one of several that I had. And I thought, "Oh, yeah. He's right. I do like scarves. I know this about myself. I like them because I like them and not because anyone told me to like them but because I do. I may not know anything else about myself, but I know that." And from that one thing, I began the process of stepping back into myself. Or rather, a more authentic self than the one I had been living previously. As I recall, I also went and bought five new scarves that day.

LMM: That's great. I have another patient who was anorexic, lying on the floor, dying. She had spent twenty years of treatment for anorexia and was down to about seventy pounds. Her great-aunt—who happened to be a ninety-eight-year-old nun—called her up on the phone and said, "There's a demonstration against nuclear weapons, you've got to come with me!" And my patient thought to herself, "Hmm, why not? Why am I lying on the floor?" So she got up, ate something, went to the demonstration, and was never anorexic again.

HSW: Something about her great-aunt calling propelled her out of that twenty-year-old rut. Very cool.

LMM: Something clicked. Just like your friend reminding you that you like scarves. There she was, thirty-something years old, wanting to die, having no meaning or purpose besides losing weight, and here is this ninety-eight-year-old nun who is full of meaning and purpose saying, "Get up and come demonstrate with me!" Who knows why that clicked for her. It's one of those mysteries of the universe. It is an exciting mystery. What is that moment in which worlds change? What is that shape-shift that people experience in their lives and how do we get them there? Or at least, how do we get them close enough so that it can happen?

HSW: It sounds like what clicks in is the soul's purpose. The "Why am I here?" question. Perhaps it is to see every bird species on the planet. Or, out of all the days in your life, perhaps it is that on that one day you go to that demonstration.

LMM: I have another patient with metastatic breast cancer. She was spending every moment of the day in some form of alternative healing and it wasn't working. The doctor said she had less than a year to live. Through our work together, she decided to stop all attempts to heal and instead to take her kids to see every warm, sunny beach in the world. She figured she would die on one of them and that would be that. Four years later she is still looking at beaches! Figure that one out.

HSW: Perhaps when the dream gets shifted from the illness to something else, the illness is no longer given as much energy?

LMM: It's a new dream. It's just like people with one of those rare dissociative identity disorders—formerly called multiple personality disorder—who have a disease in one personality, but not in the other. The disease is a part of the state of mind, not the body. And if you can make a radical shift, sometimes the new state of mind doesn't include the disease. How that happens is amazing. I wish I could make that happen on command. But I can't. I just observe it happening. There is clearly a science to it that we are trying to discover. The science of transformation.

HSW: What would you do if you found out that you had, say, a cancer?

LMM: I've thought about that and I have to say honestly that I don't have a clue, because I don't know where I would be. I know that I wouldn't do only Western medicine. I don't know that I would even do *any* Western medicine. Of course, I don't know that I *wouldn't,* either. I really don't know what I would do. I know that I would feel like I needed to make some sort of fundamental shift. To give up my way of living and try something new. Maybe I'd do something that I'd never done before. Perhaps I'd go to the Amazon and take *ayahuasca.* Something like that.

But I know that I am trapped by my culture as well. I believe in Western medicine as much as I don't believe in it. It was part of the story that I grew up with. And so it has some power to me, although at times it has no power. Once I got this really bad infection working in the ICU, and I decided to take Cipro. I was terrified of taking Cipro because of all the side effects. I said, "Well, I'll take one." And that did it. I was a lot younger and less experienced at what I do. I wasn't able to heal myself without the symbol of the one Cipro. I needed that symbol of Western medicine. And somehow that made me strong.

HSW: I read somewhere once that there isn't really a lot of conclusive evidence that any Western medicine really works. That there is a good possibility that all of it just works on the placebo effect. Nothing more than that. The power of mind and soul may be our greatest medicine.

Malidoma Patrice Somé

Magic is like any knowledge. When you get to know it, it just looks like another department of science. A remote control is a magical device. The difference is that Western culture has made a distinction between what is real and what is not real, while in my culture there isn't any subdivision.

—Malidoma Patrice Somé

Born to the Dagara people of Burkina Faso in West Africa, Malidoma Patrice Somé began his life in a culture rich in ritual and connection with the unseen worlds. At age four, Somé was abducted by missionaries and taken to a Jesuit seminary school where he was taught to reject the teachings of his native people and to accept Western ideology. Sixteen years later, he returned to his people, only to discover how alienated he had become from the ways of his native tribe.

"The knowledge I had been exposed to in Western schools left a wide range of experience unexplored," Somé recalls in his book The Healing Wisdom of Africa. *"It was up to the wise people in my village to help me learn to open up to all the realms of knowledge of which I, at the time, was ignorant."*

To help him reintegrate into the community, the village elders decided that the young man should undergo the traditional initiation rites appropriate to boys who were on the verge of puberty. Hoping to find the connection that he had lost, Somé underwent an excruciating and extraordinary monthlong initiation ritual that reawakened his deadened senses to the world of spirit and magic that he had been forced to leave behind years before. The remarkable story of Malidoma Somé's initiation is available in his spiritual autobiography, Of Water and the Spirit.

Ironically, not long after his initiation was completed, Somé was told that in order to fulfill his destiny, he must leave the village and go back to the white man's world. Today, as a healer, lecturer, and teacher, Somé truly walks between worlds, thereby fulfilling the prophecy of the name "Malidoma," which in the Dagara language means "be friends with the stranger/enemy." Somé is the author of a number of books, including Of Water and the Spirit, The Healing Wisdom of Africa, *and* Ritual: Power, Healing and Community.

Hillary S. Webb: You have said, "A community that doesn't have ritual cannot exist." Why? What is the function of ritual?

Malidoma Patrice Somé: What I am suggesting is that ritual is food for the spirit of a community. When it is not there, you cannot really speak about a community, only about a bunch of individuals who happen to live in the same geography, and who more often than not are suspicious of one another. Ritual is a kind of weaving agent that really gives roots to a community.

It also means that without ritual, what happens is that Spirit does not feel officially and collectively invited. Without that, what happens is that very quickly there is a longing and a desire for Spirit, but since the consciousness does not know what it is missing, it transfers that longing onto things that it can consume. The community then disappears and is replaced by a kind of ghost community in which individuals are busy trying to consume because there isn't a spirit that is taking that space of fulfillment.

HSW: Unlike in tribal communities, in the West we all come from such diverse spiritual and cultural backgrounds. How would Westerners best make use of ritual? Do we take one from another culture, or do we make one up on our own?

MPS: Just as importing religions has not been beneficial to any culture, imported spirituality—especially when it is copied verbatim—cannot serve a good purpose. The spirituality of other cultures can only be used as a starting point for the reinvention of the spirituality of one's own ancestors because these things don't travel. Anywhere that you go, there are certain powers that are native to that place and need to remain there. If you are connected with them, you are supposed to become exclusively sedentary. That is why certain shamans don't go anywhere.

And transplanting spiritual teachings can be very damaging.

HSW: Damaging, how?

MPS: Physically and spiritually. I've seen people who have tried to replicate the Dagara Dagger of Fire Ritual and ended up with blisters and burns all over themselves. Then what happened is that the person who got the blisters started thinking that maybe the spirits didn't like him; that maybe something went wrong in the ritual. Well, of course something went wrong! If everything worked right, they wouldn't have blisters!

There is also the possibility for spiritual damage when a ritual works *too* well. The person becomes aware that the kind of thing that he or she has been hungry for all this time has finally been discovered, but then the person is left in this kind of high-pitched vibration state and has to return to a community that doesn't have a spiritual base with which to support them. The individual is completely awakened into the Spirit, but everyone around him looks at him like there is something wrong with him. Consequently, the person begins to feel like a piece of hair in the middle of a cup of coffee. That kind of isolation and alienation can be just as sobering as physical damage.

HSW: Okay, so let's say I am involved with a group of people and we would like to get together and do ritual. Should we just create our own from scratch and, if so, how? I guess what I'm asking is, what makes a ritual a ritual?

MPS: There are four main parts in the structure of ritual. Preparing the ritual space is the first step. This is the time when you build a shrine or an altar around which you will focus the ceremony, and set up the choreography—for example, if a person must walk from one particular place to the altar, which direction should that person take, how should that person go there. All of that is a part of the preparation of the space.

Next comes "invocation." The invocation is an opportunity to clearly set the tone or the intention of the ritual. It comes as a simple prayer, a prayer that acknowledges that if Spirit does not get involved, we won't accomplish anything, because we don't know how to make anything happen by ourselves. More often than not, during this time, you allow as many voices to chime in as possible. That way, it doesn't become the burden of one person to deploy creativity that encompasses all the intentions of people.

The third part—what I call "healing"—is the actual choreographic unfolding of the ritual that takes you from where you are to the sacred altar and back. These are the healing gestures. The return is almost like an odyssey, because the person who went to the altar was a person on a quest for healing, and the person returning, at least by assumption, is a healed person. The healing section is really the apex of the ritual process.

The closing of the ritual is a simple formality aimed at saying "thank you" to Spirit. Because now that you have been helped, can't you say "thank you"? The closing is an opportunity to say, "We really feel grateful because we know that if you weren't here, this would not happen." That's it.

HSW: And the rest would be up to the imaginations of the participants?

MPS: Well, there are basic things about ritual that are not necessarily culturally related—basic ingredients that inspired all the traditions of the world.

For instance, the four elements are known in every culture. Now, the understanding that you may have, may be inspired by one culture's specific approach to these elements. For instance, if you want to reconnect with ancestors in the Dagara tradition, you use fire, because fire is the combustive energy that brings about an emotional connection with such things.

Let's take the case of the water. We know that, universally, water is a cleanser. Now this raises the question as to what is it that you want to cleanse in your spiritual self, in your emotional self, in your soul. The gesture of cleansing can therefore affect the soul directly, particularly when it is done with other people and with someone administering water onto your body in a manner that is not common. You can feel the effect of that upon your psyche.

It's the same thing for the Earth. The Earth is a home for all of us—the place where we all look for comfort, for recognition, for empowerment. So how about calling in the Earth and relating to her in this manner, allowing everyone to be touched by the Earth in a way that is different from us just stomping on her?

This is what I call the engagement of one's imagination in the practice of ritual. Any symbolic gesture has an effect upon the soul. The spirit therefore begins to feel liberated, free to engage the conscious imagination. That is the piece that can lead you to becoming a ritual creator instead of a ritual consumer.

HSW: What about intent? Isn't that the main ingredient in any symbolic gesture?

MPS: That is true to a certain extent, but not to all the extent. Intention has to be the basic departure point in any ritual. In that way, even your own clumsiness can be corrected, such as in a case in which the person was supposed to come down on his knees, but sits down instead. That kind of thing can be corrected by a clear delineation of the intention at the beginning.

When your intention does not match the symbolic action, however, that intention is canceled out by an equally powerful counter-intention. That is where trouble starts to happen. Let's say, for instance, that someone does a fire ritual as a way of getting rid of some kind of blockage that is hindering them. In order to release that blockage, that person has to materialize it in some symbolic form. And since that symbolic form is going to be burned, it must be combustible. If you put into the fire something that cannot burn, that person will end up going home with the same blockage, only intensified. Instead of getting rid of it, it has been given even more potency.

HSW: Which, again, might lead them into a spiritual crisis and doubt, thinking, "I did what I was supposed to do, why do I feel worse than before?"

In your books, you also talk about using ritual as a way of increasing awareness of and expanding perception into the spirit world.

MPS: If we know ourselves as cosmic beings—not just a product of biology—then we realize that we must be coming here from somewhere else. And there is a natural longing in all of us to return to that place. So, from that point of view, imbedded in every human being is a certain spiritual homesickness that could be confused with the desire to find a physical home on this Earth. If you push it further, you can see that throughout the history of mankind, religious aspirations, spiritual development, and all of that have been influenced by an intrinsic desire to reach out to that home that is the cosmos.

The creation and invention of ritual allows for an individual to remain connected with the transcendent self that is innately present in every human being. That is the part of the self that is like a bird—capable of flying and occupying a wide horizon of space and time. Indigenous people have developed the ritual process as a way of allowing the other world to constantly participate in this world in the interest of enriching the life of the individual.

HSW: Is the use of magic part of this enrichment? The Dagara people are well known for being able to do amazing feats of magic, such as making things appear and disappear. In one of your books you tell the story of your grandmother who had problems walking and would turn herself into a dog to get from place to place. Is there a practical aspect to magic?

MPS: Magic is important because it is useful to understand how something happened and why. In that way, you can work with it, you can direct it, you can plan it, or you can be consciously involved in the planning of it. For instance, when you travel a long distance, it's almost like a lottery. When you get into your car, how do you know that you are going to come back? It is better to know that there are certain things you can do in order to remove this uncertainty—such as creating a talisman—so that you can be certain that you will come back.

Magic is like any knowledge. When you get to know it, it just looks like another department of science. A remote control is a magical device. The difference is that Western culture has made a distinction between what is real and what is not real, while in my culture there isn't any subdivision. Your dreams are just as real as any concrete thing you can touch, smell, and sense. Your intuition, your imagination—all of these things are a part of a reality that is as concrete as anything else is. Anything the human imagination has access to is just as real as anything else. The modern world is going to have to get to that place sooner or later, one way or another. That's just the way it is.

HSW: Do you think that we in the modern world are prepared to handle the power that magic brings with it?

MPS: The danger is in the management of power. "Power" is understood here in the West as something that distinguishes you from the other, something that makes you big and the other small. This results in a greater ability to manipulate others. The kind of power that I raise a flag against is the sort of power that comes into the hands of someone who is basically an adolescent and can go on a rampage with these things. But when it is bestowed on a person with wisdom, that same power can turn that person into a servant, working for the betterment of the culture, the village, the society. The more power you have, the humbler you must become. In my culture, the most anonymous people are the ones that have the most power. Whereas, the ones that have a great profile and visibility don't.

HSW: *It's like the saying, "Power over people is so dangerous a thing that only those who do not want it can be trusted with it."*

MPS: That's right. You've got the point.

HSW: *In a tribal situation, only certain specially chosen people are given access to this knowledge. Here, anyone who can pay for a workshop can learn this stuff. There really isn't a system of checks and balances set up.*

MPS: That's true. The commodification of shamanism and spirituality is very obvious here in the West. It's certainly not like that in the village, where you can have all the money in the world, but certain things are not for sale—period. I mean, they would take your money, but they're not allowed to give you the power you want to buy, because they themselves are going to have a serious problem if they do that. In the West it is assumed that, basically, everything is for sale—that you can buy magic.

HSW: *As a teacher, do you get nervous about dispensing this kind of knowledge to the masses?*

MPS: I do get very nervous about that, because it's never obvious whether the person whom you are sharing Spirit with is the person who has the capacity to be wise about the utilization of it. I get so many people who come to me saying that they have seen in a vision that they have to work with me. When I check them out in divination, I realize, no, they are after something else. I cannot just tell them to go to Hell, because that's not very nice, but eventually I find myself in this strange quandary of having to gently give them the kind of thing that they *are* ready for. You cannot put a gallon of water in a twelve-ounce glass. It just doesn't work. Even at the level that I am at, there are certain things that I just can't handle. I get introduced to them, but I realize that living in two worlds really disqualifies me from being a keeper of certain kinds of things. So I try to do my best to fill people up to the level they are at and leave it at that.

HSW: But despite the potential dangers of this kind of thing, you still believe in passing on the knowledge?

MPS: I do. I think, just as anything else, there is an evolutionary aspect to this work. Eventually the current state will be transcended onto something much more responsible and much more concerted. Once the spiritually awakened person grows out of the consumer thrust, what is left is something that is much more grounding. Which is why I still think that this work is hopeful.

HSW: Let's shift gears from the magical to a more mundane subject: money. Having been exposed to and brought up in both worlds, do you really believe it is possible to create a society that has the material abundance of the West with the spiritual and ritualistic abundance of indigenous cultures, or is this just a utopian ideal?

MPS: Of course it is possible. There is always a tendency to believe that you can't be spiritual and still be associated with the material, but in reality, matter and spirit are not antithetical to one another. There is spirit in matter and there is matter in spirit. And so it certainly indicates that spirituality and materialism can shake hands somewhere in order to create balance. Balance is the key, because the culture that is materially advanced is proportionally spiritually scarce, and the culture that is spiritually advanced lacks the material—at least in the sense that the material world knows about.

So this raises the issue about abundance. Abundance is obviously something that constitutes a challenge to mankind, because modern economic philosophy is not based on abundance, it is based on scarcity. As a result, there are First Worlds, Second Worlds, Third Worlds. What that means is that when you exclude spirit from matter, then you get matter that is really not fulfilling. Equally, when you delete matter from spirit, you get spirit that really drains your body and sends you out. It is only those communities that are capable of striking a balance between these two that are able to find the kind of abundance and prosperity that is healthy and long-lasting.

HSW: A trend that has been happening lately is for different organizations to bring indigenous shamans to the Western world, to provide healings and teachings for the people here. In their villages, these healers use a barter system, a small token of thanks for the shaman's assistance. When they come here, however, they are paid cash—often as much as one hundred dollars per session. What can, and oftentimes does, happen in cases like this is that once the shamans are exposed to this kind of money, they begin to refuse to work for anything less. I've heard story after story about shamans who are ostracized from their villages soon after returning to their villages because they come back with a new attitude and a pocket full of cash.

MPS: I see your point. I really, really do. The balancing is not an easy thing, because just as spirit comes with a character, matter has its own dynamic as well. If someone who is buried in spirituality for a long time becomes abruptly introduced to matter, typically that person loses his head and becomes completely intoxicated. Similarly, when I've taken people from this culture to my country and introduced them to the spirituality there, it is just as intoxicating. I have noticed that there is indeed a need to come up with a gentle process of familiarizing one with the other. You've got to come to a place where you are familiar enough with both in order not to have the kind of attachment that imprisons you. So far, we haven't reached that level yet. The question is how we get there. I don't have an answer to it yet. I think this is the kind of question that we have to collectively unite our imaginations to come up with an answer to.

HSW: Are you optimistic that we can find a way?

MPS: Oh yeah. Without optimism, there is no reason for existing here. There are too many bad things. If we are not hopeful, then life really sucks.

Spirituality really can influence a society for the better. It is basically the source of inspiration for a new economy, a new society, because of this connection to community and to healing.

Eventually, if the current economic philosophy is going to change, that change must be influenced by spirituality. My sense is that, as things stand, with the kind of frenetic consumption mold that humans are in, one day the Earth is going to be depleted. So how do you create a society from outside of a consumer spirit? For one thing, it will have to be a community with a whole lot of spirit in it. To me, that is the piece that is inevitable.

Larry Peters, Ph.D.

© John Tasker

Shamanism, as with all the higher spiritualities, looks beyond the opposites. It moves beyond the categories of things like that. For example, light and dark, up and down, good and evil, male and female, subject and object—those are distinctions that you and I have been educated in as a part of assembling reality, when in fact, all these opposites predispose and suppose each other. One couldn't have light without darkness. You'd never see the stars in the sky unless it had a dark background. Foreground and a background, convex and concave—remove one, remove the other.

—Larry Peters, Ph.D.

Dr. Larry Peters is a licensed psychotherapist and an initiated shaman in the Tibetan Bön tradition. In the process of finishing up his undergraduate work in his late twenties, Peters became deeply involved in the Buddhist path, specifically, the Tibetan tradition, which led to a parallel interest in the workings of the mind and the teachings of Carl Jung and other spiritually minded psychologists.

In graduate school at UCLA—at a time when Toltec initiate Carlos Castaneda was completing his Ph.D. and lecturing there—Peters combined his spiritual and psychological pursuits with studies in anthropology, eventually receiving a grant to go to Nepal to do further research on the Tibetan Buddhist path. There he began his integration into the culture of the Tamang, a Tibetan people and one of the largest ethnic groups in Nepal, who live primarily in and around the Katmandu Valley.

During his time studying with the lamas and other Buddhist mentors of the area, Peters began to hear stories about certain healers in the village where he was living who supposedly were able to perform miraculous feats of healing. Intrigued, Peters began attending the native ceremonies, and watched as a local shaman performed healings that had miraculous effects on the people who came to him.

"People who would come in unable to walk would walk away from the healing on their own two feet," Peters recalls. "There was one case where a woman had become totally blind, whose sight was restored. This man could do remarkable feats of magic. For example, he had achieved mastery over fire. He could swallow live coals and put his hands in boiling oil, pulling them out unscathed."

Soon after, Peters began an apprenticeship with the shaman, who turned out to be an expert in Tamang mythology and healing practices. Other teachers followed, and Peters eventually was initiated as a shaman in the Bön tradition. He shares the wisdom he has gained from his experiences with the Tamang shamans with others throughout the world, conducting workshops on Tibetan shamanism across the United States, Europe, and Asia, as well as leading experiential initiation journeys to Nepal. His many articles have appeared in numerous magazines, including the quarterly journal Shaman's Drum.

*Hillary S. Webb: Nepal is a crossroads for some of the world's most
embraced spiritual philosophies. Both the Hindu and Buddhist civilizations were born in Nepal. Buddhism was brought to Tibet by way
of Nepal, and many of the Buddhist saints are said to have received
enlightenment there. How do the Tamang shamans cohabit with two
such influential and enduring religious traditions?*

Larry Peters: In reality, Tamang shamanism is not a distinct religion
from Buddhism or Hinduism. In Nepal, they've all essentially
become one, even though, intellectually, they are in many ways
quite contrary to each other. Early Tibetan Buddhism was able to
integrate a lot of the shamanic beliefs of the Tibetan people into its
teachings. One could say that Tibetan Buddhism is really a synthesis between the old Bön shamanic animistic belief systems that
existed long before the arrival of Buddhism in Tibet and the teachings of the Buddha.

There are a number of Tibetan legends that tell of the con-
frontation of the early Bön shamanic religion by Lamaism. In the
Tamang myth, the Buddhist saint Guru Rinpoche and Nara Bon
Chen, the first shaman, were arguing about whose religion should
be the Tamang religion. In an attempt to resolve the conflict, the
two decided to race up a mountain—winner-take-all, so to speak.
Nara the shaman played his drum and flew up the mountain
towards the peak. Guru Rinpoche got on a vulture, the biggest bird
in Tibet, and flew up high into the sky, tripping the shaman as he
flew by. Not to be beaten, the shaman played his drum again and
sent a swarm of bees to attack Guru Rinpoche. The bees stung his
face, but being a good Buddhist, Guru Rinpoche would not flick the
bees away because they might be harmed. So Guru Rinpoche fell
down to the bottom of the mountain as well. Out of respect, the
shaman healed the lama's wounds, and since neither of them had
made it to the top, it was decided that the lamas would be in charge
of handling funeral rites while the shamans would be in charge of
healing the sick.

That myth sort of shows the division, although those lines are
not entirely pure. For instance, there's a whole branch of Tibetan
medicine that the lamas practice, although the shamans handle most
levels of spiritual healing. And also in some places, the shamans

conduct funeral rites. So these distinctions are myth distinctions and ideals. When I was doing my dissertation on Tamang shamanism, I used to do a lot of mental gymnastics of trying to throw things into nice, neat, intellectual categories. This is Buddhist, this Hindu, that shamanic. But in the shamanic folk religion, overlap makes no difference. To the people, the Hindu deities, Buddhist deities, and shamanic deities are incarnations of each other. Thus Shiva and Guru Rinpoche, like Vishnu and Buddha, are manifestations of the same soul.

HSW: But these gods and goddesses are viewed somewhat differently in each of the spiritual traditions, aren't they?

LP: The difference is that in Buddhism, the deities have transcendental qualities, while in shamanism, the gods and goddesses and the spirits continue to play their role in the environment. They are in the mountains; they are in the trees. They reside everywhere, and the shaman, who is in communication with them, comes to know about the inner workings of their world. Buddhist processes are more concerned with what I'd call "psychological spirituality"—nirvana and self-liberation and compassion and all that.

HSW: I've heard before, or perhaps I read this in one of your articles, that the Buddhist lamas in that area are a bit wary of the practices of the shamans, seeing them in some ways as being rather sinister and somewhat dangerous.

LP: Well, because the shamans in a sense play with supernatural forces, and since there is always a lot of doubt whether they are doing sorcery or they are doing shamanism, some of the lamas in Nepal see shamanism as being rather dark and foreboding and illusionary. When I first arrived in Tibet, the lamas were somewhat fearful that I was going to get involved in all this "dark spirituality." They gave me all sorts of protection—made me rosary beads to have with me so that it would all work well.

That's not where the people are at, though. Shamanism continues to play a strong role in the areas where the victory of Buddhism was not as complete. I did my research in South Asia, and the shamans that I work with there hark from Tibet, the place least influenced by the Buddhist proselytism process. The folks there go to the shamans. They are very aware of the spiritual forces of the community and look upon their own misfortune as well as their good luck as a direct result of their relationship to Spirit.

HSW: Which leads nicely to my next question. The most vital part of the shaman's initiation in any tradition has to do with establishing a close relationship with Spirit. That relationship is what makes all of this work. How do the Tamang people make this connection during their apprenticeships?

LP: There are a lot of different levels to the shamanic initiation process. Different cultures experience each level in different ways, but one of those universal elements is that the first level consists of what is known as the "Calling," where you get chosen. In Bön shamanism this is called the *Ban Jankri* experience. *Ban Jankri* is Nepali for forest-shaman. The *Ban Jankri* are yeti-like creatures that reside in the forest, and who are considered half-human and half-animal. Some stories make it seem that they are the progenitors of the human race as well. Their role is to abduct the candidate and bring them to the forest where they teach them to be shamans—or rather, they will teach them if the person has a pure heart, and will refuse to teach them if they don't. During the training, the *Ban Jankri* show the candidate such things as how to leap from mountaintop to mountaintop, and then finally, how to fly. They teach mastery of fire. That's how my first teacher learned how to put his hands in boiling oil without being burned. One could say that the Calling is the element that gives one an immediate relationship to the spirits.

After that initial Calling experience, there are at least two different ways of proceeding. My current teacher, Aama Bombo, whose name means "Mother Shaman," is what they call an *aph se aph*, a self-taught shaman, because she never really had an external teacher. Her father, a shaman who had passed away many years earlier, became her guiding spirit. She inherited his memories, so to speak, and so a lot of the work that she does is a bit different from those who were educated with an outside teacher. If you do find an external guru, it is at this point that he will teach you the techniques of how to establish relationships with those spirits that you met during your Calling experience. You learn how to bring them into your body when you want them to come, and thereby come to control them so that one can use them in order to help other people.

HSW: And how is that taught?

LP: Different gurus handle these teachings in different ways. My first teacher had us do *guru pujas* and sacred pilgrimages, at least once a month, though sometimes we'd do *guru puja* as much as once a week in order to learn the secrets of healing and divination from our inside teacher, or "chief guru." During the pilgrimages, we would go to a sacred site to make a relationship to the deity and to ask for guidance and power in order to be able to receive the teachings. Pilgrimage is a main process of initiation for the Tamang shamans. It is a rite of passage. One goes to purify one's heart. One goes to remember the great deeds of the divinity. It is a way of leaving this world and then coming back with the power given by the deity to do shamanic work. This is the level of initiation that focuses on establishing a close enough relationship with the spirits and deities so that they can help you do the work of healing.

Now, there are a couple of phases inside of that. First, you have to learn how to call on the good, helpful spirits; how to invoke them and bring them into your body. Then you have to learn how to allow them to speak through you during ritual so that you can channel their spiritual diagnoses telling what the influences are that are harming the person. The second part of that involves being able to gain control over the *bad* spirits—to be able to see what role they are playing and also to be able to send them away to their proper places.

A lot of this work is done during *guru puja*, but there is also the final aspect of initiation, called *gufa*, during which the novices receive visions and learn to master evil spirits. A *gufa* is a man-made cave, traditionally built in a cemetery. While it's set up in a place of death, it is really a place of birth and transformation. The *gufa* structure stands on four stilts and is about five feet high. There's a ladder that connects to the hollowed-out frame. The ladder has nine rungs to it, and each one of the rungs represents a level of the upper, heavenly worlds. The shaman climbs inside, thereby going up to above the ninth level, the place where Ghesar, the great shaman's deity, resides. Ghesar is the ruler of the universe, the Source, the All-Father, All-Mother. One of the aspects of the *gufa* is to make a journey to Ghesar and to receive initiation at his hands. The shaman stays inside the structure and drums for three, five, seven, or nine days, depending on the teacher. While the initiates are there, Ghesar presents them with a special shaman's soul. He also gives them power to do healings, to do divinations and many other things.

That is one aspect, but the main underlying purpose of the ceremony is to establish even, honest relationships with the spirits of the dead that are caught in this world and who are the agents of misfortune and who cause illnesses. It's not that they are bad, although sometimes they're called bad spirits, it's more that they're ignorant and trapped. The shaman has to make a relationship with them in order to determine why they are causing illness, what it is they want, and how to bargain with them in order to dissuade them from harming their patient.

HSW: I'm curious as to the idea behind pilgrimages and why they are so essential to the Tamang initiation process. Why is going to a place of power any different than doing these rituals at home?

LP: Well, a pilgrimage is a journey to visit the deity at the deity's residence. One enters in the way of relationship and goes for a specific purpose. Sometimes it's for initiation, sometimes to beg for power or for healings or for guidance. You go to the residence of the spirit and you pray, you do your ritual, you call on the god or goddess. You have to approach with a pure heart—the best thing is to never ask for too much because the deities will see it as greedy. The best thing to do is to ask for others. Often one would go to specific places at special times of the year because that's when the deity is expected to be there. In Nepal, lay people who are ill or whose children are ill often go on pilgrimages to seek healing.

HSW: Do you see the act of going on a pilgrimage as something important that we are lacking here in the West?

LP: People here go on pilgrimages too. When their kids get sick, they go to places called the clinics, they go to the hospitals, they go to the Mayo clinic, they go to the cancer centers or wherever the big places of healing are. Those are pilgrimages too. Nothing stops them when they need to go, and that is a lot of what it is about.

Pilgrimages are also a way for people to participate in the mythology of the culture. For example, many of the Tamang go to the Shiva shrines at a specific time of year. There's a grand story about how the deities, whose powers were waning, got hold of a big serpent and, with the help of demons, wrapped it around the central mountain, Mount Meru, and churned the ocean in order to produce an elixir to restore their waning strength. Unfortunately, they held the serpent too tightly and its venom dripped out into the waters. They called Shiva to fix it because Shiva is the only deity that has experience in handling poisons. Shiva drank the poison from the ocean and held it in his throat, which is why one of Shiva's names is "Old Blue Throat." He ran up into the mountains, into the Himalayas, and created this great glacier lake up at fifteen thousand feet called Gosainkunda. Shiva then lay in the waters and all of his illness from the poison was released. So just like Shiva healed himself, the people go there to these places for healing. They are participating in the spiritual reality of the world. These places are special because they are enveloped in a great mythology. And mythology doesn't mean something fake. It's a reality that is lived, that is part of the belief system that underlies all culture.

HSW: *Are you saying that a myth becomes a truth once we make it a part of our belief system?*

LP: Sure, everything is that way from some perspective.

HSW: *You know, certain times while I've been discussing aspects of shamanism in the process of putting this book together, the experience can take on a very internal, psychological sound. Other times, like when discussing spirits, deities, et cetera, we approach it as if we are discussing outside forces. Where do psychology and shamanism meet? Are these things manifestations of our own psyche, our own unconscious, or are they things that exist outside of ourselves?*

LP: Shamanism, as with all the higher spiritualities, looks beyond the opposites. It moves beyond the categories of things like that. For example, light and dark, up and down, good and evil, male and

female, subject and object—those are distinctions that you and I
have been educated in as a part of assembling reality, when in fact,
all these opposites predispose and suppose each other. One couldn't
have light without darkness. You'd never see the stars in the sky
unless it had a dark background. Foreground and a background,
convex and concave—remove one, remove the other. If you have no
knowledge of good, you have no idea what evil is, because they are
like two sides of the same coin. In many ways, they determine each
other. So any distinctions we make between inside and outside,
between dream and reality come out of our own heads, based on
some sort of cultural consensus. We don't know what reality is. All
we know is the phenomenal world, and the phenomenal world
comes filtered through our mind, so it doesn't really make any difference.

As someone interested in psychospiritual integration, that is
how I look at it, anyway. I'm not looking to make radical distinctions. A good shaman and a good psychotherapist want to meet the
patient on the patient's ground. I'm just going with where they are
going and not erasing any possibilities. Some people believe that it
is outside forces that are bothering them. I'm not going to disagree
with that, but I am also going to allow them to see that a lot of what
we see out in the world is a mirror for what is inside us as well. Other
individuals are much more psychologically minded. That's fine, but
I will point out that we are very much connected to the beingness
of the environment as well.

HSW: As above, so below. It's a very holistic process.

LP: Shamanism is the essential psychotherapy. It's our first spiritual
discipline. There are a lot of truths that are there—ancient ways of
healing and ancient ways of being. We live in a really fortunate time.
Ways of understanding are opening up to us that haven't been available to us for a long time. We can see now that the world is alive
with story, alive with Spirit, and this is how we can be participants
in that world. Individuals used to be able to talk to the spirits, to see
the life and beingness of all of nature and the Earth. This was at a
time when animals and people spoke the same language; when
deities and spirits roamed the Earth. These were our golden times,

and shamanism is a reminder of that. It reestablishes our connection with those things that are beyond us.

HSW: And within us as well. I think I get it.

Tom Cowan

The shaman is someone who has learned how to live in ambiguity—who sees himself as part of the world, and the world as a part of him.

—Tom Cowan

Tom Cowan is a shamanic practitioner specializing in Celtic visionary and healing techniques. He is the author of a number of cross-cultural explorations of shamanism, including Fire in the Head: Shamanism and the Celtic Spirit, Shamanism as a Spiritual Practice for Daily Life, The Way of the Saints: Prayers, Practices, and Meditations, *and most recently,* Yearning for the Wind: Celtic Reflections on Nature and the Soul.

In the late 1970s and early 1980s, Cowan began a general questing for the "old ways" that revered nature.

"I've always had the sense that nature was filled with spirits," says Cowan. "That things were alive and that my ancestors were around, along with saints and angels, that there was this other world, the spirit world. I was raised a Roman Catholic, and so, as a child, I had a rich ritual and liturgical life. I loved the ceremony, the otherworldliness of going into a church or a chapel, but I also found that same kind of sacredness in nature and in the woods and along rivers."

Like many others, Cowan's introduction and involvement with shamanism came after taking an introductory workshop with the man considered the foremost authority on modern shamanism, Michael Harner. What Cowen discovered in shamanism was a tradition that could be practically applied to healing and transformation work. After studying the core shamanic practices through Harner's Foundation for Shamanic Studies, Cowan then adapted these teachings to reflect the beliefs of his Celtic and Northern European family roots.

Since 1996, Cowan has led tours to western Ireland and Scotland to practice shamanism at sacred sites and work with the spirits of the land. Tom is a minister in the Circle of the Sacred Earth, a church of animism dedicated to shamanic principles and practices. He lives in New York's Hudson River Valley, where he offers training workshops, spiritual retreats, and healing sessions for groups and individuals.

Hillary S. Webb: Your introduction to shamanism came through studying Core shamanism, a "modern" tradition that is distilled from the common principles and practices of indigenous shamans throughout the world. And yet, you have brought the teachings of your Celtic ancestry into your practices. How do the two traditions merge into one?

Tom Cowan: Every shaman has an idiosyncratic way of practicing. Even if you are in a strong tradition and are trained by elders in that tradition, you end up practicing in your own unique way. Part of that is the training. Another part is that, since every shaman works with his or her own helping spirits and ancestors, the power that you get comes from the spirits. So while the technical things that I do—such as how I do a soul retrieval or an extraction or a ritual—derive from core principles that tend to be the same all over the world, the way that I understand what I am doing, I understand through Celtic spirituality. In the Celtic tradition there are certain sources of power and certain sources of wisdom and certain ways of looking at the soul and the other world and the causes of health and illness. That's where my practice becomes Celtic. But the spirits that I work with are not necessarily Celtic.

I think the great part of any shaman's practice has to be with the spirits of the land on which he or she lives. For example, water is very important in Celtic shamanism. I live in the Hudson Valley, and so I work with the Hudson River and other streams and springs in the area—even with the well here on my own land. So although my practice is very rooted in the land here, I'm seeing it in terms of how the Celts see it.

HSW: For example, the Celts consider fire and water to be the most important elements in terms of transformation and healing.

TC: Fire and water are always used in Celtic ceremonies. For example, most of the Celtic feast days, such as Beltaine or Samhain, involve fire ceremonies. Since being healthy requires your own internal temperature to be 98.6 degrees Fahrenheit, it seems logical that fire would be part of healing, of making the person feel well.

Also in the Celtic tradition, water—springs, rivers, wells—is a great source of power and knowledge. There's an ancient myth that explains that all water is related and comes from the pool of wisdom in the other world. In that sense, all water is sacred, and every spring, well, river, and lake a passageway into the other world. Even today, people in Ireland go out to sacred wells to get water. And water that is drawn from the place where two streams meet to become a third is considered to be extremely powerful because of the sacredness of the number three, and the "betwixt and between" quality of a place where two streams converge.

HSW: How are these elements applied to healing according to the Celtic tradition?

TC: Well, when I do a healing on someone, I light a candle and have the client warm his or her hands with it. I then have them bring that warmth up to their face, their head, their stomach, or wherever they feel they need to connect with that heat. This brings the healing power of that element to the body and aura. Another technique is to carry fire around a person that you're working on. Back in the old cottages, as soon as a baby was born, the midwives would pass the child over the fire in the center of the floor three times in order to bless the child with the element of fire. At the spring festival of Beltaine, the Celts build two fires outdoors and then walk the cattle between them so that the fire purifies them of their winter ills before being put up into the higher pastures for the summer. So, during a healing, I try to incorporate things like smudging the person by letting the smoke of the fire go over them, or picking up the candle and walking around them with it.

When I do healing work, I always have a bowl of water around. The tradition is that if someone is sick, the healer goes out at dawn—that magic moment between night and day—and draws some water from a spring or well. That water is considered to be very powerful for healing. The healer then either bathes the person with the water or sprinkles it on their forehead or whatever part of their body is ailing.

HSW: Before getting involved in shamanism, you spent time exploring the Wiccan community, and even wrote two books with the noted witch Laurie Cabot. Having spent time with both traditions, what do you see is the difference between shamanism and other Earth-based spiritualities such as Wicca?

TC: There are differences, and yet they overlap. What I find about Wiccan traditions is that the people who practice them tend to do ritual in an almost dogmatic kind of way, with lots of rules and regulations. Shamanism is just too independent and idiosyncratic for that. Even when you have a shamanic drumming circle, everybody there tends to be an independent kind of person—much less group-oriented and less worried about "Am I doing this right? Am I accepted by the elders of the community?" The Wiccan traditions also have strong pantheons of gods and goddesses, and you have to buy into that. The shaman, however, doesn't really need that kind of structure or patterning. The shaman learns who the spirits are that are going to be of help through his or her personal journeying.

HSW: It also seems that the Wiccan notion of the god/goddess, male/female aspect of the Divine is a contradiction to the teachings of Celtic shamanism—a philosophy that traditionally rejects the concept of dualism.

TC: Right. The idea of rejecting dualism goes back to the Druids, who taught that all power comes in threes. This made perfect sense to Celtic thinking, because if you have three, you can't have two. If you have black and white, you have to have gray. If you have joy and sorrow, you have to have some state that transcends those two. Saint Patrick picked up on that when he explained Christianity with the idea of the Trinity.

We live in a really dualistic culture. As someone who teaches shamanism to a lot of people, I hope one of the positive things that comes out of all the workshops is that people learn that things are not cut-and-dried, black and white. That they are able to live more happily with the questions, ambiguities, and mysteries of life than they were before.

HSW: What's wrong with dualistic thinking?

TC: Dualistic thinking tends to create a split between you and the rest of the world. The shaman is someone who has learned how to live in ambiguity—who sees himself as part of the world, and the world as a part of him. The great shape-shifting traditions found in all shamanic cultures, including Celtic lore, defy the idea that we are trapped in our human bodies and in our human thinking. The Celtic idea of the soul is that it is a shape-shifter; that while it passes through the body, it is not trapped inside any physical form. That it is a kind of consciousness that can take on the consciousness of other beings and creatures such as animals and elements and so on.

Celtic art, such as the classic knotwork and braids, is a visual example of the whole idea of shape-shifting, of being intertwined and continually moving and then coming back. For example, in a design you might see a bird's tongue come out of its mouth and weave around and intertwine with other lines, and eventually end up as the tail of a dog. There's that sense that everything is connected and is continually being reshaped and reformed. Celtic practices tend to encourage the soul to have that freedom and joy of continual reshaping. It is a delight to realize that the soul is maybe as big as all nature, as big as the universe. The soul can then merge with other things and experience this mystical sense of oneness with other things and places and people.

There's a great old Celtic poem from very ancient times that says, "I am the wind that blows across the sea. I am a wave of the deep. I am the roar of the ocean. I am a hawk on a cliff. I am a lake on a plain. . . ." It goes on and on. It's the shaman's boast about how the soul can be in all those different things in nature and become one with them. It's that sense of oneness that has to overcome dualism.

HSW: The idea of rejecting dualism certainly does go against what most of us in this culture have been brought up with. Most of us have been raised on the Christian viewpoint of good versus evil, God versus the devil. Such extremes don't leave much room for anything in-between.

TC: Exactly. In the ancient Irish myths, the Fomorians—the socalled evil gods of chaos, of destruction, of "unmaking"—are not evil in the sense that they should be destroyed. You don't necessarily like what they do, because they're always destructive and violent, but there is a role for them. You have to learn to work with them. They are part of the Shapers.

HSW: Shapers?

TC: In the Bible, the Genesis story says that God created us out of nothing. The more Celtic way of looking at it is to say that God created us out of himself. In fact, *Cruthaitheair,* the Gaelic word for "Creator," really means "Shaper." It's the sense that there are powers, or maybe one divine power, who are continually shaping and reshaping all things of nature and our world—including us. So even the destructive aspects of nature, like the Fomorians, come from that same source.

HSW: Is this what you mean when you say, "At some point in the shaman's initiation, the candidate must meet the dark side of his or her consciousness"?

TC: In each of us there is a Fomorian strain that might be the cause of our anger, our resentments, our blowups, and our self-destructive impulses. But because the shaman is concerned with healing power, he or she will, at some point, discover the power that exists within this part of us as well. The shaman must then decide how to transform this so-called negative energy so that it can be made to work towards the whole, towards healing, and for doing good work.

Tom Cowan

HSW: Earlier you pointed out how Celtic artwork depicts the transformative nature of the soul. In your book, Fire in the Head, *you use Celtic myths extensively as a way of illustrating the shaman's journey.*

TC: A lot of shamanic knowledge is contained in myths and folktales and fairy tales. You go into tribal cultures and you ask people to tell their stories, and they are filled with shamanic wisdom. We Europeans have the same stories, but we think of them as children's stories, as make-believe. We don't take our folktales as seriously as we would if we were listening to the Lakota tell us their sacred stories. One way to uncover the teachings of the old European shamanism is to go back and reread the fairy tales and myths. Over the centuries they have been changed a lot to become stories to tell kids, but within them is a kernel of truth that comes out of a shaman's experience.

There's a story that pops up in a lot of Celtic collections of fairy tales about a girl who goes out into the world to seek her fortune. She spends the night with an old woman who asks her to sit by the corpse in the back room, because you always have someone sit with the corpse when you have a funeral in your home. The girl agrees, and in the middle of the night the corpse sits up and says, "If you go with me through the quaking bog, the burning forest, and the icy sea, I can retrieve my soul." She does, the corpse retrieves his soul, and they marry and live happily ever after. It sounds like many fairy tales, but if you are familiar with shamanism, something inside you should tingle and say, "This is a soul retrieval."

HSW: In Fire in the Head *you refer to* The Wizard of Oz *as "one of the greatest shamanic stories in modern literature."*

TC: The story has all the components of a shamanic journey. Dorothy gets swept up into the sky with her little dog, her power animal. There she immediately meets three spirit helpers—the Tin Man, the Lion, and the Scarecrow—who assist her in figuring out how to negotiate the different powers and requirements of the strange world of Oz that she needs to learn in order to get home. The story is really a great example of an Upper World journey. It's about acquiring wisdom and discovering what that means. Which is exactly what the shaman is trying to do.

173

HSW: The whole story even seems specifically Celtic in nature. The Munchkins, Glinda the Good Witch with her wings and wand—it sounds exactly like the faerie world that is described throughout the cosmology of Celtic shamanism. In your workshops you do work with the faerie realm. What exactly are faeries, and how do they fit into the Celtic spiritual viewpoint?

TC: Celtic people don't agree on who the faeries are. If you consult books like *Encyclopedia of Faeries* or *The Dictionary of Faeries*, you always find that there are dozens of different names and descriptions for them, for what they do and where they come from. Even in Ireland, traditions in one village about who the faeries are, are different from the village five miles down the road. But basically, faeries are spirits that live in nature. Unlike angels that come from another world, faeries are part of the Earth, part of this creation. They are in this world, involved in it. There are some faeries that are involved in maintaining nature, such as the faeries that grow the grass, the flowers, the trees, and so on. There are also faeries that are connected to the ancestors. In some Celtic lands, the belief is that when you die, you go and live with the faeries. Sometimes you even *become* them. There's also a belief that the faeries are the old gods— the old supernatural beings that were here before humans. According to the old Irish myths, when humans came, the gods sensed that their time was up; that it was time for humans to dominate the visible world. And so they retreated into the invisible world—into the trees, into the forest, into the hollow hills—and became less powerful. But they are still there, still active, and the shaman knows this. Shamans in all cultures know that these spirits are still around and still available to help or hinder us, depending on our relationship with them. There are plenty of examples where a person—not just shamans, a farmer, let's say—knows the faeries on his land. They protect his land, help provide crops and assure abundance. If he offends them, they may hinder him in some way.

HSW: In the Celtic tradition, when you go on a shamanic journey, do you seek help from faerie guides as other cultures might seek help from spirit guides?

TC: The faeries tend not to be the same as spirit guides. The spirits that I usually work with in my journeys are my power animals or ancestors. The faeries tend to be too independent for that. You have to get to know them, to be invited to see them and be with them. In workshops, I never have people actually journey into the faerie world for a number of reasons. One is that you have to be invited. Part of this tradition almost everywhere is that you don't just barge in. There is also the fear that some people don't come back—or when they finally do come back it is three hundred years later. So I tend to stay away from that.

HSW: So how does one become invited into the faerie world?

TC: The more common notion is that people stumble into the faerie world by accident or are lured into it by an attractive faerie. A lesser-known belief is not that you are actually going into their world, but that you are *becoming* faerie.

HSW: "Becoming faerie"?

TC: According to the Christian tradition, angels were created to praise and celebrate the power and the beauty of God in Heaven. One theory about the faeries is that they were created to do that on Earth—to celebrate and praise the goodness, love, and yearning of God in nature. So if you can shape-shift your soul enough to become the goodness, love, and yearning of, say, a waterfall or tree or moss-covered stone, then the faeries see you as something they should praise and celebrate.

Changing consciousness is something that we are working with all the time in shamanic workshops. If you can change your consciousness to become the consciousness of the world of nature, the faeries will make themselves known to you.

HSW: Would this be physical seeing, or in more of an intuitive manner, such as seeing with the third eye?

TC: Usually you see them with the third eye, or "second sight," as it is called in the Celtic traditions. You sense them, get little glimpses. But there are also plenty of examples of people who see them physically. It's not always like seeing a physical body—mostly they see lights or movement—but sometimes they do see what looks like physical shapes.

HSW: Here's a quote from Fire in the Head *that really struck me: "This may be, in the final analysis, the greatest gift of shamanism to the history of human spirituality: the ability to find pattern and structure in death and to render it familiar and acceptable."*

TC: In shamanic traditions and tribal cultures, death is not seen as just the end to everything. Most shamanic traditions would say that the soul doesn't just disappear completely. Shamans always feel connected to the people who have lived before, because the ancestors really haven't gone anywhere. Their spirits are still around, or can be around if we call upon them. As people who practice shamanism, the work we do is, in many ways, preparation for death and dealing with the question of what comes next.

When you ask people who have been working in shamanism a long time how has it changed their lives, one of the things that has come up over and over again is that they feel less fearful of the universe and, therefore, less fearful of death. The "something" that happens after death is a part of the other world that the shaman journeys into and comes back with information and stories about. It's not quite as unknown as it is to people who are not involved in this kind of work.

HSW: My personal belief is that fear of death is responsible, albeit unconsciously, for most of the pain and suffering in the world. Greed, anger, jealousy, all seem to stem from the basic fear of our own impending mortality.

TC: That really is true. Shamanism can provide hope for people that death is not as disastrous or as final as it might seem. And if the shaman can cast some new light on the questions of life and death, that might be one of the greatest contributions anyone can make.

Elena Avila

My weeping soul was huddled in a corner dying of neglect.
I retrieved it with a dozen red roses and sacred copal.
I lit a thousand candles and begged her for forgiveness.
I held out my arms to her and called her back to me. I
took her home and held her until she believed me.

—Elena Avila

A first-generation Chicana born in Texas, Elena Avila grew up with a mother who relied heavily on the folk-healing techniques of her native Mexico to care for her family. According to the social climate of the time, however, to believe in such old-fashioned and "superstitious" healing methods such as curanderismo was looked down upon. This pressure to assimilate into "mainstream" culture eventually brought Avila to discount her family's practices and pursue a degree in nursing.

In one of the most touching moments in her book, Woman Who Glows in the Dark: A Curandera Reveals Traditional Aztec Secrets of Physical and Spiritual Health, *Avila describes the moment when, for her, the teachings of Western medicine fused with the teachings of her family's "backward" medicine tradition.*

During her first year of nursing school, one of her professors asked her to do a report on curanderismo. She agreed, though begrudgingly.

"When my professor asked me to talk about curanderismo, I felt ashamed, insulted, and bewildered," Avila writes. "What was it she saw in me, I wondered. Did she see my ignorance, the superstitions of my culture? Over the years, I had come to associate curanderismo with everything that was primitive and backward.

"Since there was no way out of this embarrassing situation," Avila continues, "I went to the library with the intent of reading a couple of articles and bullshitting the class. Instead, something profound happened. In the quiet, scientific atmosphere of the school of nursing library, I found tangible evidence [for the teachings of curanderismo]."

Now, with degrees in both nursing and mental health, Avila herself works as a curandera, guiding her clients on their path to health. She is also a gifted poet who uses the power of words, especially poetry, as healing tools for everything from soul loss to a variety of emotional and physical problems.

Hillary S. Webb: You have written, "In curanderismo . . . the mother tongue is poetics. The healer is an artist." When you write a poem, are you calling it to you from the same place as you do a healing?

Elena Avila: Very much so. The poetry comes from my soul, my spirit. My soul and my spirit encourage me. For instance, I have been sick. I developed hepatitis C after I was given blood transfusions during the birth of my twins. I decided to take the chemo to treat it. It made me so sick that after six weeks I had to stop. I still feel tired. The other day I wrote a poem and after I wrote it, I felt good that day. I call this poem "Let Me Cry." It goes like this:

> *Dejame llorar,*
> let me cry
> The tears coming down my face are
> *agua clara,*
> clear water,
> unpolluted by the past.
> I cry because I feel good.
>
> If you ask me today, are you still sick?
> I would say no. For the first time in weeks
> I feel that the ailing times are behind me.
> I won't chase them down, these times can stay behind.
> I won't ask what eternity is or if my spirit will keep on
>   living after I die.
> It's okay if it dies with me.
> I feel it stirring within me now and that is all I know.
>
> When my spirit flies, my soul sings a
> song and my feet tap out the tune.
> I am a lover of mother-father God,
> all living things and last,
> but never the least, me.
>
> I did not want to cheat myself of heaven, so I make my
>   heaven here.

HSW: Beautiful.

EA: The next two days after I wrote that, I didn't feel good. But I looked at that poem and I got the message from my own soul that said, "Yes, honey, it is not going to be all black and white like you would like, but eventually you will feel good."

HSW: Your soul becomes your best teacher.

EA: It truly has become my best teacher. It truly has. The mind has so many limitations. It is so imprinted by trauma-drama, by the way we were raised and what we were told and not told, how we were validated and not validated throughout our lives. We develop some ways of thinking that truly impede us. When I work with people, I start with a *platica*—a heart-to-heart talk. I listen to the language of the soul. I also listen to the language of the mind and I start to pick out the distortions that people have.

There is a poem that I call "Collecting Thoughts." When I read this to people who come to see me in a *platica*, sometimes they cry. Many times they say, "That's me. You have written about me."

This is "Collecting Thoughts":

I accept my death.
I no longer wait for it.
It will happen in a day I cannot mark in a calendar
so I rejoice this moment
and release the death of a million paper cuts.

Distorted parasitic thoughts born from a past trauma-
    drama
have a sharp and dangerous edge that slowly cuts,
cunningly restricts
and deviously shrinks the wings of your soul.

One day you watch a hawk soar and notice tears stream-
    ing down your face.
When was the last time you transcended the conflict in
    your mind?

Challenge those thoughts for if unnoticed
they will cascade on your feelings
and your soul will become musty from lack of use.

Feeling emotions from distorted thoughts
is like believing that the world is flat.

Anticipating fear over what will never happen
is like a boxer punching his own face,
but the bell never rings to stop the fight.

Chasing flight is just as silly. You can run
but you cannot hide from the blood-sucking leech
planted in your mind.

Thinking of your future is
like rehearsing a play that will never go on stage.

Stop feeding it. Let it die of starvation,
open new cubicles in your mind and soft love
will flow into the arteries of your real life.

The vampire will have to find a new source.
I hope it dies of hunger.

Be an unsociable host to the parasite of your mind.
You will know when it dies
when you find yourself soaring alongside a red tail hawk
without even thinking about it.
You will know it when you choose to live until your
      death day arrives.

Peace of mind is my new dream and my gift to my soul.
I opened new cubicles in my mind and discovered
my true thoughts and feelings.

My weeping soul was huddled in a corner dying of neglect.
I retrieved it with a dozen red roses and sacred copal.
I lit a thousand candles and begged her for forgiveness.
I held out my arms to her and called her back to me. I
took her home and held her until she believed me.

The divine mother, *virgen de Guadeloupe*, welcomed us home.
With her robe of a million stars she rubbed us with stardust
and my fragmented soul sneezed itself back into my
      "standing by" heart.

Split became united and an inner wedding was the frosting
      on the cake.

Are you letting your mind control the path of your soul?
      Stop it.
Xipe, goddess of spring,

break through the frozen ground of self-defeat
so that hope-filled shoots can break through
and grow with the sun.

I lean on my spiritual door and let the butterflies in.
My casa is not your casa.
This door is opened just for me.
I softened my heart to peace and stillness
and collect thoughts that reflect the desire of my soul.

I am a collector of the innocent thoughts I had before
    the bomb fell.
Listen. My heart is ticking.

HSW: That's very powerful.

EA: I started healing and then poetry started to come out. The soul is so creative. It speaks in dreams and art and in creative ways. And each one of us has a unique soul, which needs to express itself. That's what I believe. Our soul is who we are, not what we were molded into. The Aztecs call it our *Yolitzin*, which means "knowledge of my essence." That is, my good and bad and ugly. My talents and everything else. Everything about me. That's my job—to know all of me. And to *accept* all of me. We want to find the language of the soul, because the mind is so limited and so full of parasites because of the way we were raised, that it is very hard to know your truth from your trauma-drama.

HSW: You have to untangle it all and figure out which is which.

EA: Exactly.

HSW: As a writer, I find that it is in that creative mind-set that my intuition starts flowing at its best.

EA: This medicine is very intuitive. Practicing at an intuitive level has made me very intuitive. And as it made me more intuitive, it also started to open up my creative self. For me the best way to express myself is through poetry.
    Here is one called "Women Make a Life Outside Their Bodies":

I made my life, a life outside my body,
my soul wrapped round my lover's heart like roots do
     when they take hold of soil.
I made myself a home outside the beating of his heart.

My spirit could not reach my body,
so it danced around it like a shadow
on a tango dance floor.

Ruminations without exit cycling nowhere
is the price to pay when women make a life outside their
     bodies.
The space between my heart and mind kept me busy
     with useless thoughts.

I was like ice cream in the sun.
I knew how to love you.
I even knew when to leave you.
I just don't know how to forget you.

I can't do it anymore—loving you more than me.

My soul is caught in the shadows of good-bye
and I think of you with every gesture my body makes
as it lets go of you.

A good place to be—in our bodies and out of our minds.

HSW: Wonderful.

EA: Women can relate to that. It's like, "Yeah. I've done that."

HSW: Listening to you recite your poetry, the way you speak, its sounds almost like a prayer.

EA: It very much is that way. My poetry is like a prayer because it comes from Spirit. I really feel that my work is aided by Spirit. I evoke the gods and the goddesses, and when I do recite that poem, it is in my body.

HSW: When you are doing healings, do you ever recommend that your clients start to do some sort of creative act themselves?

EA: Yes, I do. It comes naturally. Hidden talents start to come out. They start letting me know that they are starting to paint or starting to catch their dreams. It's a natural process since we are creative people.

HSW: *A healing in shamanic view is about taking away blockages. Once those blockages are removed, creativity can flow freely.*

EA: It really does. The whole medicine is quite creative. During a healing, I like to pop in a poem without introducing it first. All of a sudden I will perform them. It catches the client by surprise. And I always make it a point to make the poem simple enough so that they can understand what I am saying. Many times they laugh. Or they say, "You just opened my heart. I have been in denial for so long about what I am supposed to do. I've been in denial about how much I drink or how much I envy the skinny women or whatever, and you just woke me up to that."

HSW: *It reminds me of the koans in Zen Buddhism—simple questions used to clear the mind and act as a vehicle for an awakening experience.*

EA: I will give you a part of a poem I call "Mending Wings and Building Bridges."

> You tell me that the burdens of your spiritual path have
>   reduced you to embers and you long for the inno-
>   cence of ignorance.
> I hear you.
> I'll be a temporary bridge for you
> but you take your own ass across the waters of your doubt.
>
> You are too big to be carried so do not pretend to be asleep.
> What do you want from me?
> Freshly minted divine ambivalence to test the limits of
>   your god?

When I tell people that, I am saying, "Take responsibility for your healing." If you think that a *curandera* has a magic eagle feather and she is going to sweep everything away, you are either going to go to a charlatan who will take all your money, or you are fooling yourself. You've got to take responsibility for your own health. I'll work as hard as you, but you've got to work also. It's a *co*creation.

HSW: That can be a radical way to think in a culture brought up on the magic pill. We want to put the power onto someone or something else.

EA: Because I am a *curandera*, people tell me all kinds of things that they wouldn't tell anybody else. One of the things is, "Have I been cursed?" I tell them, we are always cursing ourselves. Doctors will curse you and give you death sentences. Other healers, other people will curse you, saying, "You'll never amount to anything." But you have a responsibility in accepting that curse or not.

Sometimes people get disappointed and say, "Oh, I was hoping you would find a curse and take it away so I don't have to do anything else." I've been working in psychiatry and as a *curandera*, so I know human behavior. So people can come to me and I could fool them into thinking that I am this powerful psychic and take advantage of them. And I point that out to them. I say, "If I was a charlatan I would ask you for four thousand dollars and you would probably give it to me." I see a lot of people wanting a magic cure. They want someone else to take away their problems. I don't know why we have gotten to that place, but that is what I see.

HSW: One would think that we would want to claim our own power, but for a lot of people that is an extremely terrifying prospect.

EA: Because they are so used to their distorted thoughts. I gave one of my clients homework. I told her to write down all her thoughts and told her we were going to go through them in our next visit and point out the distorted thoughts that come from her trauma. But she didn't do it. She asked me, "Why didn't I do it?" She said, "I don't know what I am afraid of." I said to her ,"How long have you carried around all these thoughts?" She said, "Since I was three." I said, "If we take away all these distorted thoughts, who are you going to be?" And she burst out crying. She said, "That's my fear. I'm afraid I don't know who I am going to be."

HSW: We identify ourselves with our pain?

EA: Yeah. Except that it is not real. But there is that choice to hold on to it or not. I say, if you want to live a false life, then that is your choice, but don't bullshit yourself. Do it with awareness.

HSW: How would one work at getting rid of those false thoughts and reclaim one's power?

EA: It depends on each individual. Each individual comes with their own incredible uniqueness. My job is to figure out how best to work with them, to get the mind to cooperate, to get the body to cooperate, to get the soul to start feeling hopeful that the true essence of who we are will now take priority. And since we are all so unique, it is hard to say, "Do it this way. Do it that way." But I always incorporate ceremony and *limpias* and cleansings. We do *platicas* so that they understand what it is they need to release—for instance, "I am going to let go of this particular false belief system." Then when they come for the ceremony they have an awareness of what they are releasing. It is not some doctor or so-called healer that is saying, "I see this inside of you and I've determined what it is and I am going to take it away from you because I am magic." It's a lot of work.

HSW: I would imagine the process of figuring out what the issue is, is a fundamental part of the healing.

EA: It is. I believe in empowering them. I don't want them to be dependent on me. I want them to learn so that they can apply it to situations in their lives. My work is intense. It really goes to the root.

And so I go spontaneously into a poem:

I am a third-world woman, God worshiper.
Running along the path of the sky
wearing my starry skirt and
tripping on myself as I make the sign of the cross.

Yes I am different, but there is enough space in the
universe for paradoxes.
And I like being pyramidal, cruciform and human
simultaneously.

I swish the ancient prayers in my mouth like holy gargle
but I don't spit them out at you
or to you.

I rub the sacred egg over your body to help you give
 your wounds to God.
Don't be chicken.
Let the chicken be the instrument that picks out the
 cosmic caca
from your bodies. Who did you think you were?
 Superwomen? Superman?
I swallowed the myth like consecrated wine
because the Earth is going to Heaven when it dies.
You can do whatever you want.
I just want to go to Heaven on Earth's last sigh,
And I need your arms to fly.

HSW: There is a wonderful line from a poem by El Salvadorian poet Roque Dalton that says, "I believe the world is beautiful, and that poetry, like bread, is for everyone."

EA: Poetry can just explain it all, right? We need each other, no matter who we are or where we come from or what religion we belong to. So you can do whatever you want and I will too, but at our last moment we need each other. We are not as separate as we would like to think.

Evelyn C. Rysdyk and C. Allie Knowlton

People would not do to each other some of the things they do if they realized that you and I are one. It just wouldn't happen. Kids would not be killing kids at school if they had a sense of being connected to the kids they killed. There's a desperate need to find a way to reexperience that we are connected to everything. It's like a spider web—when one part moves the whole thing moves.

—C. Allie Knowlton

C. Allie Knowlton is a former pastor of small churches in rural Maine who later became a licensed clinical social worker. Despite the deep connection to Spirit she herself had formed through love of nature, she says, "I saw so much hunger in the people I worked with, hunger that I knew was not being fed by traditional, mainline church life. I felt there had to be some way to support people to experience spirituality firsthand."

After a series of life crises, Knowlton met up with a man who trained her in shamanic journeying.

"From the moment I did my first journey, it was like coming home for the first time in my life," she says.

Evelyn Rysdyk was working in an advertising firm in New York when she found herself in the midst of "one of those screeching depressions where everything that came before no longer had any meaning." Looking through an Open Center course catalog one day, she came across a listing for Michael Harner's workshop, The Way of the Shaman. She sent in her deposit, and over the course of the weekend learned the shamanic journey process. The effect it had on her psyche, she says, was extraordinary.

"Depression has this effect of really closing life down, as if you're wearing blinders," Rysdyk says. "Everything gets closed down narrower and narrower. The journey experience opened it all back up again."

Trained in both Core shamanism and indigenous practices from Siberia, North America, and South America, the two women met during a course sponsored by the Foundation for Shamanic Studies in 1991. A year later, they cofounded Spirit Passages, in Yarmouth, Maine. As teachers of shamanism, they offer workshops on the shamanic journey process and advanced shamanism across the United States and Canada. They have presented their work in very diverse venues ranging from hospitals to the International Conference of Science and Consciousness in Albuquerque, New Mexico. Allie and Evelyn have also helped thousands of people take control of their health through connecting with Spirit. The two are cofounders of True North, a unique, integrated health center where, as shamanic healers, they collaborate with medical doctors, psychiatrists, and complementary health practitioners.

Rysdyk is the author of Modern Shamanic Living *and a soon-to-be-published book on shamanic healing.*

Hillary S. Webb: You call yourselves "shamanic practitioners" as opposed to "shamans." Is this just semantics, or do you see a difference between the two terms?

Evelyn C. Rysdyk: "Shaman" is really a tribal word. It comes from a context where there is some kind of process within the tribe whereby somebody earns the name of "shaman." And while similar processes may happen in this culture, I feel like we "practice" shamanism. I don't think you ever get really good at it. You practice it your whole life. So, in someone else's eyes this may be semantics, but to me it feels like not being someone who is ripping off someone else's culture.

HSW: I always find it interesting how people in this culture find their way onto this path. I mean, in an indigenous setting, there are elders to guide the process, who can recognize when the spirits have "chosen" someone to begin the training. Most people in this society aren't brought up to recognize physical or mental illness as a shamanic initiation.

C. Allie Knowlton: The spirits have to work really hard to help people in this culture to get on this path! Spirits have to use a lot of different ways to direct the path until it becomes clear. One thing that Michael Harner says when people ask him "How do you know if this is a good shamanic practitioner to go to?" he says, "Spirit will guide that. If there are good results, then people will continue going to that person. If not, no matter what kind of training they have, if they are not following Spirit, eventually people just won't go to them." There's a kind of natural selection process in the Western world that has to make up for the tribal thing that we don't have.

ECR: There is a voice inside all of us that has a longing for completeness. A longing that niggles away at us. If that feeling is going along with an illness, or going along with a feeling of discontent in one's life, or depression, I advise people to seek out others who are involved in spiritual traditions. Unlike in a tribal situation where the elder may recognize you and mentor you through the process, in this culture we have to find our own mentors.

It's really important to pay attention to that little voice that knows there's something more. When we look at it in this culture, everything gets translated into consumerism. That "something more" turns into "I need a better car," "I need a better job," "I need a better house." But still, there's always that feeling of not being quite satisfied. For me at least, the spiritual work has satisfied a place in myself, and also continued to want to make me grow.

CAK: The shamanic spiritual path is very rigorous. I think a lot of people may not want to commit as much of themselves as you have to in order to develop a shamanic practice. It isn't that you can't have fun and enjoy life, but it's not the same as some of the spiritual paths where the practice of it goes alongside your mundane life. Shamanism *becomes* your life. That weeds out some. And also calls some. Part of the calling is that as you become more and more involved, it becomes clearer and clearer that you either can't live without it or can't wait to get away from it. There doesn't see to be a middle of the road after a while.

ECR: The degree of return is concurrent with the degree of investment that you put into it. If you feed your spiritual life and strengthen your connection to the spirits that you work with, your life changes. And you become willing to make any change that will continue to make things fit together. The way our lives are set up in this culture and the way that Spirit operates sometimes are quite convergent. And I think having a strong spiritual life makes us want to pull more and more of the threads into harmony. And this requires work. You have to let go of some previous conceptions about what you are, who you are, what's important, what's not important, and what's worth working for.

We have an extraordinary possibility to be electrically alive all the time. But in order to do that, you have to open up to the possibility of it and continue to move anything in your life out of the way to allow it to be there. You have to work through your fear. You have to work through your doubt. You have to work through your anger, judgment—all those things that would interfere with the purity of the experience and still be grounded here in the Earth plane.

HSW: That can be a tricky balance.

ECR: It *is* a tricky balance! But it is so worth it to be really, really alive every day. To never have a day where you are just sleepwalking your way through anymore.

HSW: It often occurs to me that making a commitment to Spirit is like accepting a marriage proposal. How does one know if they are ready for that kind of commitment?

CAK: It comes back to personal responsibility. Am I willing to take personal responsibility for working through all the stuff that I've got in my life so that there is more room for my body to receive the input from Spirit? Because this is a working partnership between Spirit and our own physical container. The stronger our own physical container is, the more that Spirit can work through us. It's a place of deciding, do I really want to commit myself to continue working on my stuff the rest of my life so that when someone comes to me for a healing, I'm not in the way of Spirit moving through me?

ECR: And it will be amazingly clear what your "stuff" happens to be! As you pull in power, as you work with Spirit, you will bump square into whatever your little pile of poo poo is. It'll stop you in your tracks. Now I have to decide, do I want to plow through that pile? Do I have the courage? Do I have the stamina to work through my own stuff?

It's an ongoing process. It's a big process. But it's worth it.

HSW: In your practice, you get a lot of referrals from doctors, psychotherapists, and so on. What is missing from these "modern" healing methods that shamanism fills in?

ECR: Most practitioners like doctors and chiropractors and osteopaths work in the physical world, the visible world. We address what is going on in the invisible world, in the world of Spirit. Through the doorway of Spirit, we are able to work on those physical issues or mental health issues or emotional issues. There are lots of practitioners who attend to the physical body and attend to doing practical therapy. We are attending to the spirit, and through the spirit, we can help those other changes happen.

CAK: A powerful part of our work is attending to somebody's spirit in the way a midwife attends to a pregnant woman who is about to give birth. I think there's something really powerful in attending to somebody's spirit. In assisting that spirit to become strong.

HSW: You both started down this path once you learned the journeying process. How would you describe what happens when you take someone through a shamanic journey?

ECR: Journeying means taking your consciousness from this reality to the spirit world, the world which Harner calls "Non-Ordinary Reality." I love that expression because they are just both as real.

Going from this reality to the other reality literally takes us out of the confines of the world we live in and brings us into a state of expanded perception. A part of the spiritual growth that happens in journeying is that you begin to live more and more with the understanding that you are in that expanded place all the time, even though your perception isn't always. It's a matter of moving the blinders out more and more, so that you recognize that you are in this unfathomable miracle that we live in all the time.

CAK: The most amazing thing to me is that the whole purpose of journeying is to be able to manifest the life that you want to live here and now. It's not about going off some place and escaping this reality. It's really that in that expansion process you open up so that everyday life can be more joyful and more fulfilled and healthier.

HSW: Learning to journey can be a difficult process for a lot of people. How does one get past those mental blocks that invariably pop up?

ECR: When we teach, I have several different explanations that I use to explain the process. The first thing we'll tell you is that you're going to move your spirit from this place to another place. For those that don't like the "s" word, I talk about the experience of the consciousness achieving other states. For others, I say we're going to use the drumming and the imagery to shift us out of our left brain, the symbolic language mind-set that you use every day, and journey across the corpus callosum into that global thinking, visionary experience of the right brain.

It's up to us when we teach to find the little keys that work in all the different locks so that people can open up to the experience, without any preconceptions or judgments that come up around it.

CAK: A lot of people bump up against the wall of letting go of control. A lot of us have survived through controlling, particularly through our minds. And so it's challenging for some in the journey process to let go, to allow something to happen that their brain isn't orchestrating, or mandating, or defining. So that's why we use different ways of describing the process—so that people can connect with one of those.

ECR: I also remind students that journeying is in our genetic codes. Your ancestors, no matter where you are from on the planet, at some point in their evolutionary experience were hunter/gatherers. And this is the spirituality of the hunter/gatherer. In your DNA, you've done this before. So all we're trying to do is to help you remember what you already know.

HSW: One thing that drew me to this path is that, unlike many religious traditions where you have an all-powerful being or beings pulling the strings, in shamanism there seems to be more of a working partnership between those of us in the physical world and those on the spirit plane.

ECR: Absolutely. Grandmother [Evelyn's primary teacher in the spirit realm] says, "Don't just abandon your free will to what Spirit says. The spirits have a different perspective than you have, but you also have a valuable perspective because you're here on the Earth plane. Instead of thinking that we have all this higher knowledge and you don't have any, think that we're in the same stadium. You on the Earth sit down close to the playing field where you can see the subtle expression on the players' faces. I am up in the high seats in the stadium where I can't see the players faces, but I can see the overall patterns in the game that are invisible to you."

She does that to continue to break through any possibility of me turning my power over to her. Which is so easy to do. But it's important to remember that this is about collaboration, this is about a relationship. We have gifts of the physical that the spirits don't have.

HSW: Evie, in your book you talk about the need we have in this society to reconnect with our "inner hunter/gatherer." You say that "We need the hunter/gatherer's wise guidance to shift toward a more meaningful, joyful and fulfilling life." How so?

ECR: In our culture, people are really drawn to studying shamanism, studying different kinds of spiritual traditions. I think this comes from a longing to reconnect with that ancient part of ourselves that knew our connections firsthand. Hunter/gatherer people don't ever see themselves as separate from their environment, separate from other human beings, separate from the animals. And in this culture, we have had the luxury to think of ourselves as somehow separate from the way the Earth does its thing. Part of learning the way of the shaman is about losing that misperception; getting back to the sense of being part of both the physical world and the spirit world. That inner hunter/gatherer character is the part of us that knows what it's like to perceive the animals as fellow travelers; to see all the plants around us as having power. You can't possibly see yourself as separate when you're in that hunter/gatherer mode because you are always a hair's breadth away from not surviving. You see that you have to honor the spirit of the animal's life that you just took, because that death is feeding you so that you don't die. You see the circle.

We are so taken away from the circle of life in our culture. Our food is hermetically sealed in the supermarket. When you ask a kid in the city where beans comes from, they say, "Shop & Save." They don't think that it comes from a plant. Reconnecting to that part of ourselves that has that basic understanding helps us to remember our own connection and the sacredness in all things.

HSW: And if we don't?

ECR: Then we get trapped in that longing place. Most people in this culture aren't happy. If you were to ask most people how they really feel, many people feel unfulfilled, they feel depressed. At the very least they feel disconnected. There's this sense of "I have everything I want and I still seem to need more."

CAK: People would not do to each other some of the things they do if they realized that you and I are one. It just wouldn't happen. Kids would not be killing kids at school if they had a sense of being connected to the kids they killed. There's a desperate need to find a way to reexperience that we are connected to everything. It's like a spider web—when one part moves the whole thing moves.

ECR: When I talk about reconnecting with the inner hunter/gatherer, it's not about going back in time and gathering fruits and nuts and living in a cave. It's about coming full circle. We've had the experience of being separate from one another. We've developed agriculture, developed the ability to change the face of the Earth, to dominate animals, to dominate plants. And that has given us many things. The idea is not to throw that away, but to reclaim some of the gifts that we've lost along the way and bring them into changing how we're doing things today.

HSW: Do you really think it's possible for society as a whole to do that at this point?

ECR: I wouldn't be doing this if I didn't.

CAK: We see miracles all the time. Teaching journeying is one way; in the body, healing is another, where people experience their own sacredness. They just feel it. And I think the challenge is to find ways to reinforce it so that it becomes so much of a person's life that they can't conceive of it otherwise.

ECR: I'll keep going back to what Grandma says. She always reminds us that everything that we do goes out a thousandfold. So each person that gets a sense of their preciousness is transforming a thousand other people. Because when you have a different sense of yourself, people relate to you differently. It just happens. It's not like you have to go out on a soapbox and say, "We're all precious!" As you feel it, you interact with people differently. You're different in the world and the world is changed.

HSW: Because we are all one.

ECR: Exactly! You can't help it. I find I'm more optimistic now than I ever was when I was younger. I have a much better sense that change is possible.

HSW: That's great to hear, especially since things can seem very bleak at times. It can be frustrating.

ECR: There is nothing as powerful as simply doing your own work. Making your own connections. Because as you are different, you change the world around you. And while you can't see how you are literally connected to, say, Columbine, Colorado, and the tragedy that happened there, the world does change as each person moves through. I really trust in that process that when enough people have an idea, a critical mass is achieved where it becomes universal. And wouldn't it be extraordinary if the universal idea was that everyone and everything was precious!

Simon Buxton

© Naomi Lewis

This is so important because this material absolutely, definitely, and desperately needs to be out in the world. It is a way of seeking to heal the splits that divide our world, a vital tool for healing, for leading us back into a way of learning to walk lightly on what is our only home, our Earth. It's our only home. There isn't another one.

—Simon Buxton

Simon Buxton is the founder of the Sacred Trust, a center for shamanic studies in Cornwall, England. Towards the end of our conversation, Buxton told me, "All the great shamans that I have met—whether indigenous shamans or modern shamans in the Western world—are the ones who are also poets, whether they are energetic poets or people who have an incredible ability with language."

While I can't speak to the former, the latter is certainly true of Buxton. Talking to him for the first time, I was immediately struck by his poetic nature, the way in which he was able to articulate the teachings of his particular shamanic path—the little-known Bee tradition—through his lyrical and metaphorical explanations.

In discussing his journey that brought him back to the path after time away from it, Buxton says, "Most of those years had been spent searching. For what? I suppose for connection and communion once again with the elemental forces of nature and for the truths that had been whispered to me through the trees. My eyes had been opened all those years before by my teacher—by his ability to change destiny and outcome through the power and will of nature. And so I was on a quest—a passion to understand and comprehend and be a part of that world. That world was very different from the one I saw around me every day, the one in which working people willingly boarded trains to spend the day in the compounds of work and desks and offices. I was part in and part out of that world, so I knew something of the trap of the modern world. Enough to know that I never wanted to be trapped within it myself. I was young, but I was attempting to find the human key to the inhuman world around me, to connect the individual with the community, the known with the unknown, and to relate the past with the present, and both of them to the future."

His tradition, called the Path of Pollen, is but one of the Bee tradition's many manifestations across the globe. Not many have heard of this shamanic tradition—one so well hidden by its practitioners that it has, until only recently, remained unreported within both academic and spiritual circles. Buxton is the author of what may be the first book on the subject, The Way of the Bee.

Hillary S. Webb: What are the characteristics of this tradition? What is the "Way of the Bee"?

Traveling between the Worlds

Simon Buxton: The members of this ancient tradition represent a company of highly committed people able to work in ways that would be considered to be outside, or rather beyond, the laws of science. Their activities were transformed into cosmic events that could influence the world around them and nourish the inner life of each generation.

The formal initiation into the tradition is done by the use of the bee venom. The bee venom from the bee sting is considered to be one of the great secrets of this tradition, and is known as the "sacred fire." Bee shamans over hundreds, thousands of years have mapped out ways of working with the bee stings much in the way that the needles are used by the modern acupuncturist. In fact, if you travel to China you will find that some of the acupuncturists over there still dip their needles into bee venom before inserting them. There is some resonance there, some echo of the past when the bee was used. Yet unlike acupuncture, where one is largely working with predefined meridians, the process is slightly different within the Bee tradition because one is operating in concert with the bee, operating in an altered state of consciousness.

Within the Path of Pollen, the sting is used not only as a therapeutic tool, but also as a tool for creating certain altered states. Much of my training involved learning how to apply bee stings not only for therapeutic use and healing—because of course healing is central to the role of the shaman the world over—but to produce particular altered state experiences. The primary initiation into the tradition involved being stung on certain key parts of the body, which then induced a certain threshold experience. One is stung on certain points in concert with the communion that the shaman has with the hive to induce an experience that brings about a move from this world into the world of the hive. Essentially, one is reborn into the hive, and that initiates a symbiotic relationship with the hive itself, which, if successful, is never broken. In other words, a marriage is made between the human and our most ancient allies in the world, the honeybee. It is rarely disputed that the bee is our most ancient ally. They have been on the Earth since the Cenozoic period, which is some fifty-five million years ago! And if you look at the images in the civilizations of Old Europe, you will discover that next to ser-

200

pents, bees are the creatures most often depicted. There are certain things that they have in common—both live in small, dark places, both carry venom, and both issue forth from the hole at certain seasons of the year. But whereas snakes might be depicted as symbols of both good and evil, bees were almost always regarded as beneficent.

It is the bees that direct the healing itself. No prior information is needed about the person, even about what their ailments are, because the bee is considered to be all-knowing. They are not to be considered all-powerful, which is why they need the partnership of the shaman himself or herself. If they were all-powerful as well as being all-knowing, then there would be no need for human interaction. This partnership is really the basis of all acts of shamanic work. The bee shaman learns to push the ego aside, to become the empty reed or the hollow bone. In that state, the shaman is able to merge with the hive. The healing is then directed by the wisdom of the hive. The hive will dictate where, how often, and how the individual is to receive the venom to assist in their healing. That's a key part of the healing process. There are also methods that are used that are more cross-cultural, as one would expect within any legitimate tradition—concepts such as removing spiritual intrusions that are causing blockages in the person's body, or the concept of the loss of essence or soul of the person. In this case, however, all of it is dealt with in communion with the wisdom of the hive.

HSW: Then nothing is done without consulting the hive first?

SB: Absolutely right. Absolutely right. The first stage for anybody stepping into this work is actively working with the hive. Any young initiate, any young apprentice, is going to begin by learning how to become a beekeeper!

A further aspect of the work that is absolutely central is the use of what in the modern world would be called "toxic honey." It's not a very pleasant term—it sounds like something from a nuclear waste site, doesn't it? The toxic honey is actually a honey that has been derived from the nectar and pollen of plants that are psychotropes. Within the Bee tradition in the British Isles there is a small island—unique as far as I have researched and traveled—that is made up, more or less exclusively in terms of its flora, of certain plants that are used for creating psychotropic honey. The plants in particular are a British *Datura*—known as thorn apple—henbane, and belladonna, or deadly nightshade. These plants are extremely toxic, and when taken in an unprepared way, can kill. But by allowing the bees to collect the nectar and produce the honey, it allows a level of toxicity that is safe to ingest. But the process is even more poetic than that! The senior shaman—known as the Bee Master—introduces the initiate to the bees and informs them that this is the probationer who is going to be ingesting the potion. The bees then make up the honey that is in accord with the needs of that student.

HSW: How beautiful.

SB: It is. It is very poetic indeed. You see, the bees, as with all of nature, are seen as a manifestation of the visible face of Spirit. That's the term that you will often hear—"the visible face of Spirit" or "the visible face of the gods." Within the training itself, one is taught how to commune with the hive. Here one begins to see the shamanic principles behind certain common superstitions that are held within beekeeping around the world. One of the common superstitions that you hear is that you must tell the bees everything. In the old days, the common beekeeper would know of the tradition of "telling the bees." This meant that anything significant in the life of the family or the community or the village would be told to the hive. This is an example of something that has leaked out from the Bee tradition itself. In the Bee tradition you tell the bees everything of note. The reason this is done is because the hive is considered to be the repository for the lineage. But telling the bees is only half the equation. You also *listen* to the bees. You learn to hear the bees, and therefore you are able to be a recipient of all the teaching that has been placed there by previous generations, which means that nothing is ever lost.

HSW: So the bees are looked at as the elders, the keepers of the wisdom.

SB: Exactly. I take any key realizations that I have around the work to my own bees. That means that in due time, those who come in my wake will be able to be a recipient of all the information that I have given to the hive. Not only mine, of course, but also all the information that all the previous teachers within the path of pollen placed into the hive.

HSW: How does the shaman communicate with the hive?

SB: The primary way of communing with the hive is with the aid of a tool—which again has become part of folklore, superstition within beekeeping—called "tanging," which is basically banging on a piece of metal! If you read old books on beekeeping, you'll read how people used to do this tanging thing. The superstition was that if there was a swarm, by "tanging" you'd be able to get them to safely land on a particular branch and then you'd be able to access them and bring them home and establish a new hive. The hitting of this object is something that is in complete accord with the way that percussion is used in many shamanic traditions. You beat a drum, or in this case you bang this special object called a "tanging quoit" at a certain rhythm which is usually four to seven beats a second, and that puts the shaman into a shamanic state of consciousness. And it is in that altered state that the Bee shaman is able to commune with the hive. He is able to speak to and receive wisdom from the hive. The hive itself is both physically, metaphorically, and energetically a repository for a body of teaching.

I think that there is one other theme that may be of interest to people reading about this tradition, and that is that the men and women are taught separately. The Bee Master teaches a single male apprentice at a time. His opposite number is known as the Bee Mistress, but the Bee Mistress teaches six women at a time. Although the principles communicated to the men and the women are the same, there are certain teachings that are given only from the Bee Mistress to her own female students. These women are known as the *Melissae. Melissae* is a term from ancient Greece that was adopted by these women. In ancient Greece, at the Temple of Demeter and Aphrodite—who was also known as Melissa—the priestesses were called *Melissae,* which means "bees."

It was some time after my training began before I met the Melissae. There were six female apprentices taught by a formidable woman known to me only by her formal title of Bee Mistress. It was perhaps hardly surprising that as a young man, I was utterly enchanted by these mysterious women. They were never ever seen without their veils. The veils were ostensibly to protect their eyes and their faces from the bees, but also had a secondary function, which was to create a certain kind of aura of mystery around them. Of course, I would bombard my teacher with my questions about these women, but he refused to shed much light on the matter. It took months for me to discover the most basic information about these women. Of course, I now realize that this was all planned in advance. I finally said in a very kind of exasperated way, "What on earth is their purpose? Do they actually have one?" I'd almost given up altogether. I remember very clearly what he finally said: "The knowledge of destiny and the ability to inspire are the two central powers of these women." He went on to say that the knowledge of destiny is much more than simple folk magic. It is actually the innate knowledge of *type*. It includes the ability to educate and guide a type of person according to the sort of power that that type is meant to have.

This itself was pretty enigmatic to me. I thought, "What on earth is a type?" I assumed that it is a form of personality or human behavior which differs among people, and that the *Melissae* could somehow tune in to this in order to offer guidance and instruction of some kind which was most suited to that individual person. The Bee Master went on to say that the *Melissae* are women who live in a country that is "east of the sun and west of the moon, to which there is no known map." He said that we, men, are guests of the Bee tradition, and that the *Melissae* are the hosts, because bee society represents the zenith of feminine potency of nature. We men are simply the drones, and we'd better bloody remember that!

The teachings of masculinity and femininity are vitally important within the Bee tradition. The basics of masculinity and femininity have not changed much for a million years or more. The female consistently does more of the reproductive work. The male is, in many ways, just a parasite upon their partners. Women may be the last thing to be civilized by men—thank heaven! These women in particular, the *Melissae*, will never be civilized, I was told, and those who have fallen into their arms rarely do so without falling into their hands—as I was eventually to learn, to my cost. Well, this was enough to send a shiver down my spine and want to meet them desperately! But despite the drama and all of that, I sensed what was being said was not the complete picture. Rather, it seemed to me—and was later verified—that the role of the Bee Master and the Bee Mistress, the connection between them, was not based on who was the superior of the two. Both roles were distinct and of equal importance. Their function, when taken together, performed a kind of corporate responsibility. The *Melissae* are the physical representation of an ancient sisterhood known as the Sisterhood of the Hive. They are transmitters of an archaic impulse, which is central to the path of pollen.

HSW: What archaic impulse?

SB: Melissa was the goddess of intoxication and sexual passion. Both of these are used as doorways to a communion with all of life. It is this archaic impulse that the *Melissae* continue to transmit.

I remember the first time I met one of the *Melissae*. I was standing in the apiary studying a single bee as it moved upon a flower—this was one of many instructions designed to hone my practice of observing and of entering the world of the bee so that I could understand their rituals and their energy. I was so focused on this task that I hadn't noticed that one of these mysterious women that I'd heard about had entered the orchard. I felt her presence, her gossamer lightness in the back of me, before I ever saw or heard her. She quietly made her way over to me. Clearly, she had watched in silence as I had continued my observations. Very lightly she whispered to me, "Is the flower the food of the bee, or is the bee the genitals of the flower?" That was my introduction to them, and that says a little something about what they were carrying and teaching.

HSW: They sound very otherworldly.

SB: Yes, quite right. The *Melissae* were and are very fascinating women. Later the Bee Master instructed me to meet up with the Bee Mistress, and she said, "Well, the Bee Master has sent you so I suppose I'd better take a look at you!" We moved into the orchard where the apiary was located. I remember it so distinctly. As I closed the gate behind me and turned, I felt truly as if I was being spun into a myth. In the orchard there were figures moving, figures of women at work among the hives. They were wearing the gowns that they always wore. They were all wearing their protective bee veils, so I could only hazard the dimmest guess at what the faces looked like beneath them. An occasional ripple of laughter broke this busy silence. Several of them were singing. One of their favorite chants was the "Song of Songs," which goes like this:

"The taste of honey is on your lips, my darling. Your tongue is milk and honey for me. I've entered my garden, my sweetheart, my bride, gathering my spices and my myrrh. I am eating my honey with honeycomb, I'm drinking my wine and milk . . ."

It goes on like that. Another one of the *Melissae* was painting a hive, covering it with images sacred to the tradition. I was introduced to them on that occasion very formally, and then later I was brought to meet the Bee Mistress properly. She began to give me some of the teachings that were given to the women, because ultimately on this path, the men are introduced to the women and the women are introduced to the men.

The women within the Path of Pollen are fully empowered. They are not empowered in the way that many women are in this day and age, in which in an attempt to regain power that was taken from them, they will simply imitate men. Look at nature. The Sun and the Moon don't compete—they are opposites. The *Melissae* are said to fall within two distinct groupings, two primary types drawn to the work. There is the maternal type and the magnetic type. The *Melissae* incline in varying degrees to one or the other of these extremes.

HSW: How would you describe each of these types?

SB: Well, if she is purely of the maternal type, she will ask very little save to fecundate her year by year and protect and provide for her offspring—which might be a ritual, it might be a project, or it might be a child. If she's of the magnetic type and true to the law of her nature, she will deny herself to no one who calls upon her in the name of the tradition. Understand?

HSW: Well . . .

SB: Remember, this was given to me in metaphor.

HSW: As so many of these teachings are.

SB: Yes, exactly. You have to unlock them. Let me try to give it to you as a metaphor, also. There is one sort of bee that moves from flower to flower, sipping nectar from each luscious blossom, picking up pollen from this bloom. She deposits it from one to the other, circulating pollen everywhere, fertilizing all the flowers. As a result, the garden flourishes. Back in the hive she deposits the pollen-rich nectar into the communal vats which, in the fullness of time, will ripen into dark, rich, sweet honey. This is a visible offering to the visible face of the Spirit.

There is another type of bee who also moves from flower to flower but does not sip nectar. Rather, she devours the blossom with all of her senses, inhaling the fragrance, savoring the taste, absorbing the color, and so on. She imbibes the song of joy evoked by the sunlight hitting the petals. Back in the hive she also shares her bounty with the community. As they gather together, each bee will dance an expression of the blessings that she has gathered—dancing the joy, dancing the splendor, dancing the delight. One by one, all the bees add their share to fill the cauldron in the center and then they all dance together, encircling the cauldron and singing the praises of the visible face of the Spirit. The resulting blend will ripen and ferment into honey, which is also rich and sweet, and to most people utterly invisible. As a walker on the Path of Pollen, I was told that it is my right as the Bee Master's final student to seek out this honey and imbibe it if I could find it. I was told that one single drop would change me forever.

So there we have it. Ultimately the *Melissae* are split down the middle between two types, between the magnetic and the maternal, into two groups of three sisters. Mythically, if you like, they were like the Northern Fates, or the Wyrrd sisters. They carry a function of priestess. And they produce sweet elixirs, both literally and metaphorically, to ensure fertility in the greatest sense of that word. At the same time, they retain their autonomy and their control of their own sexuality and therefore of sexual reproduction. So the female teaching is a vital body within the tradition.

A fair bit of the book details that information. I really feel that even though I only received this information—I didn't experience it, because I am a man—that I have a responsibility of sharing some of this information because I consider it is something that will be enormously relevant and empowering for women to read.

HSW: I can understand that. There seem to be so few female teachers in this work, at least ones that are choosing to have their voices heard, to put their knowledge out to the world. Many more men than women seem to be the figureheads of this path. I discovered this as I was compiling a list of people to talk to for this book. And beyond being a writer, as a woman I have certainly felt the lack of female teachings in my own exploration of the path.

SB: There are so many good ones out there. The teachers that I think are really doing the work are the ones that are not just repeating information they've received. Anyone can make a living doing that. The trick is in recognizing that shamanism is an art form. It's a spiritual art form.

HSW: How so?

SB: Shamanism is a dance of energy. The shaman is someone who has a palette of colors, but instead of it being the artist's palette and the easel, it's a combination of extraordinary colors of the Spirit. The trick is how to bring these together into patterns and designs and dances that inspire others. All the great shamans that I have met—whether indigenous shamans or modern shamans in the Western world—are the ones who are also poets, whether they are energetic poets or people who have an incredible ability with language.

This is so important because this material absolutely, definitely, and desperately needs to be out in the world. It is a way of seeking to heal the splits that divide our world, a vital tool for healing, for leading us back into a way of learning to walk lightly on what is our only home, our Earth. It's our only home. There isn't another one.

HSW: Then rather than being entirely literal, the Way of the Bee can be seen as a metaphor for learning how to walk lightly on the Earth and in balance with the realm of Spirit?

SB: Yes, that is a good question. It's like: "Are you expecting that everyone is going to go out and buy a beehive?" Let's put it this way. Yes, it would be wonderful if it does inspire people to step into a relationship with our most ancient allies. The number of beekeepers in the world has diminished. In Britain just after the Second World War there were eighty to ninety thousand beekeepers. Now it is thirty to forty thousand. We need more bees to keep the world a fertile place. I certainly would adore this to inspire a revival of beekeeping. But yes, let me be clear: the Path of Pollen is not a metaphor, but is a very real, vibrant, living shamanic tradition, although its teachings are richly metaphorical. The teachings contain information and inspiration to push people back towards who they really are, or who they were before they were told who to be by their parents, their teachers, their society, their culture. This path is all about learning to actually embrace who you really are, and daring to step into that fully and unconditionally.

Brooke Medicine Eagle

© Anne Wennhold

Our hearts are always connected to the Source of all things, to the truth of all things. Thus, that wisdom and knowledge are available and can be stimulated. Our challenge is to get there. I think when you have really strong elders guiding you that it is an easier path. But we do not all have those. Seek out and work with the highest and finest master teachers and those teachings that you can find to help you listen to Source through your heart. This can stimulate another level of possibilities.

—Brooke Medicine Eagle

Brooke Medicine Eagle is an intertribal métis *(mixed blood) teacher, ceremonial leader, sacred ecologist, and visionary. From an early age, Brooke found herself with a deep hunger to live with Spirit. Although she was raised on the Crow Reservation in Montana, her family seldom made it out of the backcountry to participate in any of the gatherings or ceremonies of her people. When her family moved off the reservation to put her in better schools, she lost even those few spiritual gatherings.*

When she was twenty-eight, Brooke's father got remarried to a Cheyenne woman who one day took her to meet her new "Grandmother," a medicine woman named Stands Near the Fire. Despite the fact that Brooke did not speak Cheyenne, a bond was created between the two. Thus began Brooke's relationship with the woman who awakened her into an ancient visionary tradition. The story of her spiritual awakening is documented in her first book, Buffalo Woman Comes Singing.

Today Brooke blends Native American traditions of her heritage with Earth-wisdom teachings from around the world. When asked what she would consider to be her tradition, she states:

"One time I was questioning Spirit about what form I should follow, and Spirit said to me, 'Your form will be the formless form, which breaks through form into Spirit.' I certainly follow my Native background and try to awaken myself more and more to the old ways of seeing and understanding, yet I really find that I have also become aware of the deep truth behind every tradition." Her most recent book shares prophetic wisdom from around the world, and offers profound information for living well in this challenging time and for doing one's part to create a Golden Age on Mother Earth. It is entitled The Last Ghost Dance: A Guide for Earth Mages.

Medicine Eagle is the founder of Song of the Nations, a series of learning opportunities, gatherings, councils; and Wakantia, an intensive training program in the practices of Earth magic and service. Her most recent focus is on FlowerSong, which promotes a sustainable ecology and, as Brooke says, creates "a flowering of Mother Earth and All Our Relations for seven generations of children." She has created a breakthrough CD (Gathering: The Sacred Breath) *and her Dance Awake the Dream summer camp in the Montana wilderness.*

Hillary S. Webb: In your teachings, you refer to the work we must now do as "magical service." How would you describe this term?

Brooke Medicine Eagle: First of all, magic is an economic, ecological way of doing things in less time, using less energy—a sustainable way of approaching our challenges. To me, magical service means becoming what I call an Earth Mage, or Earth magician. That is, someone so tuned in and connected to their own heart and to the deep wisdom of Mother Earth that they are able to bring about the magic that is needed for the healing of the Earth. This kind of spiritual action is the level at which we must work.

I have just started an in-depth training program called Wakantia. *Wakantia* is a Lakota term that reminds us of our need to be protectors of our sacred lodge, Mother Earth. This program is about creating groups of dedicated people who will work together over time to become Earth Mages. Becoming an Earth Mage means stepping out of our material daily existence, stepping up a level into Spirit, towards source, to a place where our energetic actions and intent can echo very magically back into the physical, manifest world of our everyday lives. The actions of Spirit and magic go to a much deeper level than just at the outer structure of things, so this is where real change will take place.

HSW: Ecofeminist Starhawk talks about magic as being first and foremost an inner shift which then produces effects in the outside world.

BME: That's it. It's an inner shift and an inner acquaintance with our enormous and magnificent power. One of my teachers used to say, "You are all magnificent and trying to be okay." Our schooling is just terrible in that way. It says to us, "You don't know anything, and you're damn well going to get in trouble if you don't say exactly what I tell you to say." After eighteen or twenty years of that, it's very hard to find yourself again, to find your own worth and your innate abilities and connection with Divine guidance. You haven't trusted it for so long that it becomes quite lost from you.

Finding ourselves again, finding Spirit alive within us, and discovering the amazing gifts that we have to bring forward is where the magic will come from. I recently cotaught with a wonderful

Dagara shaman, Malidoma Patrice Somé. His tradition encourages each individual to seek out, in themselves and in others, the person that they truly are from the womb until they die and to continually bring forth their gift, because it is an incredible gift for each and every other person.

That is so contrary to what we see in the life that we live today. Our goal, then, is to peel away a lot of cultural conditioning and really touch into that magnificence. Because, really, what else is there to do in this life but to step forward into our highest and best self and do our highest and best work? If we don't, we are in very deep trouble. It's not like we can la-di-da along—we are either going to make a magical shift or we're going downhill and over the cliff.

HSW: Of course, try to tell the average person on the street that magic is the answer and, at best, they may write you off as a total flake.

BME: Oddly enough, magic seems to have a bad reputation in this world. The belief is that you can't get there from here by doing it the easy way; that there is no magic carpet. If something can be done very quickly and magically, nobody wants to count it. I've been learning a new way of working with trauma through a process called Thought Field Therapy, an energetic technique that creates cures for phobias, trauma, and emotional issues by working through the body's meridian system. This is a much more magical way of working with trauma than we've had in the past. With it you can cure phobias—sometimes in just five minutes. Still, people find ways to discount this kind of thing, even if it totally cures them. Instead it's like, "That couldn't have worked because it only took five minutes." That way of thinking is limiting us from using many of the incredible possibilities we have.

HSW: It also seems that the expediency, the instant results, that magic gives us is needed more now than ever before. We have brought ourselves to a place in which we are teetering on the edge. According to many people—scientists, ecologists, environmentalists—we don't have twenty more years to try to fix things using the usual means. It has to be done now.

BME: That is exactly what I would say as well. You're right—we don't have the money, time, energy, or commitment to wait twenty years for everybody to get their act together. We are right on the balance here. We have pushed ourselves up against the place where we have to find our magic.

Every one of us needs to make major shifts. Even those of us who are relatively conscious and aware were still raised in a culture that gave us many negative ways of thinking about ourselves and of relating to our world.

HSW: Could this be why we are experiencing such a surge of interest in spiritual and magical practices lately? Perhaps some deep part of ourselves knows that this may be our final option.

BME: Absolutely. I really believe that the Great Spirit is calling out to us and sending some very powerful ways of working. We must allow ourselves to touch into those and let them be a part of our lives. Not to be silly and fall for anything foolish, but to really take hold of those things that do create magical results.

HSW: So how exactly do we "find our magic" once it has been beaten out of us by culture?

BME: First and foremost, I think it is really important for people to find a way of silencing the mind, of stilling the inner voices that are constantly jabbering and calling for attention—that chatter which keeps us hooked into old ways of thinking. In my new book, *The Last Ghost Dance*, I talk about a technique of silencing. The idea behind it is to get you to stop talking to yourself; to stop paying attention to the voices that say, "Sit-down-shut-up-you-don't-know-anything-you-shouldn't-do-that-this-is-too-hot-this-is-too-cold-no-there-aren't-fairies-there-aren't-elves-there-aren't-devas . . ." These thoughts really interfere with our ability to live magically.

HSW: And when we hear them over and over from childhood, they become part of our patterning.

BME: *Yes.* An interesting thing that I've heard is that some time during our teenage years there is a kind of acid bath that passes through the brain and wipes out anything that isn't strongly held. So, say if you see fairies as a kid but no one reinforces that or gives it any usefulness, those perceptions just get washed away.

HSW: Gone forever?

BME: Well, gone forever unless you are around someone who acknowledges its importance and teaches you to see again. Our hearts are always connected to the Source of all things, to the truth of all things. Thus, that wisdom and knowledge are available and can be stimulated. Our challenge is to get there. I think when you have really strong elders guiding you that it is an easier path. But we do not all have those. Seek out and work with the highest and finest master teachers and those teachings that you can find to help you listen to Source through your heart. This can stimulate another level of possibilities.

HSW: Which is one of the reasons for this book. To highlight the various teachers that are available out there, and to give them the opportunity to share the philosophies of their particular traditions.

This leads me to a question I have about the ethics of sharing one's tradition with people of differing descent. Many Native Americans maintain that their teachings should not be shared with nonnatives. As someone of Native American descent, what is your position in this debate?

BME: In many ways it's understandable. Native Americans have lost pretty much everything they had to an outside group. So of course, we are sensitive about losing our most precious thing: our spirituality. Asking tribal people to share these teachings is like saying, "Forget that the ancestors of the dominant culture committed genocide murder on you. Forget that they ran poles through your pregnant women and beat your kid's heads out on trees and killed your old people. Forget all that and teach them what you know." I mean, that's a very big order. Native people really remember. The memory of what happened many generations back is set deep in the energetics of the culture.

HSW: Can we heal this split? What's more, should we?

BME: Yes, we must. It's one of the things that I address in *The Last Ghost Dance*. The big challenge for all of us right now is to figure out how we can come into cooperation and sharing, wholeness and integrity with each other, offering our greatest gifts. Only in doing that can we make a decent life for *any* of us.

The main thing that needs to happen on the Native American side is that we don't cut off our nose to spite our face. If we "own" something that is magical and powerful, we'd better be giving it away and teaching everyone how to do it, because we need every bit of help we can get. We need to share the teachings of *all* cultures and peoples so that we all wake up. White Buffalo Woman has told me that we will cross into the new time on a bridge of light, a rainbow bridge of all colors, all beings. We won't get there without it. So, do we pout and hold back our gifts because we are mad at the person that injured us a generation ago? Or do we say, "Hey, it's not worth it. All of our children are going to be gone if we don't all cooperate." As Native Americans, we have often been sort of tribal, parochial, small group, small clanlike. We really need to take that big leap to get to that level of brother-sisterhood where we can honor and respect the gifts of all our relations and be in good relationship with one another.

On the nonnative person's side, I think it is important to differentiate between core shamanism/core Earth wisdom, and the specific teachings that individual tribes have developed. If some Native American says, "You can't drum because we own the drum," that's not even sensible. People all around the Earth have had drums, probably from the time monkeys started taking sticks and beating them on hollow logs. The same goes for sweat lodges. Practically everyone in the world does some form of purification lodge like a sweat lodge. However, there *are* some very specific kinds of rituals and things that certain tribes or groups have developed, and these things they really do own in a sense. The Lakotas do a West-facing healing sweat lodge. That is a very specific thing that they have developed and been trained in. In that case, yes, absolutely honor that rite as a part of someone else's tradition, and leave it alone unless you are specifically invited to learn it.

I think people are getting much more wise and aware about that. Still, a lot of people—and not just Native Americans but people all over—get into this victim-persecutor mode. They have a lot of anger about being victimized in the past, which then leads to a certain amount of possessiveness. Yet I truly believe that the Great Source has sent forward the energy we need to make the leap to heal that split.

HSW: The organization for Support and Protection of Indian Religious and Indigenous Traditions (SPIRIT) is calling for a boycott of your workshops and teachings. They are accusing you of misrepresenting and abusing the spiritual traditions of the Crow people. What is your response to these accusations?

BME: I have a Crow background and I belong to the Crow tribe, but I've never taught Crow ways, because the Great Spirit gave me a Cheyenne teacher. Of course, the Crow hate the Cheyenne, so that is a good start on why they are angry. And the Crows don't like half-breeds, which I am. I have never gotten much of a welcome from my Crow elders. Many of the medicine people that I have approached are very closed, so I've never gotten hooked back up. In some ways, I haven't been drawn to. I don't especially want to go back and spend time with the people whose energy is like that. I don't consider that high medicine in any way, shape, or form.

My practice is to look at this feedback and say, "Is there anything true about this? Am I doing anything I should be ashamed of? Is there any way I can use this feedback to correct the way I am being in the world?" I ask my elders and guides to help me clean up anything I may have done wrong. Yet, I actually see very little that has been negative or harmful to anyone. My teaching has benefited everyone and taught people to honor and be open to the wisdom of native peoples. I don't think I would still be a popular teacher after twenty-five years if I had not been doing something very positive. Indian people have always been fighting in some way, and when someone steps out there like I have, it's going to draw some fire. Unfortunately, it seems to go along with the territory when one says, "Hey, I am willing to listen to a deeper drum than any one individual or any one tradition. I am really listening to my heart here." If

217

that takes me into a bit of controversy, then, golly, that doesn't really thrill me, but I'm not going to stop the positive work I am doing for the world.

I think the main thing for me is to try to listen deeply and ask myself, "Is there anything I should do differently?" When I first got this kind of feedback, I did realize that I should change the wording of some things. For example, in my brochures, to not say that I am from the Crow tribe, but say, "Although she is a member of the Crow tribe, she bases her teachings in globally centered Earth-keeping wisdom." I try to make it very clear where I am coming from. I can't do much more than that. So if anyone can point out anything specific that I can do differently, then great.

On another level, my work is to forgive the people who judge without knowing. One of the Crow elders once said to me, "I can't believe you are getting six hundred dollars a person to teach people for a week." Well, I get fifty dollars a person—the rest goes to facilities and advertising and this and that and so on. So some of the negativity is ignorance about what is really going on.

HSW: The ethics of charging people for spiritual teachings is another heavily debated topic. Some believe that spiritual teachings should be given out for free. On the other hand, even in indigenous communities, apprentices pay to receive their teachings. The difference is that there the apprentice may pay in chickens instead of cash. And, in those situations, the shaman is often supported by the community in exchange for his or her services. Here, you are dependent upon how many people show up at your workshop; there is no guaranteed income.

BME: Exactly. Teachers who go out on the road don't have a retirement plan. We live our lives without family, out of a suitcase. It's a very stressful lifestyle. We are not making a million dollars. Sometimes there is the experience of buying an expensive ticket to Chicago because there is supposed to be a teaching there, and five people show up. There may be a little basket out for contributions to support the teachers, and what comes is fifteen dollars for two weeks of your life, which doesn't even pay for the ticket.

It's not quite as glamorous as it looks from the surface. And most people have an extremely limited experience of what really goes on.

There's a Native American elder that teaches at Eastern University who has been critical of my work. I've written to him and said, "What is it that you object to? You get paid by a college to teach white people about our ways. You've got a guaranteed job. I lived on the road for twenty years and had people come to me. If they didn't like my work after two or three times, they dropped out. If I hadn't done good work, I wouldn't have made it past the first two or three years. So what is the real complaint?"

I think there is an enormous amount of integrity in this work. I don't make any money unless I do good work and people come. In my work there is no guarantee. I have to be judged day to day on what I am doing.

HSW: The idea that you were talking about before—of constantly questioning yourself—sounds like something that you said in Buffalo Woman Comes Singing, *that "the spiritual warrior takes responsibility for all that comes her way and lives an impeccable life."*

BME: Well, I'm certainly giving it a good go, anyway. That's always the challenge. I'm clear that this is what *all* of us are being called to do. We're in a time when we need to listen very deeply and follow our hearts and not be beckoned by outer approval or the surface of things. While it's important to look deeply for any lessons we need to learn from feedback, we must continue to move on the path of our own heart.

It has been an interesting thing to practice walking the path of keeping my heart, mind, and soul open to Mother Earth and Father Spirit. My goal is to listen deeply to what my gifts are and to bring them forward to do what needs to be done. My heart knows that as each of us brings forward the rare and unique gift Creator gave us, we will transform our world into a place of harmony, peace, beauty, and abundance for all our relations.

Sandra Ingerman

In this culture, pretty much all of us steal souls, but we are not aware of what we are doing. Perhaps we are attracted to somebody's energy. It looks like this person has a lot more power than we do, and we think that if we could just have some of that, our lives would be better, so we take a piece of their soul. The difference is that here most of us steal souls out of ignorance. If you said to someone, "Do you realize that you are stealing that soul?" they would look at you like you were crazy.

—Sandra Ingerman

In indigenous cultures throughout the world, the near-death experience is often viewed as a sign that an individual has been chosen by the spirits to walk the shaman's path. In these societies, elder shamans are available to explain the significance of the occurrences to the young initiate.

Sandra Ingerman's "sign" came in the form of not just one near-death experience, but three. At the age of seven, she was hit by lightning. At age nineteen, she came close to drowning. And at twenty-seven, her car veered off the road and tumbled down a cliff.

Perhaps if she had grown up in a shamanic culture, the call to the path of shaman might have been clear to her earlier on. As it was, not until she entered graduate school did Ingerman become aware that these "accidents" might have a spiritual significance. This time, the spirits used a more direct approach to get her on the path.

One day, a school friend of hers told her that "some man" was coming up from Connecticut to teach a weekend workshop, and that she could get two easy units of college credit for attending. Without even looking at the name of the workshop, Ingerman put her name on the list. As it turned out, the "man from Connecticut" was the "Grandfather of Modern Shamanism" Michael Harner, who had come to teach his workshop, The Way of the Shaman.

"I just had an incredibly profound experience in that workshop, and it literally changed the course of my life," Ingerman says. "I am still working on those two 'easy' units. I was tricked by the universe into my new life path."

Sandra Ingerman travels the world teaching workshops on shamanic journeying, healing, and reversing environmental pollution using spiritual methods. She is the author of Soul Retrieval: Mending the Fragmented Self, Welcome Home: Following Your Soul's Journey, A Fall to Grace, *and* Medicine for the Earth: How to Transform Personal and Environmental Toxins.

Hillary S. Webb: Back in the 1950s, your mentor, Michael Harner, traveled the world studying the similarities between shamanic techniques from culture to culture. His research revealed that all shamanic practices share consistent beliefs and practices, such as the technique of going into a "shamanic state of consciousness," called "journeying," in order to access information from the spirit world. Based on these findings, he developed the practice of Core shamanism, a system that takes shamanism down to its bare bones by getting rid of its culture-specific trappings and focusing on those techniques that are common to shamans throughout the world.

I'm going to play devil's advocate here. While these may be the "bare bones" of shamanism, doesn't the practice lose something when you take it out of its cultural context?

Sandra Ingerman: It's a tricky issue. I definitely meet some people who say you lose a lot by taking shamanism out of its cultural context. But the goal of Core shamanism is to give people a spiritual practice that they can easily adapt into their life. It's true that those things that come from being involved in a tradition that has been passed down for many years is something we can't bring through in this system. But by adapting the different healing methods to address the issues of our culture and our time, we can bridge these ancient techniques into a modern-day culture.

And really, it's the people in our culture who are insecure in their own spiritual practices that make a judgment that "you're doing it wrong, and I'm doing it right because I studied this particular way." I think a lot of this attitude comes from our fear of really feeling the confidence in ourselves to have direct revelation. What I feel good about with Core shamanism is that we are giving people a way to get spiritual information for themselves. The journeying method opens up a door so that all people can have direct revelation. If somebody is telling you that you are getting direct revelation wrong, then you just started your own organized religion, which is not what shamanism is about. The whole purpose of shamanism is that there is no right or wrong. The only place where there is a right or wrong is that you never want to use these methods to hurt anybody else. They're only here to heal and to help.

HSW: You have been called a "specialist in the human soul." How does shamanism define the soul? And how is soul different from "spirit"?

SI: The soul is our essence; it's our life force. It's that part of ourselves that keeps us alive. Actually, the definition of soul that I use not only comes from a shamanic point of view, but comes straight out of *Webster's*.

The difference between soul and spirit is one of those issues that you can have endless conversations about. I have never been able to find agreement on this one, whether I have talked to shamans or philosophers. Personally, I make a real distinction between spirit and soul. My belief is that the body contains both the soul and the spirit. For me, the soul is that part of us that evolves over time. We have lessons, we go through life, we learn things, and we grow through our life experiences. The spirit, however, is the part of us that is absolutely pure divinity—a reflection of the Creator in its purest form.

HSW: In your book Soul Retrieval, *you talk about soul loss as a spiritual illness that causes emotional and physical disease. This isn't a concept that many people in our world are familiar with.*

SI: In psychology, we talk about "dissociation," but in psychology we don't talk about what dissociates or where the thing that dissociates goes. In shamanism, we say that whenever we experience an emotional or physical trauma, there's the good possibility that a piece of our soul might separate from our body in order to survive the experience. The types of things that would cause soul loss in our culture would be any kind of abuse, surgery, accidents, wartime stress, being in a natural disaster, death of a loved one, divorce, illness, addiction. Really, anything that creates shock to the system could cause soul loss. A soul can even be stolen by another person.

Soul loss is actually a survival mechanism. If I am going to be in a head-on car collision, the very last place that I want to be at the point of impact is in my body. Our psyches can't endure that kind of pain, so we have this brilliant self-protect mechanism where a part of us leaves the body while the pain is occurring so we don't have to get the full impact of it. The problem is that many times, the soul doesn't return on its own after the pain is over. Since the universe can't stand a void, an illness might come in and fill that space. In this case, it actually takes another person to search through nonordinary reality to track down where the soul has fled to and then to bring it back. The role of the shaman is to go into an altered state and, through the help of the shaman's helping spirits, track down that soul and return it to the body again.

HSW: *You mentioned that a soul could be stolen by another person. Are there people who are consciously going out and stealing a soul for one reason or another, or is this an unconscious thing on their part?*

SI: It's both. In many shamanic cultures, soul stealing is done on a very conscious level, as a form of psychic warfare. The East Indian term for soul stealing is "psychic vampirism," because when you steal somebody's soul, you attempt to take some of their energy.

In this culture, pretty much all of us steal souls, but we are not aware of what we are doing. Perhaps we are attracted to somebody's energy. It looks like this person has a lot more power than we do, and we think that if we could just have some of that, our lives would be better, so we take a piece of their soul. The difference is that here most of us steal souls out of ignorance. If you said to someone, "Do you realize that you are stealing that soul?" they would look at you like you were crazy. Soul stealing can happen when we don't want to let people we love out of our lives.

HSW: *Then how would we avoid either stealing someone else's soul or having it stolen from us?*

SI: It's all about learning to become conscious about what you do with your own energy. Back in the early 1980s, a bunch of us were having a discussion about how to protect ourselves psychically. A Chumash medicine woman who was there talked about a method of seeing yourself surrounded by a translucent blue egg as a way of keeping out harmful energies. Blue is my favorite color, so I began to work with that visualization. I found it worked so well that I started to teach my clients and students it. I get tons of feedback that it's a great way of working. It is important to remember that it takes two to tango in soul stealing. Somebody can't steal your soul unless you let them take it.

To make sure you are not stealing anybody *else's* soul, you again have to be conscious of what you are doing with your energy. If you're in a room and you think that somebody looks like they have a lot of power or a great presence or you are envious or jealous of them, there is the possibility that you might steal a piece of their soul.

It's also important to remember that you are not helping yourself at all by stealing someone's soul. In fact, now you're being burdened by unusable energy. It's a lose-lose situation. Nobody wins with soul stealing.

HSW: Looking at it from an energetic perspective, it is frightening to think how many people are running around dumping their negativity, completely unaware of how energetically powerful they and other people are. What are we doing to each other?

SI: We're making a mess. Seriously, we have been focusing on soul retrieval because that's what one of my books is about, but in shamanism, one of the causes of illness is spiritual intrusion—the symptoms of that being localized pain or illness. So, cancer, a chronic neck problem, chronic anger, or chronic depression could be caused by a spiritual intrusion that enters the body. And spiritual intrusions come from negative thought forms.

Indigenous cultures are more conscious of energetic communication. In our culture we don't understand the difference between sending our emotions to other people and learning how to express them consciously. So we walk around city streets dumping our anger, our frustration, our depression in the airwaves thinking that they're just going to magically disappear. But from a shamanic point of view, this actually *creates* an energy that can cause sickness. That is one of the reasons that we might be seeing so many different forms of illness today. We're not working with our energy consciously—we're just dumping it.

And the solution to this is not to not have emotions. We know from all the cancer research that you can cause a spiritual intrusion inside of yourself by not expressing them.

It's really about not feeling guilty, because we all do it in this culture. It's learned behavior. The answer is in learning to work with your energies in a conscious fashion. What I do—what my helping spirits have asked me to do—is that when I do get angry and start venting, I acknowledge that I am having this emotion, but ask the spirits that it be transmuted into healing energy and not to harm anyone. It all sounds like a lot of words, but you can do it in a matter of seconds.

HSW: Sounds like the answer to all this lies in working on keeping our egos out of the way.

SI: Yes, absolutely. In order to grow spiritually, you have to learn how to get your ego in check. The nature of the ego is to think of itself as separate—I am separate from you, I am separate from God, I am separate from the spirits, I am separate from the trees, I am separate from animals. Spiritual growth has to do with remembering that you are connected to everything. The ego will never acknowledge that, because if you say that you are connected to everything, then the ego has to die.

HSW: What place does the ego have, then?

SI: My belief is the place of the ego is to be able to experience space and time. When I drive a car, if my ego isn't intact, I don't know how fast I am going. In our culture, though, instead of having the ego being able to perceive space and time, the ego actually thinks it is running the show. Which means we have to compete, we have to hate—all the things that go along with seeing ourselves as separate.

In order to be a good spiritual healer, you have to bring Spirit through your body. If you're in a real ego state of consciousness, there's no room for Spirit to move through you to do the work. This is one of the places where, in indigenous societies, the shaman's dances and songs come in. Being able to dance and sing helps move the ego out of the way so that the power of the universe can come through the shaman. If you watch shamans working, they dance and sing for three hours before doing their work. Some indigenous cultures down in South America use vision plants, which totally blast the ego. That's where the miracles happen.

HSW: So when you, Sandra Ingerman, do healing work, do you feel as though you have achieved that state of egolessness?

SI: I do. I'm gone. But I spend a lot of time in preparation. I really believe that preparation is more important than the actual healing work. If I can get out of the way and let Spirit through, the spirits are going to heal.

I find singing does it for me more than dancing. I'll sing for at least twenty minutes before I start doing any kind of work. My heart bursts open and I have unbelievable amounts of compassion. I mean, I had compassion for my clients before, but it's coming from a different place. It allows me to let my thinking mind go so that the spirits can actually do their work.

Dealing with the ego is a constant struggle, but as a shamanic practitioner you can't stop working on yourself, because practitioners who don't work on themselves are usually not of great help to other people.

HSW: Do you see any danger in this recent shamanism craze with everyone jumping on the bandwagon and becoming "shamanic healers"?

SI: I definitely have a lot of concerns about what is happening with shamanism today. The reason that I *like* seeing it getting so popular is that it is an indication to me that people want to grow on a spiritual level and are willing to take responsibility for their own life. Where I get nervous about it is that you see a lot of people dipping their little fingers in the water and thinking, "Oh I know what it's all about." Shamanism is a discipline. It is a life path. It's something you do your whole entire life, not something you do on the weekend. Shamans who started working when they were fifteen years old and practiced shamanism until they died in their nineties still felt that they were babies in the work. I've been practicing shamanism for twenty years and have worked with and trained thousands of people, but I still say that the door has only just slightly been opened for me. In our culture we are into such fast-food spiritualism that people take a weekend workshop and they think they know everything. Also, we are spiritually lazy. People often won't take the time to really practice shamanism—to, say, journey on a regular basis. There is no danger in that kind of thing, but the work will eventually lose power. A lot of people that come to workshops are dabbling. They are not serious. To me, that is a loss of vitality.

The other challenge of bringing shamanism into this culture is that because we are a culture founded on materialism, people will say, "Oh, that looks like an easy way to make money, I think I'll go for that," instead of, "Is this my heart's desire to really help people? Am I being called to this path?" In a traditional culture, there were different ways that people were called. Michael Harner does talk about cultures where a person pays a shaman to have their information passed down to them—in that way, it's similar to what we're doing here in this culture—but oftentimes there is some kind of calling that happens for people. It's not even that you have a choice, it's a destiny thing. With a lot of the shamanic practitioners that I've trained, I absolutely know that they are in a destiny situation, as I feel I am. But I've also met people who think that this looks like an easy way to have a business. You see a difference in the quality of the work.

But really, I don't believe that shamanism is going to get that huge. I think it is self-regulating because of the fact that you have to believe in spirits. People can study yoga, they can study meditation, and it's not going to impact their spiritual beliefs because there is no talk about spirits in these systems. Whereas in shamanism, you are going to work with spirits, and so that wipes out another huge part of our population.

HSW: And those people who don't work with the spirits? Are they as effective, in your opinion?

SI: The spirits are working with us whether we know it or not. If you're not journeying, it doesn't mean that you don't have spirits. From a shamanic point of view, you have spirits around you whether you know it or not—you don't have to be initiated into shamanism. But by having an actual relationship with them, by finding ways to communicate, the spirits are able to do their work in a conscious partnership. Which means they can do their work better when they don't have to constantly hit you on the head to get your attention.

HSW: What is their work?

SI: It's hard to get too philosophical about it, but from my point of view, the spirits are the intermediaries of the power of the Universe. When I had my near-death experiences, I went to what I consider to be "God." And God is just complete love. He did not see me as an individual; he gave me exactly the same amount of love as he would give a murderer standing next to me. I was not an individual; there was no separation. In terms of the healing work, though, I find I can't really go to God or the Divine Force and say, "I'm having a problem with this client, could you help me?" because all I would get back is love. Which is wonderful, but I need more practical advice like, "Okay this person needs to change their diet." Whereas, through the spirits who are intermediaries of that power of the universe and that oneness, I can get practical direct information.

HSW: That's where I tend to lose my confidence during journeying. I'm never quite sure when to trust what is a true message from Spirit and what is just ordinary mind chatter.

SI: It's all about experience. As I said, shamanism is a life practice. One way to stop the mind chatter is to see all the synchronicities that come up within the journey. Too many synchronicities have happened in my life and other people's lives that I could never have made up. Another is that, for me personally, the spirits use a vocabulary with me that is different from my own. When I hear my own intonation and wording of things, I know it's me, since the spirits use very different wording.

HSW: Which, I would imagine, is why practicing the journey process is so important to anyone who wants to be a practitioner. As with any working relationship, there is an initial "getting to know you" stage, before a successful partnership can really unfold.

SI: That is the key. This work takes time. It really does take time.

Tenzin Wangyal Rinpoche

© Janine Guldener

Shamanic practice is a causal vehicle, our support toward higher realization. It's not the end. The end of something is always the beginning of another thing.

—Tenzin Wangyal Rinpoche

"I grew up strongly connected to the power of the natural world," writes Tenzin Wangyal Rinpoche in his book, Healing with Form, Energy, and Light: The Five Elements in Tibetan Shamanism, Tantra, and Dzogchen. *"The way we lived required it. We didn't have running water or electric stoves. We carried all our water in buckets from the nearby spring, heated our buildings with wood fires, and cooked over an open flame. We had a small garden patch where we grew vegetables—onions and tomatoes—and so we put our hands in the earth. The summer rains meant both flooding and water for the rest of the year. Nature wasn't preserved in parks or kept on the other side of the window, and contact with the elements wasn't for pleasure, though there was pleasure in it. There was a direct relationship between our lives and the fire, the wood, the water, and the weather. We were dependent on the raw elements of nature for survival.*

"Perhaps that dependence helped our culture, like most indigenous cultures, understand the natural world to be sacred and alive with beings and forces, visible and invisible. During Losar, the Tibetan celebration of the new year, we did not drink champagne to celebrate. Instead, we went to the local spring to perform a ritual of gratitude. We made offerings to the nagas, *the water spirits who activated the water element in the area. We made smoke offerings to the local spirits associated with the natural world around us.*

"Beliefs and behaviors like ours evolved long ago and are often seen as primitive in the West. But they are not only projections of human fears onto the natural world, as some anthropologists and historians suggest. Our way of relating to the elements originated in the direct experience by our sages and common people of the sacred nature of the external and internal elements. We call these elements earth, water, fire, air, and space."

The founder and director of the Ligmincha Institute in Charlottesville, Virginia, Tenzin Wangyal Rinpoche is one of the few Bön masters living in the West today. He brings to his teachings a lifetime study of the Bön tradition, a practice that encompasses not just one, but three methods of relating to spirit—a shamanic focus, a tantric focus, and the highest teachings of Dzogchen. In Tibetan Bön, these three disciplines come together to inform all the various aspects of the individual's spiritual journey. In addition to Healing with Form, Energy, and Light, *Tenzin Wangyal Rinpoche is the author of* Wonders of the Natural Mind *and* The Tibetan Yogas of Dream and Sleep.

Hillary S. Webb: You have described the Bön tradition as being made up of three levels of practice: the first being shamanism; the second, tantra; and finally, what is called Dzogchen. *Could you explain a little bit about them? What is their division, and what is their relationship to one another?*

Tenzin Wangyal Rinpoche: You see, the different levels of spiritual practice in our tradition can be explained in terms of the elements. When a practice emphasizes the external elements—meaning the gross elements and the spirits of the gross elements—it is seen as a causal vehicle, or shamanic, approach. You recognize the spirits of the gross elements, you work with them, and you try to control them or you make friends of them. You utilize their energy to heal the disturbances of people in the family, in the village, and in the world. In the Bön tradition, even the common villagers have a strong, basic understanding of shamanism. They know how to do the rituals and they relate in a deep way to the mountains, to the rivers, and to the spirits. It is part of their way of life. But if you formally ask someone, "Are you a shaman?" they will answer, "I am not."

In tantra, which is the second level of practice, you are working with the subtler aspect of the elements, the subtler aspect of mind. Here you are evoking and connecting with a deity who is more enlightened than, say, the spirit of a rock or of the Earth. When you are working to achieve realization through the blessings of the enlightened deities and receive protective powers from them, either on behalf of yourself or other people, that is tantra. In tantra, you must have a teacher and engage in study. It is much more complicated than shamanic ritual.

Finally, when you are working with the subtlest form of the five elements, with the most sacred, most subtle mind, that is the practice of *Dzogchen*. This involves a very pure awareness of consciousness. Here you are not working with a spirit or with a deity, but with pure light, the essence of nature and manifestation. Here you are working with the qualities of space and openness within yourself, and with the purest form of the elements. *Dzogchen* practitioners are the yogis. They go up into the mountain and just do sky or sun gazing and rest in the nature of mind. They don't concern themselves much with the deities or the spirits. They are in pure meditation.

In all three levels of practice, you are working with the elements—either the external elements of the spirits, the internal elements of deities, or the sacred elements in practices of the mind.

HSW: So, in a way, each practice has its own goals.

TWR: Yes.

HSW: What would be the goal of the Bön shaman, then?

TWR: Unlike in *Dzogchen* practice, the shaman's goal is not to achieve a rainbow body, nor is it to attain the realization of the deity, as in tantric practice. The shaman's ultimate goal is much more about being able to live in harmony with the spirits and forces of nature. When somebody is sick, the shaman will do a soul retrieval. If someone's business is not going well, the shaman will go up in the mountain and invoke the mountain spirit and put up prayer flags in order to raise the energy, or *chi*, of the universe. When shamans do that, they are not thinking about enlightenment or liberation. They may only be thinking about overcoming sickness, about making it rain or stopping hail.

HSW: In other words, the goal of shamanism is not to transcend the material world but to use the forces of nature and spirit to make the physical world a more balanced place.

TWR: Yes. When there is no war, when there is no hunger, when there is health and prosperity and so on—this is the intended achievement of the shaman for his society.

HSW: You make a distinction in your book that in the Bön tradition there is no word for "shaman." Instead, shamanism is called the "causal vehicle." What is this distinction?

TWR: The reason it is called the "causal vehicle" is because these practices can be seen as a preparation for understanding the subtler form of elements, for understanding the higher forms of deities. The intent is not just to commune with the gross elements and spirits, but also to evolve and grow from that way of relating so that one may work with the subtler forms of the elements. If one does shamanic practices with that intention, they become a vehicle of causation.

HSW: What is it about the elements—you list them in your book as earth, water, fire, air, and space—that is so vital to these teachings?

TWR: The five elements are very important because everything that exists in the universe is based on the elements. Time and space are based on the elements. The environment is made up of elements. We are made up of elements. Just as everything manifests because of the elements, spiritual growth also happens through the elements.

HSW: You write, "The living experience of being is a display of the pure elements interacting with awareness."

TWR: Every experience that we have is a display of the different forms of the elements. Think about your own body, about your own existence. What is your body? What is your soul? What is your life force? According to the Tibetan teachings, they are all a display of the forces of the elements. In a very deep sense, our five emotions of anger, greed, ignorance, jealousy, and pride are all related to the five elements. What brings negativity, darkness, and deception is a lack of awareness. When ignorance interacts with the elements, these dark forces come.

On the other hand, when awareness is involved with these five elements, it brings positive qualities, light, and enlightenment. As our awareness becomes perfected, eventually our own physical body will completely dissolve back into the subtlest energetic form of the elements. Then the energetic form will dissolve into the light form of the elements. When it does so, one has achieved what is called a "rainbow body"—a body of light. That is the *Dzogchen* practitioner's greatest achievement, and the greatest achievement comes because of awareness of the elements.

HSW: How about this: "With a deep understanding of how the apparently solid world is actually the play of pure elemental light, peace can be

found even in a troubled world, problems can be eradicated before they manifest, and ultimately the nature of the mind can be fully realized."
That is a huge statement. How can we as people on the spiritual path achieve that kind of understanding?

TWR: It is all about understanding causes and conditions. For example, before a very destructive action occurs, it is caused by a state of mind, such as anger. Anger in itself really has no power unless you give it energy, or *prana*. And if you catch it in its earliest stage, you can work with that energy before it actually becomes anger, before it can manifest as a destructive action. If you think about the destructive quality of anger, it arises in five stages, just like the arising of the elements. Its initial movement is like the flow of air. In its fire-like stage, it is getting more solid. In its water stage, it is becoming even more solid. In its earth stage, it becomes very solid. At that point it is already destructive.

So, you have levels of subtlety. The subtler something is, the easier it is to transform or eliminate. If you are getting really angry, you can look inward at your mind and see that what the anger really wants is to destroy itself. Try to look at how you are feeling and just breathe. Take a half an hour of deep breathing, and the anger will be gone. You take it back to air, to its subtlest form.

Any problem is easier to work with on its most subtle level. Why does ritual serve a function and have power? Ritual is like a form of language that has a power to catch issues when they are on the subtlest level. When only the causes of obstacles and disease are there, the ritual has more effect. By the time disease has already physically appeared, ritual will be less effective. By then, I think it is good to go to the doctor.

HSW: You had made a distinction in your book that while all things on the material plane are an illusion, you also say that if you stand in front of a truck you are going to get run over. How does Bön, especially the Bön shaman, hold both truths at once? That is, that it is all an illusion and yet a very tangible illusion.

TWR: Basically, that balance has a lot to do with personal realization. There might be a fully realized person who could stand in front of the truck and not be run over. But if an ordinary person tried to do that, then that person would die because he or she is still within the boundaries of conventional reality. Standing in front of a truck is an extreme example, but there are a lot of other things you can look at in this way. Some people approach life with much openness and flexibility. Others experience their life and the world in a very strict, narrow way. So in a way it is very personal.

HSW: I find it interesting that Bön is inclusive both of the shaman, who is dedicated to working with the material realm very purposefully, and of the practitioner who seeks to achieve enlightenment, a release from the illusion of the physical world. It seems the two might contradict.

TWR: Well, to some degree they do contradict each other. But let's clarify this. In a way, these views are really very much integrated. Bön is not about separate traditions; it is one school with three ways to relate to the world. All three levels of practice offer different ways for people to grow. Because of their ability or their level of realization, some people feel more connection with the first level, not the second. Some people feel more connection with the second, not the third. Regardless of their level of realization, everyone has a body and must live in and relate to this world, to the gross elements, the spirits, and so on.

HSW: I like the fact that your tradition is very inclusive. It has something for everybody, no matter what the focus of their particular path.

TWR: I also find this very, very important. The tradition has something for everybody, yes, but it incorporates everything as one. It allows for growth. Whatever practices you are connecting to, you can grow from there to higher understanding. That's what I try to emphasize.

HSW: Which is the goal of any spiritual practice. How about the shaman in particular?

TWR: Shamanic practice is there for us to learn to become harmonized with the environment, so that the environment is very happily supporting us. But once we have a healthy society, a prosperous society, and everything is in balance, what do we do then? We have to grow from there. Shamanic practice is a causal vehicle, our support toward higher realization. It's not the end. The end of something is always the beginning of another thing.

Contact Information

Elena Avila
EAvila9234@aol.com
www.Elena-curandera.com

Simon Buxton
The Sacred Trust
P.O. Box 183
Penzance, Cornwall TR18 4EE
England
mail@sacredtrust.co.uk
Tel: (+44) 01736 331825
www.sacredtrust.org

Tom Cowan
www.riverdrum.com

Ken Eagle Feather (Ken Smith)
www.BIOESYSTEMS.com

OmeAkaEhekatl (Erick Gonzalez)
P.O. Box 90

Glen Ellen, CA 95442
(707) 280-7033
ajqij@jps.net
www.mayanshamanism.com

Sandra Ingerman
P.O. Box 4757
Santa Fe, NM 87502
www.shamanicvisions.com/ingerman.html
For a list of shamanic practitioners trained by Sandra, you can
write to Sandra at the above address or e-mail Ruth Aber at
aruthabelle@aol.com

Serge Kahili King, Ph.D.
Aloha International
P.O. Box 223009
Princeville, HI 96722
(888) 827-8383
www.huna.org

Brooke Medicine Eagle
PMB C401
One Second Avenue E.
Polson, MT 59860
(406) 883-4686
brooke@MedicineEagle.com
www.MedicineEagle.com

Lewis Mehl-Madrona, M.D.
University of Arizona
Program in Integrative Medicine
P.O. Box 245153
Tucson, AZ 85724-5153
(520) 304-6898
madrona@email.arizona.edu

Oscar Miro-Quesada
2639 Mohawk Circle
West Palm Beach, FL 33409
(561) 471-7378
heartofthehealer@aol.com
www.mesaworks.com

John Perkins
Dream Change Coalition
(561) 626-5662
www.dreamchange.org
dreamchang@aol.com

Larry G. Peters, Ph.D.
1212 Old Topanga Canyon Road
Topanga, CA 90290
(310) 455-2713
lpshaman@aol.com

Christina Pratt
Last Mask Center for Shamanic Healing
2343 SW Cedar Street #7
Portland, OR 97205
(800) 927-2527 ext. 02586
lastmaskcenter@earthlink.net
www.shamansense.org

Gabrielle Roth
The Moving Center
P.O. Box 271
Cooper Station
New York, NY 10276
(212) 760-1381
ravenrec@panix.com

Evelyn C. Rysdyk and C. Allie Knowlton
Spirit Passages
www.spiritpassages.com

Brant Secunda
Dance of the Deer Foundation
Center for Shamanic Studies
P.O. Box 699
Soquel, CA 95073
(831) 475-9560
(831) 475-1860 (fax)
info@shamanism.com
www.shamanism.com

Malidoma Patrice Somé
malidoma@earthlink.net
(530) 894-0740

Alex Stark
270 5th Street, Room 1D
Brooklyn, NY 11215
(718) 840-2820
(718) 832-1787 (fax)
alex@alexstark.com
www.alexstark.com

Geo Trevarthen, Ph.D.
www.celticshamanism.com
tuath@celticshamanism.com

Tenzin Wangyal Rinpoche
Ligmincha Institute
313 2nd Street SE, Suite 207
Charlottesville, VA 22902
(434) 977-6161

ligmincha@aol.com
www.ligmincha.org

Hank Wesselman, Ph.D.
P.O. Box 2059
Granite Bay, CA 95746
hank@sharedwisdom.com
www.sharedwisdom.com

Rabbi Gershon Winkler
Walking Stick Foundation
P.O. Box 1865
Cuba, New Mexico 87013
(505) 289-3344
www.walkingstick.org

About the Author

© Carl A. Hyatt

Hillary S. Webb is the author of *Exploring Shamanism: Using Ancient Rites to Discover the Unlimited Healing Powers of Cosmos and Consciousness.* She is a longtime student of shamanism and other Earth-honoring spiritual traditions. Her intent for her writing and practice is to continue to "push the envelope of consciousness," to "uncover the boundaries of the human psyche and crack them wide open." A native of Salem, Massachusetts, she currently resides in southern Maine.

About the Cover Artist:
Susan Cohen Thompson

Journey Into Ancestors

Visionary painter Susan Cohen Thompson says, "When I go into the woods, into nature, I realize how much wisdom there is to be found there. I see nature is alive and feeling, and that humans are made of earth. I feel passionate about relaying this oneness in my art."

The painting *Journey Into Ancestors* was inspired by an experience that Thompson had while hiking in British Columbia. "In an old-growth forest, the elder, fallen trees provide nourishment for younger trees that grow on top of them. As we walked through the forest we could see giant ancient trees in the land-form of the ground—all the ancestors—in the forest floor. They were providing the nutrients for living trees that were growing out of them. *Journey Into Ancestors* is the recognition of how much we ourselves are nurtured and built by what comes before us. It is my way of expressing this camaraderie and connection with nature."

Thompson has just moved to Camano Island, Washington, from the Boston area. She has been painting and exhibiting her work professionally for 25 years. Her paintings have shown in galleries and nature sanctuaries around the Americas. Her Web site is filled with her vivid and exotic images and information about her work. Contact the artist online:

www.ThompsonArtStudio.com
www.art4earth.com
susan@ThompsonArtStudio.com

green
press
INITIATIVE

Hampton Roads Publishing Company

. . . for the evolving human spirit

Hampton Roads Publishing Company
publishes books on a variety of subjects,
including metaphysics, health,
visionary fiction, and other related topics.

For a copy of our latest catalog, call toll-free
(800) 766-8009, or send your name and address to:

Hampton Roads Publishing Company, Inc.
1125 Stoney Ridge Road
Charlottesville, VA 22902

e-mail: hrpc@hrpub.com
www.hrpub.com